The Japanese Way of Tea

茶經卷上　　唐竟陵陸羽鴻漸撰

一之源

茶者南方之嘉木也一尺二尺迺至數十尺其

巴山峽川有兩人合抱者伐而掇之其樹如瓜

蘆葉如梔子花如白薔薇實如栟櫚葉如丁香

根如胡桃瓜蘆木出廣州似茶至苦澁栟櫚蒲

葵之屬其子似茶胡桃與茶根皆下

孕兆至瓦礫苗木上抽其字或從草或從木或從木并

當作茶其字出開元文字者義從木當作搽

搽其字出本草草木并作茶其名

Chajing, The Classic of Tea, opening section. Ming dynasty edition. From a collection of historical works on tea, the *Chashu* (Jp., *Chasho*; Tea Writings), compiled by Yuzheng and dated Wanli 40 (1612). Woodblock print. Konnichian Library archives.

The Japanese Way of Tea
From Its Origins in China
to Sen Rikyū

Sen Sōshitsu XV
Translated by V. Dixon Morris

University of Hawai'i Press
Honolulu

Publication of this book was assisted by a subsidy from Professor Emeritus George Akita in remembrance of Akiko Akita (1927–1992) and Shinobu Akita (1960–1965).

03 02 01 00   5 4 3 2

Library of Congress Cataloging-in-Publication Data

Sen, Sōshitsu, 1923–
    [Chakyō to waga kuni chadō no rekishiteki igi. English]
    The Japanese way of tea : from its origins in China to Sen Rikyū /
Sen Sōshitsu XV ; translated by V. Dixon Morris.
        p.   cm.
    Includes bibliographical references and index.
    ISBN 0–8248–1897–0 (alk. paper). — ISBN 0–8248–1990–X (pbk. :
alk. paper)
        1. Tea—Japan—History.   2. Japanese tea ceremony—History.
I. Title.
TX415.S4613   1998
641.3'372'0952—DC21   97–23843
                                                                  CIP

University of Hawai'i Press books are printed on acid-free paper and meet the guidelines for permanence and durability of the Council on Library Resources

Jacket and cover illustration: "Cha" (Tea). Calligraphy by Gotō Zuigan, Zen mentor of the author.

Designed by BookMasters, Inc.

Contents

Color plates follow page 84

Foreword

The *Chanoyu* of Sen Rikyū

There is no more revered personage in the history of *chanoyu* than Sen Rikyū (1522–1591). Perfecter of *wabicha* (*chanoyu* based on the *wabi* aesthetic), national tea master and arbiter of taste, personal adviser to the hegemon Toyotomi Hideyoshi (1536–1598), Rikyū is a towering figure not only in the cultural records of the late sixteenth century, when he lived, but also in those of *chanoyu* through all the centuries that have followed. In the Edo period (1600–1867), Rikyū was deified as the god of tea, and from at least Tokugawa times all tea schools have traced their lineages, either in genealogical fact or in spirit, back to him. Even today, tea masters and others in *chanoyu* are inspired above all by Rikyū. In many ways, Rikyū is *chanoyu*. Surely there are few arts anywhere that have been as dominated as *chanoyu* by the example, ideals, and spirit of a single person.

Yamanoue Sōji (1544–1590), one of Rikyū's disciples, stated that "[A]s a tea master, [Rikyū] freely transformed mountains into valleys, changed west to east, and broke the rules of *chanoyu*. But if the ordinary person were simply to imitate him, there would be no *chanoyu*."[1] And the contemporary historian Kumakura Isao, commenting on the high period of Rikyū's career, the decade of 1582–1591 when he served Hideyoshi, has observed that "[During that time, Rikyū] ignited explosions in every aspect of *chanoyu*."[2]

These are startling judgments, made by men separated by four centuries, that Rikyū was a person who, in his unorthodoxy, extremism, or both, shook the very foundations of the world of tea and perhaps even the aesthetic order itself. People today are likely to think of *wabicha* as the epitome of tranquility, social harmony, and aesthetic re-straint—as something hardly to be associated with the "transformation of mountains into valleys" or the "igniting of explosions." But histori-cally *wabicha* was a radical offshoot from *chanoyu*'s main line of devel-opment. It was, above all, a product of the Sengoku age (age of provincial wars, 1467–1568), a time of great disorder throughout Japan when "those below overthrew those above" (*gekokujō*). Taken from Chinese history, *gekokujō* is an apt term for describing the upheavals of Sengoku life, including peasants rising against landlords, warrior vassals betray-ing their chiefs, and tea masters defying or "overthrowing" traditional social distinctions and established aesthetic standards.

    Wabicha was a product of social *gekokujō* in part because it was the creation of a parvenu class, the rich merchants of cities such as Sakai, Kyoto, and Nara. This class, having accumulated much wealth, aspired to elevate itself culturally. Since its members could not aspire to partic-ipate significantly in many of the established arts, such as *waka* poetry, still largely the protected preserve of the Kyoto courtiers, or the *nō* the-ater, which was patronized by the warrior elite, they turned to a new art, *chanoyu*. And in shaping *chanoyu* as *wabicha* they engaged in both aes-thetic and social *gekokujō* by, on the one hand, rejecting many tradi-tional aesthetic standards and seeking a "*wabi* beauty" in such things as misshapen and cracked tea bowls and rustic "grass huts" (*sōan*) and, on the other hand, waiving class and status distinctions at tea gatherings.

    As discussed in this book, tradition tells us that Murata Jukō (or Shukō; d. 1502), a merchant from Nara, was the originator of *wabicha*, that Takeno Jōō (1502–1555) of Sakai developed it further, and that it was brought to perfection—or to its extreme—by Rikyū, also from Sakai. There is perhaps irony in the fact that *wabicha*, one of the great artistic and aesthetic achievements of the medieval age, was actually "perfected" in the next age—in the Momoyama cultural epoch at the beginning of the early modern age. The transition from medieval to Momoyama and early modern brought extraordinary change to Japan: change, for example, from warfare and disunion to peace and unity, from social upheaval to a closed class system, from otherworldly spirituality to an absorption with life in the here and now, and from an art (painting) whose mainstream favored quietistic, monochromatic landscapes to one boldly depicting scenes of great variety and energy in gold and other brilliant colors.

    In stark contrast to the brightness and vigor of most of Mo-moyama culture and art is the two-mat tea room Taian, built by Rikyū, that is the supreme artistic masterpiece of *wabicha*. Presently attached to Myōkian Temple not far from Kyoto, Taian has been called the North Pole of Japanese aesthetics. Of an almost irreducibly minimum size (less than six square feet of seating space), dimly lit, and with darkened mud and straw walls, Taian possesses an unworldly, "cold" (*hie*) and "with-ered" (*kare*) atmosphere that exemplifies *wabi* taste both at its finest and its most extreme. Hideyoshi, we are told, directed Rikyū to build Taian. A devotee of *wabicha* under Rikyū's guidance, Hideyoshi also had an-other rustic tea room—perhaps similar to Taian—installed at his prin-cipal headquarters in Osaka Castle.

Chanoyu of the Sen Family after Rikyū

Many theories have been advanced to explain why Hideyoshi ordered Rikyū to commit suicide by disembowelment in 1591. A particularly interesting theory, in line with the present discussion, is that Rikyū was condemned to death precisely because he "transformed mountains into valleys" and "ignited explosions in every aspect of *chanoyu*"—that is, because he engaged in *gekokujō*.

In any event, when Rikyū committed suicide in 1591, the lead-ing members of his family undoubtedly feared that their careers in *chanoyu* were over. But surprisingly, Hideyoshi allowed them to resume those careers within just a few years, and during the seventeenth cen-tury, after the founding of the Tokugawa military government or Shogu-nate, the Sen family rose to high eminence in the world of *chanoyu*, especially under Rikyū's grandson Sōtan (1578–1658), the family's Grand Master (*iemoto*) from 1614 until his death in 1658. Three of Sōtan's sons established the three schools of Sen-family tea, Urasenke, Omotesenke, and Mushanokōjisenke, that remain in the forefront of *chanoyu* in Japan today. The author of this book, Dr. Sen, is the fifteenth Grand Master of the Urasenke school (counting Rikyū as the first Grand Master, his son Shōan [1546–1614] as the second, and Sōtan as the third).

In the last years of the seventeenth century there occurred a great revival of the ideals and spirit of Sen Rikyū. Sōtan, known as the "Beggar Sōtan" because of his devotion to *wabicha*, was a forerunner to this revival, which reached its climax in the discovery about 1691 of *Nampōroku*, a text purportedly written a century earlier by a disciple of

Rikyū that is now regarded as the "bible" of Rikyū's way of tea. Rikyū himself emerged at this time as the god of tea, and the Sen schools were recognized as the principal bearers and transmitters of his traditions.

After having flourished greatly during the Tokugawa period because of widespread public interest in *chanoyu* and the patronage of those territorial warrior rulers called daimyo, the various tea schools, including the Sen schools, were hard hit by the Meiji Restoration of 1868, which brought an end to the feudal government of the Tokugawa and thrust Japan, almost willy-nilly, into the Western-dominated modern world. A number of the traditional arts were at a low ebb at this time, making it even easier for many Japanese to abandon them in a rush to embrace the arts of the West as part of a powerful, widespread movement of Westernization that was labeled a quest for "Civilization and Enlightenment" (*bunmei kaika*). Deserted by their patrons, the daimyo, who were dissolved as a class by the new Meiji government, and by many of their other supporters and students, the traditional schools of *chanoyu* fell upon difficult times indeed.

Within about two decades, however, the *chanoyu* schools began to recover. The most important step taken in this recovery, which was led by Urasenke, was the adding of *chanoyu* to the instructional curricula of public schools, especially women's schools. Before, *chanoyu* had been almost entirely a male pursuit. Viewed from this time as an essential means for training young ladies in proper etiquette, bearing, and aesthetic taste, it became mainly an activity of women.

Sen Sōshitsu, Fifteenth Grand Master of Urasenke

Dr. Sen was born in 1923, the first son of the fourteenth Grand Master of Urasenke, Tantansai (1893–1964). Tantansai was the first of the Grand Masters to take a professional interest in the world outside Japan. He traveled extensively through the United States and Europe, where he lectured on and gave demonstrations in *chanoyu*. In 1947, after the end of World War II, Tantansai affirmed his commitment to the dissemination of *chanoyu* overseas by establishing the International Chadō Cultural Foundation. Tantansai's wish to disseminate *chanoyu* abroad has been enthusiastically shared by his son, Dr. Sen. Indeed, transforming *chanoyu* into an international culture, devoted above all to the promotion of world peace, has been one of Dr. Sen's most cherished dreams and also one of his most important achievements since suc-ceeding Tantansai as Grand Master in 1964.

After a busy childhood and youth that included an active inter-est in sports as well as training in *chanoyu*, Dr. Sen entered Dōshisha Uni-versity of Kyoto in the spring of 1941, choosing to major in economics. In December of that year the Pacific War began, and in April 1943 he entered a trainee program for hydroplane pilots that enabled him to con-tinue his studies at Dōshisha. In December 1943, however, Dr. Sen left Dōshisha and joined the Japanese Navy, where he was assigned to pilot training in the Special Attack Unit. He was awaiting orders to fly a sui-cide mission when the war ended in August 1945.

Dr. Sen has written poignantly about his service in the Special Attack Unit: "Among the experiences I can never forget was the time I served tea during the war as a member of the Special Attack Unit of the naval air force. Since I was told that they wanted everyone to have a cup of tea before setting out on a mission, I performed *chanoyu* using my special box of tea utensils. All the pilots drank the tea I prepared, sitting cross-legged in their flight uniforms. Finishing with words of ap-preciation for the tea, many of the group departed on their mission. My comrades launched their attack the following day, and I thought that perhaps I might be obliged to do the same the day after."[3]

Returning to Dōshisha, Dr. Sen completed his interrupted stud-ies there, receiving a B.A. degree in economics in September 1946. In 1949 he took Buddhist vows at Daitokuji (Zen) Temple in Kyoto; and from 1952–1953 he studied art and philosophy at the University of Hawai'i, establishing a relationship with the university that remains strong today. Each year in February when Dr. Sen, who received his Ph.D. in philosophy from Nankai University in the People's Republic of China in 1991, makes one of at least two annual visits to Hawai'i, he takes time from an extraordinarily busy schedule to participate in the activities of the History Department, where he holds a professorship, by visiting and lecturing to students in one or more classes. Since I joined the faculty of the History Department on a full-time basis in 1994, Dr. Sen has lectured twice each February to my class on the history of the Way of Tea. He is a fine lecturer who never fails to impress the students with both his knowledge and his enthusiasm. In regard to enthusiasm, I remember especially the time a student asked him about the proper way to sit in Buddhist meditation. Promptly kicking off his shoes, Dr. Sen hopped up on a table to demonstrate both the half- and full-lotus positions for seated meditation.

Dr. Sen has visited more than fifty countries, establishing Urasenke branches in many of them. He has received countless honors, awards, and decorations. The governments of Brazil, Finland, France, Germany, Italy, Peru, and Thailand have honored him for his work in promoting goodwill and cultural exchange between their countries and Japan. He has received the Medal of Honor with Blue Ribbon eight times from the Emperor of Japan, and in 1994 the Emperor bestowed upon him the Order of the Rising Sun, Second Class. In 1989 he was named Person of Cultural Merits by the Japanese government, and in 1995 he received both the Japan Foundation Award and the Foreign Minister's Commendation.[4]

The Japanese Way of Tea: From Its Origins in China to Sen Rikyū

Few subjects in Japanese cultural history compare in importance with *chanoyu*. Taking its basic form during the medieval age, from the fourteenth through sixteenth centuries, *chanoyu* has drawn upon and, at the same time, has influenced many spheres of culture, art, and religion, including architecture, interior room decoration, ceramics, painting, calligraphy, flower arrangement, and Buddhism, especially Zen. Because of its involvement with so many spheres, *chanoyu* itself is difficult to define. Some, for example, have described it as a performing art, others as a means of artistic display, and still others as a path to religious enlightenment. In the late sixteenth century, as we have seen, tea masters such as Sen Rikyū were leaders of the world of art and culture in Japan, and some even influenced the course of government. Today *chanoyu* is, among other things, a repository of traditional Japanese taste and etiquette, a medium for intimate, formalized social intercourse, and a continuing source of spiritual inspiration.

It is surprising, in view of *chanoyu*'s great role in cultural history, that it has, until recently, received little scholarly attention in the English-language literature on Japan. Okakura Kakuzō's *The Book of Tea*, published in 1906, was a brief attempt by a prominent Japanese art historian to introduce *chanoyu* to the West. Okakura, however, doubted that Westerners were likely to appreciate *chanoyu,* commenting: "The average Westerner, in his sleek complacency, will see in the tea cere-mony but another instance of the thousand and one oddities which constitute the quaintness and childishness of the East to him."[5] In fact, Okakura himself may very well have contributed to the impression that *chanoyu* is "quaint," if not "childish," by his exaggerated and theatrical presentation of the subject in *The Book of Tea.*

The only major effort by a scholar writing in English before World War II to explain *chanoyu* and its history was Arthur Sadler's *Cha-no-yu,* published in 1934. Sadler's book remains a valuable source of information, but it is arranged more as a reference work than a bal-anced analysis of *chanoyu* and its history. It is not a book for the general reader, nor is it suitable for use as a classroom text.

Much of the scholarly writing about *chanoyu* that has appeared in recent years has been a result of the patronage of Dr. Sen and Urasenke. *Chanoyu Quarterly,* a journal launched by Urasenke in 1970, comprises an invaluable collection of articles by both Japanese and non-Japanese writers on *chanoyu* and its related arts. And *Tea in Japan: Essays on the History of Chanoyu* (1989), edited by Paul Varley and Kumakura Isao, which emerged from an Urasenke-sponsored confer-ence on the "History of *Chanoyu*" held in Honolulu in 1982, contains essays by Japanese, American, and British scholars that cover *chanoyu's* development from earliest times until the modern age. For a description of the actual functioning of *chanoyu* as an art, I recommend *An Intro-duction to Japanese Tea Ritual* by Jennifer Anderson, an anthropologist who studied tea at Urasenke in Kyoto.

Dr. Sen's *The Japanese Way of Tea* has previously appeared in both Japanese and Chinese. Its publication now in English is an event of major importance for students of Japanese cultural history. For one thing, it is the first book-length writing on *chanoyu* in English that pro-vides a detailed discussion of the Chinese origins of the Japanese way of tea. In particular, Dr. Sen's analysis of Lu Yu's classic *Chajing* (*The Classic of Tea*) provides, for the first time, a coherent historical expla-nation of what "tea" had come to mean culturally to the Chinese on the eve of its introduction to Japan about the beginning of the ninth cen-tury and of what, apart from a new beverage, the Japanese actually got when they brought it to their shores. But, to my mind, the greatest value of *The Japanese Way of Tea* lies in the authority with which Dr. Sen has been able to describe the evolution of the way of tea in Japan from its beginnings to the age of Sen Rikyū. Basing his writing on extensive research into the primary historical records, he tells his story both as a historian and as one of the leading practitioners of *chanoyu* in Japan and the world. In this dual role of historian and leading practitioner, Dr. Sen is able to deal with *chanoyu* with a sensitivity and insight not likely to be found in the writings of others. *The Japanese Way of Tea* will surely take its place at the forefront of writings in English on *chanoyu*.

Paul Varley
Sen Sōshitsu XV Professor of Japanese Cultural History
University of Hawai'i

Author's Preface to the English Edition

I have frequently been asked by universities outside my home country to present lectures on Japanese culture centering on the Way of Tea. The lectures have been quite fruitful, in that I have been able to communicate something about the *fūryū* or "romantic" spirit of the Japanese and the kind of spiritual repose that the people enjoy because of it. The Japanese have developed a special setting and mode of engaging with others and with nature, pervaded by the spirit of *fūryū*. I refer here to the "living art" of the Way of Tea, which has exerted a profound influence on many of the finest aspects of Japanese culture. In my encounters with people from other lands who are attracted to Japan, I have found that they are eager to gain an understanding of the philosophy underlying this veritable art of life. This interest, I am convinced, reflects a universal human instinct—the need to seek out that which will truly soothe and enrich the soul. Especially as humanity becomes increasingly engulfed in the materialistic and technological concerns of modern civilization, we become keenly aware of this need.

Nearly a decade and a half have passed since my book enquiring into the connections between Lu Yu and the Japanese Way of Tea was originally published in my native language. My pleasure in now having it appear in English translation from the University of Hawai'i Press is immense. This English edition would not have come to pass without the enthusiastic urging of Professor George Akita of the University of Hawai'i, together with Professor Paul Varley, who serves as Sen Chair at the University of Hawai'i, and Mori Akiko, my own manager for international projects. Of the many individuals who have been involved in this English edition, I wish particularly to thank Dr. V. Dixon

Morris, who rendered the text into English, supplying additional bibliographical notes for the international audience.

Mastery of the Way of Tea requires thorough understanding of the moral and spiritual principles underlying it, erudition in terms of its literary, historical, and artistic foundations, and the ability to pull all these together in one's training and actualize them in one's practice. It is my sincere hope that the present book sheds light on some of these points and will bring the reader to a closer understanding of the philosophy that gives this art its timeless relevance.

Translator's Preface

"Translation," asserts Okakura Kakuzō in *The Book of Tea,* "is always a treason," and translators understand their own culpability as well as anyone. Striking the right balance between a literal rendering of the original and a freer, more easily comprehensible version is always a challenge, certainly, if not the treason that Okakura charged. Many of the citations here are in the almost painfully terse classical Chinese of the Tang and Song dynasties, and expressing them in the prolix English style of the late twentieth century involves fleshing out bare bones, making explicit the nuances that were only implicit in the original. Medieval—and sometimes even modern—Japanese entails similar additions as well as a glossing over of elements like status relationships, which Japanese readers would expect to find. As a consequence, readers of the English translation need to understand some of the general principles and conventions that this edition employs.

The most common editorial change here has been to pare away elements in the original that would seem redundant in English. In general, the Japanese version takes the form of a citation of a primary source from China or medieval Japan, followed by an explication and interpretation in modern Japanese. To have translated the original citation into English followed by an English-language interpretation would soon become tedious for the reader, as both would be essentially the same. (To have cited primary sources in the original languages would probably have sent readers running for cover! That was never an option.) As a guideline, readers can understand that material enclosed in quotation marks or indented is intended to be a reasonably close paraphrase of the original. In addition, Japanese readers seem to have a greater appetite for long, direct quotations than English ones do. The original,

consequently, has a number of extended citations. These have been reduced in length, with the balance taking the form of a summary in
a narrative style. The translation similarly reduces long quotations in
the notes.

The translation is also a revised version. With the author's bless-
ing, the new edition combines chapters 1 and 2 of the original. The
chapter on tea contests is considerably shorter here, on the advice of
the readers for the University of Hawai'i Press. In the latter chapter, especially, notes have replaced quoted material.

The biggest addition to this version is reference endnotes. The
original identified its sources parenthetically in the conventional style
of scholarly Japanese writing. English-language scholarship normally
requires greater detail in citation, with the material in footnotes or endnotes. To conform to this standard, the translation includes endnote
references to cited works as well as a bibliography with publication data.
Unfortunately, after the lapse of a decade and a half since the first writing, the original notes were no longer available. It was impossible,
therefore, to know with precision which of several versions of various
works the author may have used. In a few cases, therefore, multiple versions appear in the notes. In others, the version that the author was
most likely to have used was the basis for citation. The majority of notes
cite works that are in the author's own library and archive, Konnichian
Bunko. *Chadō Koten Zenshū*, a twelve-volume collection of primary
sources for which the author was general editor, for example, served as
the definitive source for notes to works included in it. Where works are
not in Konnichian Bunko, the translation generally cites editions available at Kyoto University and the Kyoto Prefectural Archives.

Readers may note that the translation includes a number of citations to English-language works or to works that appeared after the
publication of the original. Such sources would not or could not have
been in the original. The translation supplies English citations as a con-
venience for readers of that language. Some Japanese sources that appeared after publication have also been cited because of their
availability. Readers who perceive problems with the citations should
lay them at the translator's door rather than that of the author.

A couple of further comments about the notes may be in order.
A number of citations direct the reader to traditional East Asian publications. These have printing, often using woodblocks, on one side of a
sheet of paper, which is then folded with the unprinted side in. The

loose sides are bound at the spine, and the fold is out, opposite the spine. Page numbers (if any) appear on the fold, but these do not have a uniform page numbering system. When endnotes have cited such traditionally printed and bound volumes, page numbers refer to the entire folded sheet, called "*chōme*" in Japanese. Modern photo reprints of such works usually have sequential page numbers in addition to the original page numbers. Citations are to the sequential numbers. Where there are no sequential numbers, the page number simply refers to the order of the sheet in the work cited.

Even in the twentieth century, volume numbers of multivolume works in Japan are not entirely standard according to Western usage. Volumes labeled *jō*, *chū*, and *ge* (literally, upper, middle, lower) are cited as volumes 1, 2, and 3, respectively. Where there is no *chū*, *ge* becomes the second volume. Sometimes publishers have subdivided numbered volumes into *jō*, *chū*, and *ge*. The notes cite these as volume number plus *jō*, *chū*, or *ge*. An example would be *Gunsho Ruijū*, vol. 17 *ge*, meaning the second of two volumes numbered seventeen. The guiding principle in the notes is to direct a reasonably efficient and conscientious researcher to the work cited.

As is customary in scholarly writing on Japan in English, Japanese names appear here in their normal Japanese order, that is, family name first, given name second.

Weights and measures also require some explanation. Traditional societies often lacked the standards for measures that we are accustomed to in the modern era. It is often impossible, therefore, for historians to calculate modern equivalents, and so, when the translation supplies a modern amount for a traditional measure, it can only be approximate. The reader should understand any of the weights and measures in this volume as being subject to some margin of error.

Readers may notice here a greater than normal use of the masculine gender in reference to those who practiced *chanoyu*. Though women outnumber men in the tea art today, during the period covered in this volume the reverse was the case. Virtually all individuals referred to here were males. The use of the masculine gender for nouns and pronouns in the translation, therefore, is intentional.

Finally, dating follows conventions that seem to have become standard for writing about premodern Japan. Years are given to the closest Western date. Until the nineteenth century, the Japanese year normally began some weeks after January 1 in the West, so dates in the twelfth month in Japan would fall in the following Western year. They are given here, however, as being in the same year as the earlier months. The text abbreviates dates as year/month/day or month/day. Thus, 1591/2/28 stands for the twenty-eighth day of the second month of the nineteenth year of the Tenshō era (1591). Traditional Japan also had intercalary months as a means of realigning their basically lunar calendar with the solar year. That meant that a thirteenth month would be inserted periodically. The year 1591, for example, had an intercalary first month, which meant that there was a second first month inserted between the first and second months of that year for a total of thirteen months in the year. Such months are identified with the word "intercalary." Thus, 1591/intercalary 1/11 would be an example.

Prefaces are for thanks as well as for caveats, and I want to express my gratitude to many helpful and supportive individuals. George Akita, now retired from the University of Hawai'i at Manoa, has taken a strong interest in the relationship between the university and Urasenke and has lent his support to this translation as well. Mori Akiko, as head of the International Division of Urasenke, was my chief contact with the author during the entire period of translation. Gretchen Mittwer, editor of *Chanoyu Quarterly*, has provided logistical assistance throughout and has offered her editorial skills to improve the manuscript. Professor Shōji Yasu generously spent dozens (probably hundreds) of hours discussing knotty problems of interpretation. At the Konnichian Bunko, Yokota Yaemi and Yamada Tetsuya collected great stacks of books for me to consult, and the latter especially provided advice and helped search the rare book collection for necessary citations. All the staff at the Bunko were helpful, fueling my searches for references with dozens of servings of *chagashi* and bowls of *matcha*. Those at the Kyoto Prefectural Archives, the Kyoto University Library, Kobe University Library, and the Chinese Studies *Kenkyūshitsu* at Kyoto University also helped greatly. The young scholars at the Chinese Studies *Kenkyūshitsu*, especially, interrupted their own valuable research to dive into ranges of seemingly identical volumes of Chinese dynastic histories and emerge with just the one needed to supply a reference note. Kyōko Belachew deserves particular thanks, for she made the note search her own project, performing such miracles as finding three separate fragmentary lines in a volume of over seven hundred pages. Professors William LaFleur and Paul Varley read the manuscript in its entirety and made valuable suggestions. The latter, especially, gave several pages of detailed editorial comments. To try to express thanks individually to all who helped with particular problems would be nearly impossible, but I do appreciate their help. If, despite the support of others, I have crossed the line between free translation and outright error, I must accept the responsibility. These kind people are not accessories to my treason.

Historical Periods Covered in This Volume

Major Periods of Japanese History

Nara period	710–784
Heian period	794–1185
Kamakura period	1185–1333
Muromachi period	1336–1573
Nanbokuchō (Northern and Southern Courts) period	1336–1392
Kitayama era	late fourteenth–early fifteenth centuries
Higashiyama era	late fifteenth century
Sengoku (Warring States) era	1467–1568
Azuchi-Momoyama period	1568–1600
Edo period	1600–1867

Major Periods of Chinese History

Zhou period	ca. 1020 B.C.–256 B.C.
Qin period	221 B.C.–206 B.C.
Han period (successor states)	206 B.C.–A.D. 220
Sui period	589–618
Tang period	618–907
Song period	960–1279
Yuan period	1279–1368
Ming period	1368–1644
Qing period	1644–1912

Introduction

When I am asked about a life devoted to tea, I often respond that it is "an intellectual diversion in another world." The Way of Tea, though it is a part of real life, strives to attain a spiritual form of entertainment on a higher dimension. I should like to discuss concretely the reasons why I have defined it in this fashion.

When invited to a tea gathering, what might the guest be thinking as he or she stands in that garden, called the "dewy ground," outside the tea house? Why must I tread this dewy path as a first stage before entering the tea room? Standing among the stepping stones disposed here and there along the way one wonders if there is some meaning to their arrangement. Then, along the path the guest reaches a middle gate. Yet this gate is neither stout nor especially luxurious. Gates in ordinary life make no sense unless they serve to separate that which is within from that without, but this is scarcely more than a simple garden wicket. In the mundane sense of dividing inside from out, it is too plain, a gate in form only.

What interpretation are we to place upon this? If we presume that inside and outside lie along a common dimension and that the gate marks the boundary between the two, and if we interpret inside and outside as self and other, then there can be no more formidable gate. When one defends a territory, outside is the enemy, and one expects the gate to symbolize the recognition of the hostility that lies without and the posture of defense against it. Yet the gate in the tea garden completely demolishes that notion. This simple wicket opens without effort, and one can easily spy through it whatever lies on the opposite side. For this reason, though the wicket appears on the surface to be a gate, it is not made to function as a barrier in the common understanding of such a structure. This is because the two sides of the gate do not in fact lie along a common dimension. Though what lies beyond it is merely an extension of the same tea garden, the gate serves as a boundary to make us conscious of a world that exists in a different dimension. The Parables of the Lotus Sutra contain a well-known line, "[One] emerges from the house in flames in the three worlds to sit on the open, dewy ground." Here indeed is the key to unlock the secret of the ideal of *chanoyu* as "an intellectual diversion in another world."[1]

If we proceed toward the tea room itself, this circumstance becomes even clearer. There stands before the room a stone basin called a *tsukubai*, where the guests will rinse their hands.

As the *Nanpōroku* states in a noteworthy passage: "The first act of the host is to carry water into the tea garden, and the first act of the guest is to use that water. Herein lies the cardinal principle of the dewy ground and the grass hut. This is the basin where both the one who invites and the one who is invited into the dewy ground can wash away the impurities of the world."[2]

What we call *chanoyu* is nothing more than the occasion for the partaking of a bowl of tea. It is only the ordinary act of eating and drinking that can be seen in daily life. Nevertheless, in the requirement that we sweep away the impurities of this world, we can see the operation of an other-worldly concept that makes us conscious of having put aside the concerns of mundane life. One seeks to transcend the scorn that holds the ordinary to be vulgar.

Similarly, the *Nanpōroku* says, "Chanoyu in a small room means first of all to practice the austerities of Buddhism." Later it continues: "The teaching of the Buddha is the essence of *chanoyu*. . . . [First] we boil water and make tea. [Next] we offer it to the Buddha, serve our guests, and drink it ourselves. We arrange flowers and light incense. All of these are ways to pursue the teachings of the Buddha and his elders."[3]

Thus, even the ordinary act of drinking tea could be the means by which one rose above the ordinary and crossed over into a higher plane. The austerities that Buddhists practiced in pursuit of enlightenment treated reality as mundane and trivial, and so the aspirant sought to transcend it. The act of drinking a bowl of tea was a step toward achieving that ultimate ideal reality.

This sense deepens still further as one enters the tea room itself. The alcove no doubt contains a hanging scroll brushed in India ink.

From the kettle, escaping steam pervades the room with the sound of the wind whispering through the pines, and the fragrance of freshly lit incense suffuses the air. The space may be quite confined, and yet, seated there, one will perceive the attempt to create a different reality, a world unlike that outside. The room has been constructed of the simplest materials and is without ornamentation. The walls of unfinished plaster reveal the fiber used in their construction, and the wood of the pillars is rough-cut with its grain clearly visible. The window has an irregular shape and is scarcely more than a gap in the wall revealing the underlying material from which the room has been made. It is in any event hardly a luxurious dwelling. As far as possible it excludes whatever is mundane or extraneous and encloses a space no larger than it must be. Four and one-half tatami mats, about ten feet square, is the classic as the smallest practical size. Though its designers have made the room for the purpose of drinking tea, they have attempted to create a space that is a place apart from the ordinary. In other words, the tea room is the product of the attempt to create a venue for "an intellectual diversion in another world" in which one transcends the vulgar. This is why the *Nanpōroku* stipulates: "*Chanoyu* in a small room means first of all to practice the austerities of Buddhism. To enjoy a splendid dwelling or a meal with rare delicacies is a trivial pleasure. A house suffices if it does not leak; a meal, if it satisfies hunger."[4]

The Way of Tea has created a special culture that seeks to transcend the commonplace through the extremely common act of drinking tea. The practice of tea drinking, of course, is not limited to Japan. It can be found anywhere in the world. Nevertheless, only the Japanese have created that cultural tradition that we call the Way of Tea. How might one account for that singular development? Why have the Japanese alone made something so ordinary so very special? It is that the Japanese have tried to conceive an intellectual diversion in another world by designing gardens and building tea houses as places for the drinking of tea, by producing implements for serving it, and by having hosts and guests come together to take advantage of the materials so assembled. It is because the ordinary act of drinking tea, when it becomes *chanoyu*, comes to share with Buddhism the concepts of meditation. It is because a room, no matter how simple or cramped it may seem, when it becomes a tea room, comes to be a hall for Buddhist contemplation and is, therefore, more majestic than the most sumptuous palace of gold or jade. It is precisely for these reasons that Japan developed this culture of tea. The Japanese have given precedence above all else to the ideal that in taking a bowl of tea one flies free to this world apart. It is as if an extreme spiritualism or an intense idealism were the keynote. And it is for this reason that the tea garden and the tea house have assumed the form that they have.

How did this ideal of tea come to be? What lay behind it and contributed to the creation of its special world? For both Chinese and Japanese the source of it all was Lu Yu, the author of *The Classic of Tea,* whom both esteemed as their "tea ancestor." Several Chinese works clearly demonstrate how highly his countrymen venerated him. Li Zhao recorded in *Tang Guoshi Bu*[5] that the tea warehousemen in Jiangnan worshiped him as a god of tea. According to Zhao Lin writing in *Yinhualu,*[6] tea merchants used to set up ceramic statues of Lu Yu and pray for success in business by pouring tea over their statue's head in much the same way that modern Japanese anoint statues of the Buddha with sweet liquids on his birthday. A customer who purchased a large lot of tea utensils might expect to receive such a statue of the tea god as an extra gift. These works dated from the eighth and ninth centuries, and we know such practices continued, for Ouyang Xiu testified in *Jigulu* to their existence in the Northern Song era.[7]

In Japan as well Lu Yu enjoyed the highest esteem in the world of tea during the centuries down to the time of the creation of the Way of Tea by Rikyū. Eisai wrote of him in *Kissa Yōjōki.* In the early Muromachi era, too, *Isei Teikin Ōrai,* a copybook, noted: "The immortals sang the praises of tea, and humans enjoyed it as well. The custom [of tea drinking] did not exist until after the Han and Wei dynasties, [but] it became common during the Tang and Song eras, when it could command even a thousand pieces of gold." Whether there was no drinking of tea in the Han and Wei eras is open to question, and I shall touch upon that later, but certainly from the time of Lu Yu in the Tang, as the copybook said, tea did become popular. The copybook continues, "Tea nurtures purity and humility and allows one to join the realm of the immortals. Lu Yu and Lu Tong were [among] those who knew the virtues of tea."[8]

Lu Yu's reputation, therefore, extended to Japan as well as China. The spiritual world of tea in Japan, however, differed greatly from the world of tea that Lu Yu depicted in his *Classic.* The work of creating a systematic culture of tea fell to Rikyū, but behind him lay a long spiritual tradition that he was able to crystallize and shape. This book is about that process. We shall examine the origins of tea in China and follow tea drinking practices after they crossed over into Japan down to the time of Rikyū and the creation of the art of *chanoyu*. At each stage we shall consider relevant historical changes and the significance they held for the Way of Tea.

PART 1

The Classic of Tea

1 The Advent of Lu Yu and *The Classic of Tea*

Among the works on "tea," that which is regarded as both the oldest and the greatest is the *Chajing, The Classic of Tea*.[1] Lu Yu, its author, esteemed as the progenitor of the drinking of tea, was a Tang dynasty scholar-official of the eighth century also known as Lu Hongjian. Because of his seminal role, it is appropriate to begin a consideration of the history of tea with him. First, however, let us consider the earliest history of tea drinking in order to place Lu Yu into perspective.

The *Chajing* says, "Tea is a grand plant of the southern regions."[2] This simple statement leaves no doubt that Chinese had enjoyed tea before the time of Lu Yu. Despite considerable scholarly inquiry, there are many points still at issue with respect to the drinking of tea in China, but the accepted foundation myth of the country held that Emperor Shennong, the divine progenitor of agriculture and medicine, was the first to drink the beverage. *The Classic of Tea* may itself be the source of this account, for its seventh chapter relates, "Shennong's *Treatise on Food* said: Tea gives one vigor of body, contentment of mind, and determination of purpose."[3] In Japan as well, the *Wakan Chashi* of 1728 similarly notes that Shennong and the Duke of Zhou were among the earliest to use tea and indeed runs through a list of eminent Chinese from statesmen to Taoist mystics who had been among its drinkers.[4] A note says that "Shennong's *Treatise on Food* called the drink 'cha,' while *Erya* called it 'buds of the *jiaming* plant.' "[5] Let us, however, set these accounts aside and return to the statement that "tea is a grand plant of the southern regions."

In *Chakyō Shōsetsu* the Zen prelate Daiten cites the "grand plant of the southern regions" and then follows with a note that tea "emerged in the warm lands of the South."[6] Indeed, tropical areas such as India

Lu Yu (ca. 733–803), author of *The Classic of Tea*. Painting by Yamamoto Baiitsu (1783–1856). The artist portrays Lu Yu with a travel kit containing a tea pot, cups, water bottle, and fire fan. Photo reproduced from *All About Tea* (New York, 1935).

may be the original producers of tea. The tea that comes from the south-eastern part of the Chinese mainland, like that in Japan, has leaves that reach a maximum length of about seven centimeters and a width of about three centimeters. In central and southern China, however, conditions differ. Many plants from the southwestern area of Fujian province, Guangdong and Guangxi provinces, as well as the area from Guizhou, Sichuan, and Yunnan into northern Burma and eastern India have leaves as large as thirty centimeters long and fifteen centimeters wide, and one cannot distinguish at a glance whether they are tea or camellia bushes. There are theories that tea first emerged in areas such as these.[7] Thus, tea may have come from the state of Assam in India or from a coastal area near the island of Hainan.

In the final analysis, however, there is no way to tell whether tea was brought to China or whether it grew there naturally as a wild plant. It may well be that it did occur there, for the *Bencao Gangmu* claims that the mythical Shennong tasted hundreds of plants in a search for ones

COMPARISON OF TEA LEAVES

ISHIKAWA, JAPAN   TAIWAN   ASSAM, INDIA
mountains   BURMA   ASSAM, INDIA

cm
5
10
15
20
25

of medicinal value.[8] Of these some seven-tenths were poisonous, so he used tea as an antidote. It is also possible that tea came into China together with Buddhism as it moved eastward. In any event, the very first reference to tea in a historical source came in the Former Han dynasty (206 B.C.–A.D. 8), according to Aoki Masaru in *Chūka Chasho*.[9] The passage in question came from *Tongyue*, which appeared in 59 B.C. during the reign of Emperor Xuandi. "*Tongyue*" referred to a deed of purchase of a slave and was the title of a work of fiction by a scholar from Shu named Wang Bao.[10] It detailed the duties of a slave whom Wang Bao had purchased. The servant was to clean the house, wash dishes, purchase wine, draw water, prepare meals, and set the table. He was also to pull garlic from the garden, cut wood, prepare meat, make soup with tubers, make vinegared salad with fish, steam turtles, prepare tea, and go into the city to buy something called *tu*. We presume this referred to tea, because the Chinese character closely resembled that for tea and because previous research has suggested that it was synonymous with the character for tea prior to the Tang era.[11]

Though tea appears to have had a history of several hundred years before Lu Yu, there is not space here to explore it fully. It will suffice to say that the early history of tea contains many obscure points that cannot be resolved at this stage. It was, however, Lu Yu with his writing of the *Chajing* in the Tang dynasty that focused his world's attention on the benefits of the drinking of tea.

During the seventh and eighth centuries A.D., the Tang dynasty was at its most vigorous and China had reached a summit of cosmopolitanism and cultural florescence in its history. We know that by this time, even before Lu Yu's day, the practice of drinking tea had spread throughout north China, for there survives a passage titled "Drinking Tea" in the sixth volume of the *Fengshi Wenjianji*, which was compiled by a writer named Feng Yan who lived during the eighth century.

According to Feng Yan, tea that was picked early was called *cha*, whereas that picked late was called *ming*. These satisfied thirst and kept one awake. He wrote that people in the south had enjoyed this drink earlier and that at last during the Kaiyuan era (713–741) it spread to the north as well. He further explained that at that time there was a priest, Jiangmo, at the temple called Lingyansi in Taishan, Shandong, who was both a great teacher and a student of the Chan sect of Buddhism and tirelessly pursued its discipline. Furthermore, he took no evening meal and expected all the others similarly to refrain from eating. He permitted only tea in place of food. Each person carried his own supply and, wherever he went, prepared and drank the beverage. Still others imitated this practice until at last it became the general custom. Finally, he said, it spread from Zhouxian, Jinan, Huimin, and Hebei to the capital at Chang'an. Many shops opened in the city's markets, and there they made and sold the beverage while people of all classes paid to drink it. This tea came from Jianghuai by boat and cart and was piled in great mounds in the city, where several varieties were available at different prices.[12]

Thus, the custom of drinking tea was already widespread by the time Lu Yu appeared. It had originated in the south of China and then moved to the north thanks to the influence of Chan temples.

The man who was to be revered both as the author of the *Chajing, The Classic of Tea,* and as the god of tea was born just as the drinking of the beverage was achieving this peak of popularity. There are several accounts of his life. One is to be found in the biographical section for retired officials in the *Xintangshu*.[13] It says that Lu Yu, in addition to the name we use today, employed the various epithets of Hongjian, Ji, and Jibi and was a resident of Jingling in Fuzhou (modern Tianmen in Hubei province). The writers were unable to verify his antecedents. One theory they cited maintained that the Chan priest Zhiji of the Longgaisi Temple found him abandoned as an infant near the banks of a lake and brought him home to rear him. When he grew older, they used divining rods and consulted the *Classic of Changes* (*Yijing*) to select a suitable personal name. The rods led them to the passage "The great goose moves steadily toward land. Its wings are to be used for ceremonies." From this, he adopted Lu (Land) as a surname and Yu (Wing) as a given name. His epithet of Hongjian derives from the same passage and means "great bird or goose, steadily."

Other sources contain similar accounts. One, the biography of Lu Yu in *Wenyuan Yinghua,* says essentially the same thing about his being found and raised by a priest as well as about the source of his name, though it reverses his name and epithet.[14] Moreover, it says that he was not a handsome man and was a prolix, nervous talker despite a stammer. Another, his biography in *Tang Caizizhuan,* which Xin Wenxiu compiled in the Yuan era, repeats the story of his origins and gives substantially the same account of his name.[15]

The *Xintangshu* supplies further information about Lu Yu's life as well. It tells of the discipline that he experienced under his teachers when he was young. At one point when the teacher became angry, he forced Lu Yu to clean the toilets. As a boy he also struggled to learn to read and write. Charged with the care of thirty cows, he practiced writing characters on their backs with bamboo. He sat among other children and read aloud but was dismayed at his inability to read poems by Zhang Heng when he received them. His dissatisfaction with his scholarly skills reduced him to tears. The history says he had a melancholy disposition and went for days without working, but he had friends since people could relax around him. It also says that he joined a theatrical troupe and wrote burlesques. During the 740s he became a government official in Fuzhou and made the acquaintance of another official named Li Qi. This work even gives quite an intimate depiction of his appearance and claims that he cut rather a sorry figure. It repeats the description that he was quite garrulous despite his stammer. In about 760 he retired and took the name Sang Ningweng. His death occurred in about 804, during the reign of Dezong, which corresponds, coincidentally, to that of Emperor Kammu in Japan.

Finally, the *Xintangshu* comes to Lu Yu's connection with tea. It says that he came to enjoy the drink on a regular basis and finally wrote the *Chajing*, which contained three parts: the origin, cultivation, and tools for tea. This work contributed in turn to a general knowledge of tea and its diffusion throughout the country. The shops that sold it at the time made ceramic statues of Lu Yu and worshiped him as the god of tea. The *Xintangshu* continues that there was at that time a man named Chang Boxiong, who relied on Lu Yu's work to explain the advantages of tea. An official, Li Ji, on his way to Jiangnan as an imperial emissary, came to Linhuai, where he learned that Boxiong was famed for his tea. Li Ji summoned him to his presence. When he finally reached Jiangnan, people recommended Lu Yu to him also, and so he summoned him as well, but there was immediate discord between them. When Lu Yu appeared with his tea utensils, he was wearing his everyday clothing. Li for his part failed to thank Lu Yu, so the latter was offended and decided to write another work called *Huichalun*, "On Destroying Tea." Thereafter, the history continues, the practice of enjoying tea spread more and more until finally even the Turkic peoples of the west came into China for the first time to trade horses for tea.[16]

The biography of Lu Yu in *Wenyuan Yinghua*, mentioned above, writes further of Lu Yu's personality. It claims that though he was kind to those whom he admired, he could also be quite frank in pointing out people's faults. Naturally, many did not appreciate that and avoided him. Finally, the account lists the titles of the works that Lu Yu wrote. On his associations it comments that Lu Yu had a friendship with Shi Jiaoran of Wuxing, an older man who was a priest. Their relationship was so deep, it says, that any difference in their ages was forgotten.[17] In 756 the latter wrote of his friend and also composed several poems for the tea sage. One, headed "Poem to Lu Yu on Drinking Tea with Him," had these lines:

> Ninth day at a temple in the mountains,
> By a hedge on the east, yellow chrysanthemums in bloom.
> Ordinary people drink too much wine.
> Which of them know how fragrant tea could help?[18]

Yan Zhen, an official in Hubei, specially built a pavilion for Lu Yu at the Miaoxisi Temple in Shushan, where Shi Jiaoran resided.[19] This poem no doubt recalled the times they spent drinking tea there together. Another by Jiaoran, with the title "On Visiting Lu Yu and Finding Him Away," went like this:

> Though you've moved to a place all enclosed,
> The road in is wild with mulberries and hemp along the way.
> Close by it is a chrysanthemum hedge,
> But since it's still not autumn, no blooms can be seen.
> When I pounded the gate, not even a dog's bark answered.
> I wanted to leave but asked at the house on the west.
> They said that you were away in the mountains
> And returned each day as the sun sank low in the sky.[20]

This poem clearly evokes the image of Lu Yu's life in seclusion, for it seems to describe a visit to his retirement hermitage. The scene is one of rustic tranquillity.

Let us now return to the biography of Lu Yu from the *Xintangshu*. It indicates that he had an early fondness for letters and that allegories particularly attracted him. His works such as *Sibeishi* or *Tian Zhi Weimingfu* brought tears to everyone's eyes. In addition to the three volumes of the *Chajing,* his works included one on the bond between prince and retainer in three volumes, a thirty-volume work on the analysis of the origins of various things, many volumes of historical biographies of officials and the Four Families in South China, and a three-volume work on divination with dreams.[21] Inasmuch as this account of his scholarly output appeared in 761, some forty-three years before his death, later writers must have supplemented the list of his works. It is difficult to imagine that he would have been able to complete that corpus so early.

According to the *Fengshi Wenjianji,* Lu Yu wrote a treatise on tea in which he explained its efficacy as a beverage, how to roast and prepare it, the twenty-four tools needed to cultivate it, and how to store it. It went on to say that Chang Boxiong supplemented the work and disseminated it widely, thereby establishing in basic outline the way of tea so that there was no one among the most illustrious in the land who did not partake of the beverage. In other words, this work gives credit to Lu Yu and Chang Boxiong for the widespread popularity of tea.[22] Another work, *Taiping Guangji,* in a section on Tang miscellany, records that Lu Yu had become the god of tea for his writing of the *Chajing* and that merchants made statues of him that they worshiped in the hope that there would be a generous supply of tea and that it would sell well. It notes that when their tea did not sell, it was their custom to pour boiling water from the kettle over the statue.[23]

The accounts of Lu Yu are similar, even his so-called autobiography. We can summarize his legend in this way:

1. His origins and genealogy are unclear; he was an individual without the normal family and social connections.
2. He was physically unattractive and had a stammer. Yet he possessed a talent for speech and a strong character given to speculative thought.
3. He suffered from a sort of mania, had a reclusive nature, and buried himself in his books. He disliked detail and the company of most people.
4. His associates were poets and men of letters so that he was always surrounded by high-minded gentlemen.

5. He had a tendency to transcend the mundane and to take pride in isolation.
6. The date and place of his death are unclear.

In sum, perhaps all we can say with certainty is that he was a man of noble character who lived a carefree life withdrawn from the world. One of his poems, "Liu Xian Ge," reflects this quality.

> I covet not a golden vessel
> Nor yet a cup of white jade.
> I covet not admission to court
> Nor yet the life of grand minister.
> All I covet is West River's water
> As it flows below Jingling.[24]

This poem appeared in *Tang Guoshi Bu*, compiled by Li Zhao, as well as in the Tang section of the *Taiping Guangji*. Lu Yu had abandoned mundane ambitions like so much rubble. He paid no heed to worldly desires save only to enjoy the waters of the West River that flowed below the town of Jingling. No doubt for Lu Yu, living as he did in detached leisure, tea was his greatest companion, and water, the essential ingredient for brewing it, was the one desire that he still cherished.

Regarding the preparation of tea, the *Fengshi Wenjianji* referred to "preparing and selling tea" and to "roasting tea," while the Lu Yu biography from the Tang history spoke of "boiling tea." What did they mean? According to Morooka Tamotsu, the way people drank tea in Lu Yu's day in the area from Hubei to Sichuan was very much like the preparation of "*yamacha*" (mountain tea), which is found in the mountains of Shikoku in Japan today. This is a primitive method of parching fresh tea leaves, immersing them in hot water, and then drinking the resulting infusion. Another method widely used in Lu Yu's era was "*baifei cha*," and this, too, can still be found among Japanese farm families. It involved repeated immersion of the leaves of the tea plant in boiling hot water before drinking it.[25]

Aoki Masaru has argued that it is sensible to conclude that these methods of boiling unprocessed tea leaves are primitive and therefore probably preceded the processing and grinding of tea leaves, as is done in *chanoyu* today. As evidence he cites the note on tea in the tree section of *Erya* by Guo Pu. It says: "The tree is a shrub that resembles a gardenia. It bears leaves in winter. These may be boiled to make a broth to drink. The early leaves are called '*cha*' (tea); the later ones, called '*ming.*' Some call it '*shun*'; people in Sichuan call it 'bitter tea.'" Thus it was treated much like a sort of simple vegetable soup. The method of powdering the tea can be seen at the end of the Western Jin era in *Shunfu* by Du Yu, which referred to making tea in such a way that grounds sank to the bottom while foam rose to the top. This appears to be powdered tea, like that of modern Japanese *chanoyu*.[26]

Lu Yu's biography in the Tang history recounts that his *Chajing* was written early in the Shangyuan era. That corresponds to the Tenpyō Hōji era (757–765) and the reign of Emperor Junnin (758–764) in Japan. The work comprised ten sections in three volumes as follows:

> *Volume 1*
> > *Section 1. Origins of tea*
> > *Section 2. Tools for cultivating tea*
> > *Section 3. Methods of cultivating tea*
>
> *Volume 2*
> > *Section 4. Tea vessels*
>
> *Volume 3*
> > *Section 5. Preparation of tea*
> > *Section 6. How to drink tea*
> > *Section 7. Facts about tea*
> > *Section 8. Areas that produce tea*
> > *Section 9. Simplified manners for drinking tea*
> > *Section 10. Illustrations of tea*

The first section said, "Tea is a grand plant of the southern regions." It continued that the plant grew to a height of one to two feet and in some cases to several tens of feet. In the mountains and river gorges of Sichuan, some plants were of such girth that it would take two people to join arms around one tree, which had to be felled for plucking. The trunk, Lu Yu said, resembled a gourd vine while the leaves were similar to those of a gardenia and had the fragrance of cloves. The seeds were analogous to those of the coir palm and the roots, to those of the walnut. The tea flower was "like that of the wild rose turned white."[27]

As for the character with which the Chinese wrote "tea," Lu Yu indicated that sometimes it was written with the grass radical, sometimes with the tree radical, and sometimes with both. The *Kaiyuan Wenzi Yinyi* had it with the first, the *Bencao*, with the tree only, and the *Erya* with both. In addition to the conventional pronunciation, *cha*, there were the pronunciations *jia*, *she*, *ming*, and *shun*.[28]

The *Classic* then turned to those conditions that the plant needed to grow well and the best time to harvest it. The best soil, it said, was slightly stony, while rich, graveled soil was second best. Yellow clay, though common in China, was unsuitable, since the plant would not bear fruit. The farmer might plant and transplant it as he would the melon, but he should wait until the plant's third year before harvesting it. Lu Yu claimed that wild tea excelled garden tea, and no matter whether it grew on the better, sunny slopes or in the shade, russet leaves were better than green ones. The youngest, most tender shoots were better than buds, and tightly curled leaves, the most preferable. Open, unrolled leaves were merely acceptable. But tea grown in a valley without sun would not be worth the effort of picking.[29] He continued with a discussion of the efficacy of tea.

> Tea is of a cold nature and may be used in case of blockage or stoppage of the bowels. When its flavor is at its coldest nature, it is most suitable as a drink. If one is generally moderate but is feeling hot or warm, given to melancholia, suffering from aching of the brain, smarting of the eyes, troubled in the four limbs, or afflicted in the hundred joints, he may take tea four or five times. Its liquor is like the sweetest dew of Heaven.
>
> One must guard against plucking tea out of season, manufacturing that does not catch its essence, or adulterating it with other plants or herbs. Drinking tea under those conditions can only lead to illness.
>
> The injurious properties of tea are not unlike those of ginseng. We know that the best ginseng is produced in Shangtang, the medium grades in Boqi or Xinluo, while the poorest varieties also come from Korea. Ginseng from Zezhou, Yizhou, Youzhou, or Tanzhou prefectures is without merit as a medicine. Even worse, if the plants from those regions are not, in fact,

ginseng but something like ladybell, they can lead to the six illnesses with no restorative virtue at all. Our knowledge of the
injurious capabilities of ginseng instructs us concerning similar
ones in tea.[30]

Thus Lu Yu extolled tea's virtues. When one was out of sorts, its
flavor would be the sweetest, most splendid known to humankind.[31] If
picked at the wrong time or processed in the wrong way, however, it
could lead to illness. In referring to tea as "a grand plant from the southern regions," he no doubt meant the southern part of China, and in calling it a "grand plant" he had in mind its effects as a beverage as well as
its splendid taste, in no way inferior to the dews of Heaven. In general,
moreover, he stressed its medicinal efficacy.

In the second section, dealing with tools, Lu Yu took up each of
the devices used to produce tea. These included

ying	a basket woven of bamboo and carried on the back by tea pickers
zao	a furnace, which need not be very deep; its kettle should have a mouth with a lip
zeng	a steaming basket
chujiu	a mortar and pestle, also called a *dui*
gui	also called *mo* and *juan*, a mold made of iron
cheng	also called *tai* and *zhen*, a kind of stand or holder

Next came the explanation of the *yan:* "a cover made of oiled silk, rain-
wear, or a piece of worn-out apparel." "To make the tea, place the cover
over the holder and then place the shaper over the cover. After the tea
has set, it can be moved by lifting up the cloth cover."[32] Priest Daiten's
Chakyō Shōsetsu calls tea of this sort, brick tea.[33] In other words, Lu Yu's
description of tea processing all referred to the making of tea bricks,
which were steamed and then dried into cakes or bricks for storage. The
list of tools continued:

bili	a screen woven of bamboo like a gardener's earth sifter; used for grading and drying the tea
qi	also called *zhui*, an awl for making holes in tea bricks
pu	also called *bian*, a bamboo whip run through the holes in the tea bricks to separate them

Brick tea. Relatively modern example from China, impressed with the maker's name, location, and trademark. Brick tea is produced in a wide range of forms and grades. In contrast to the firmly molded and well-dried example in this photograph, there are others that are coarse and irregularly shaped.

bei	a tea dryer
guan	bamboo stringers placed through the tea bricks before drying them in the *bei*
peng	a wooden device placed over the dryer to dry the tea
chuan	a type of skewer
yu	a kind of basket used for storage[34]

Thus did Lu Yu describe in this second section all of the tools needed for the processing of tea.

The third section took up the tea processing itself. Lu Yu began with the season for plucking the leaves. He indicated that tea was normally picked in the second through fourth months and that one should set out for picking while the morning dew was still on the leaves. He also noted, "Do not pick on the day that has seen rain or when clouds spoil the sky. Pick tea only on a clear day. All there is to making tea is to pick it, steam it, pound it, shape it, dry it, tie it, and seal it."[35] Dry, cloudless days were best for the steaming, shaping, and drying as well. He continued with a description of the forms that tea could take:

> Tea has a myriad of shapes. If I may speak vulgarly and rashly, tea may shrink and crinkle like a Mongol's boots. Or it may look like the dewlap of a wild ox, some sharp, some curling as the eaves of a house. It can look like a mushroom in whirling flight just as clouds do when they float out from behind a mountain peak. Its leaves can swell and leap as if they were being lightly tossed on wind-disturbed water. Others will look like clay, soft and malleable, prepared for the hand of the potter and will be as clear and pure as if filtered through wood. Still others will twist and turn like the rivulets carved out by a violent rain in newly tilled fields. Those are the very finest of teas.[36]

He also described those that were not so desirable:

> But there are also teas like the husk of bamboo, hard of stem and too firm to steam or beat. They assume the shape of a sieve.

Then there are those that are like the lotus after frost. Their stem and leaves become sere and limp, their appearance so altered that they look like piled-up rubble. Such teas are old and barren of worth.[37]

Thus, he explained that there were seven steps from picking to sealing and eight types of shapes.[38] He concluded the section, however, by writing, "Discrimination between good and bad tea is a matter for secret oral transmission."[39] Why did he choose to make so striking an assertion about discriminating the quality of tea?

Though it is true that Lu Yu moved in the highly cultivated literary circles of his day, the appearance of such a statement in what is essentially a discourse on plant and soil science is nonetheless remarkable. What I mean is that, though tea may have been only a beverage for him, the life that he experienced in partaking of it and the world to which that life opened his eyes perhaps inevitably brought him to such an affirmation.

Nunome Chōfū comments on the statement "Discrimination between good and bad tea is a matter for secret oral transmission" in a note to the *Chajing* in *Chadō Koten Zenshū*. He writes, "This statement appears rather abruptly and may have been inserted into the text by a later redactor."[40] Perhaps his doubts are justified, but, leaving them aside for the moment, in light of Lu Yu's earlier manner of expression and the world of tea that he depicted, one must conclude that he believed that the ability to discern the quality of tea was not a talent that just anyone had, but was rather a natural endowment that only a chosen few enjoyed. The assertion that discrimination of tea quality is a matter for secret oral transmission seems natural for Lu Yu to have made. He explained how to differentiate among tea types with an almost pathological precision, and he did so in order to be able to make clear how to appreciate the true taste of tea. His approach was wholly different from that of a tea manufacturer. The tone throughout is a literary one, and it shows Lu Yu's true attitude.

Huang Furan, a close friend of Lu Yu, wrote the following poem in which he envisioned the writer picking tea.

> The thousand peaks await the hermit.
> Fragrant tea is growing luxuriantly.
> Lost in the act of plucking leaves,

> Alone in the mist, you are to be envied.
> Is that a mountain temple I see?
> Dining at a pure spring amid the rocks.
> Tranquilly smoke rises from a fire.
> I imagine the sound of music.[41]

The world of tea that Lu Yu enjoyed was of such beauty in the eyes of his companion that it produced this poetic expression and indeed gave one a vision of a transcendent world apart. But not only did it portray Lu Yu plucking tea; it was something more. The act of picking tea itself produced a mode of expression that made it essentially different from other ordinary acts. In a further poem titled "To Lu Yu as He Goes to Yueh," Huang Furan recalled seeing Lu Yu off on a journey.

> The farther you go, the deeper into the forest.
> River after river, traveling into a dream.
> Your course like a leaf in the breeze,
> Night turns the river islet a darker shade of green.[42]

The poem graphically depicts Lu Yu as he journeyed through the mountains buoyantly enjoying nature. Continuing his tramp, he searched for places with tea like one possessed. This makes it clear that, in terms of its underlying spiritual foundation, the *Chajing* was no mere disquisition on areas of production of tea, ways to discriminate among types of tea, or how to process it. It was far more. Lu Yu's intention was to depict directly the world that one might ultimately attain by drinking tea, avoiding the pitfall of simple explanation, and by discussing correct ways to drink it ultimately to draw the reader into that world.

One can see the hopes and aspirations he had for his work in the title he so boldly gave it. The second character, the *jing* of *Chajing,* meaning "classic," suggested his confidence that the work held a special significance.

The fourth section took up the twenty-four types of utensils needed for brewing tea. It is extremely difficult today to reproduce precisely the utensils used at that time. We can, nevertheless, perceive the underlying spiritual tone that runs through Lu Yu's description of them. The discussion of the brazier for boiling the tea provides an illustrative example. He advised that the brazier be made of brass or iron and shaped like an ancient *ding,* a vessel with three legs. His own brazier had traditional script adorning each leg, with one signifying the trigrams for water (*kan*), wind (*xun*), and fire (*li*). These were in their appropriate positions with water above, the wind for the draught below, and the fire in the center. A second leg gave the date of casting as the year after the Tang armies defeated the Mongols, and the last indicated that one could avoid disease by keeping the five elements of traditional Chinese scientific thought in proper balance. Between the legs there were three windows and another at the bottom, for the draught and for removal of ashes.[43] The trigrams signifying water, wind, and fire cast into the brazier, and the references to the harmonizing of the five elements and the avoiding of disease are noteworthy, for they demonstrate that Lu Yu's brazier had been cast in conformity with the prevailing Chinese world view that was based on the traditional concept of changes, as in the *Classic of Changes*, the *Yijing*, for example. Naturally, water, wind, and fire were essential for the brewing of tea, and these inscriptions conveyed the sense that, precisely because they were so necessary, one must pray for them from the depths of the heart. For Lu Yu the five elements of Buddhist thought, earth, water, fire, wind, and sky (the void), plus the five Chinese elements of wood, fire, earth, metal, and water melded together into a unitary whole. He believed that drinking tea provided quotidian benefit, for in doing so one balanced the elements to make the body healthy and thereby avoided the myriad illnesses. Also, in addition to the ancient script by the three windows for the draught and for the removal of ashes, there were three patterns drawn into the ash inside the brazier.

He went on to write that over each of the windows there were two more characters in ancient script. The six taken together evidently meant, "What Prince Yi was to cuisine, Lu is to tea." Finally, he wrote that there was a pattern in each window. The first was a pheasant, which represented fire. Its trigram, called *li*, consisted of three lines, unbroken, broken, and unbroken, to symbolize *yang, yin,* and *yang*. The second was a small tiger to denote the wind with its trigram, *xun*, with lines of *yang, yang,* and *yin*. The last was a fish, a water creature, with its trigram of *kan*, with *yin, yang,* and *yin*. Lu Yu explained that the reason for having the three trigrams was that wind could cause the fire to blaze so that it could boil the water. Finally, he said, he had geometric designs, linked flowers, vines, and streams. Though most braziers were made of iron, they might be ceramic as well. The ash receptacle stood on a tripod with an iron handle.[44]

This adornment allows one to see clearly Lu Yu's attitude as he prepared tea. He was not merely brewing a beverage for drinking, for in making the tea there was a spiritual dimension. As he boiled the water, he invoked the spirits that controlled the wind and those that controlled the fire and water. The tea itself became a kind of offering. This attitude demonstrates, therefore, that in terms of his underlying approach to tea, Lu Yu was determined to plumb to the heart of nature in each cup.

The poet Lu Tong, often thought of as a man of tea together with Lu Yu, expressed the ultimate of the world of tea in this way:

> The first cup fully moistens lips and throat.
> The second cup banishes isolation.
> The third cup makes one sharp and ready to read five
> thousand scrolls.
> The fourth cup brings a light sweat that draws complaints
> from the pores.
> The fifth cup cleanses to the bone.
> The sixth cup makes one commune with the immortals.
> The seventh cup would be too much.
> Refreshing breezes embrace my body.[45]

He skillfully depicts the spiritual transition that occurred as one took first one cup of tea and then another. One swept away the cares of the world, escaped to enjoy a realm of the spirits, and banished the burdens of reality. At last, after six or seven cups, one achieved a transcendental, dreamlike state of perfect concentration. One moved up to a world of dreams and spirits reinvigorated by fresh breezes in which the distinction between self and others disappeared. One can interpret this as the realm of the immortals, which the Chinese have sought since ancient times. It is plain to see that drinking tea was not something that they pursued only for its medicinal effect.

Accordingly, Lu Yu was quite thorough in his description of tea utensils.

ju	woven of bamboo and wisteria vine; a charcoal container
tanzhua	a charcoal splitter shaped like a mallet or an ax
huojia	fire chopsticks, also called *jin*
fu	a kettle

jiaochuang	a wooden stand for the kettle made in the shape of a cross
jia	pincers of green bamboo for use in roasting the tea
zhinang	a paper sack for storing roasted tea to seal in its fragrance
nian	a tea mortar
luo and *he*	sieve and lidded container
ze	a tea scoop
shuifang	a water supply jar
lusuinang	a common water filter
piao	a water ladle
zhujia	bamboo chopsticks
cuogui	saltcellar (from this we see that they salted the brick tea)
shuyu	cooling basin for boiled water [46]

After describing each of these utensils in turn, he came to the tea bowl itself, and his description reached its most vivid level.

Some say Yuezhou ware is best. Dingzhou ware is next best. After that come the bowls of Wuzhou, [a second] Yuezhou, Shouzhou, and Hongzhou. There are those who argue that the bowls of Xingzhou are superior to Yue ware. That is not at all the case. It is proper to say that if Xing ware is silver, then Yue ware is jade. Or if the bowls of Xingzhou are snow, then those of Yue are ice. Xing ware, being white, gives a cinnabar cast to the tea. Yue ware, having a greenish hue, enhances the true color of tea. That is yet a third way to describe Yuezhou's superiority to Xingzhou in the way of tea bowls. In his poem on tea, Du Yu speaks of the équipage and of a moistly glossy bowl that originated in the East. The bowl was Yue ware. Hence for him Yuezhou made the best of bowls. The lip does not curl over, but the base is round and shallow and will hold fewer than eight ounces. Stoneware from both of the Yuezhous is of a blue-green shade. Being so it intensifies and emphasizes the color of the tea. If the tea is of a light red color, it will appear as red in the white bowls of Xingzhou. If the tea is red, it will look a rusty brown in Shouzhou bowls, they being of a yellow glaze. Because Hongzhou ware is brown, the tea will look black. All of those are unworthy of tea.[47]

Just as jade excelled silver and ice surpassed snow, so Yue bowls surpassed all others. Indeed, the kilns of Yuezhou had produced numerous noted works since ancient times, but it was not merely for their high artistic value that Lu Yu praised them. Lu Yu was hardly interested in their artistry alone; the reason he esteemed them was for their merit as vessels for the drinking of tea. First, the color of the utensil had to harmonize with the color of the tea that was poured into it. If the bowl was too white, the tea would appear washed out and would not look right. He said that tea must look green, so the greenish cast of Yue ware was perfect. Decisive in the suitability of a tea bowl were its shape and color, for these needed to enhance the appreciation of the tea that was in it. The appreciation of the artistic value of a utensil was far from his mind. Lu Yu said the best utensils, the best ceramics, came from eastern Ou. Moreover, the best kiln in Yuezhou was in Ou. The lips of its bowls did not curl, and their bottoms were round and shallow so that it was easy to drink tea from them. These were the factors that influenced his judgment as to their quality. Note that this was completely different from the considerations of artistic merit that caused Japanese of later ages to value tea utensils.

He continued his survey of utensils, showing their appearance and how to make and use them for tea.

ben	a basket that would hold up to ten cups
zha	a brush made from a tubular bundle of cut bamboo, like a large writing brush
difang	a container for waste water
zifang	a container for tea dregs
jin	a napkin for cleaning the utensils
julie	a rack for organizing the utensils
dulan	a carrier for the tea set[48]

With this explanation of the utensils completed, Lu Yu reached the end of the second volume of his work. He then turned to the brewing and drinking of tea and set forth detailed requirements for the fire and its fuel as well as for the water.

He wrote that in roasting the tea brick it was essential not to place it so the wind would blow the fire toward the tea too strongly. One should frequently turn the tea while holding it near the fire.[49] About fuel he wrote that charcoal was best but that very hard wood might suffice. He enjoined his readers, however, to avoid charcoal that had been used once already, since it was likely to have a musty or greasy odor. For the same reason oily wood or old, used utensils would make unsuitable fuel. Finally, he advised that the ancients approved of the use of well-cured wood for the brewing of tea.[50]

As for the water used to brew the tea, he preferred that from the mountains but would accept river water, while he advised avoiding water from wells. Of mountain water, that rippling gently among the rocks made the finest tea, while turbulent, rushing water should not be used. He also ingenuously explained that it was best not to drink water that flowed from the mountains and sank into the ground without finding an outlet, for from the seventh through the ninth months there might be harmful poisons that have emanated from dragons there. If you must use such water, he said, first let it flow for a while and drain a good bit off before drawing from it. He also advised that when using river water it should be drawn far from human habitation and that one should use well water only after first drawing a large quantity of it.[51] In this way, Lu Yu was quite strict and detailed in his advice: "Use mountain water in preference to river water and river water in preference to well water." "Don't use water from the mountains if it is too turbulent or if it is stagnant." It was his ideal to use only the finest water if at all possible. Moreover, he did not accept that just any sort of fuel would be permissible so long as the water was right. One should never burn rotted, discarded materials to make tea or use wood with a disagreeable odor. People in olden days, he wrote, had a proverb that showed they despised such fuel for its foul taste. Charcoal was best. Lu Yu set as an absolute condition that one would employ only the finest water over the purest fire.

Next he took up the right way to boil the water, which he called the first, second, and third boil. What he called the first boil was a temperature that produced small bubbles and a faint sound, which he described as "like the eyes of fishes and with a distant voice." The second boil produced "a bubbling spring around the edges like a string of pearls." The third was like "the crashing of breakers upon the shore." Boiling it more than that would exhaust the water and make it undrinkable. Throughout, his mode of expression was rich in simile, while his attention to detail was minute. He further noted that one could add salt to taste during the first boil. At the second stage one should withdraw a ladle of water, set it aside, and then stir the center with bamboo chopsticks. At this point one put powdered tea into the center. When it started to boil again, after a time one could return the water one had set aside and reduce the boiling once more. In this way one would "nurture the flower" of the tea.[52]

Next one took it into the tea bowl, and this was terribly important. For this moment he reserved his most elegant figures of speech, relying on poetry to describe the effect. He likened it to the white of the blossom of the Chinese date floating on a pond, to the green of new grasses freshly growing in a marsh or by the shore, to scaly clouds adrift in a blue sky. He described it as the moss floating by the bank or the chrysanthemum froth on a cask of wine. Its luster was like drifting snow.[53]

At last he came to the drinking of the tea itself, and here he was no less attentive to detail than he had been earlier. One did not simply sample the taste of the tea. One had to savor it deeply in order to appreciate it properly. He dealt in detail with the number of times one drank, with the temperature of the tea, and with the speed with which one drank it. He also described the flavor of tea as like that of the elixir of the immortals. He mentioned that one should remove and set aside a scoop of water for use later in settling the boil and explained how the turbidity of the brew affected the froth that adorned its surface like a flower. The flavor of true tea, he said, is such that sipping it brings out its bitter quality, while swallowing it brings out the sweet.[54]

Proceeding to the sixth section, Lu Yu discussed the drinking of tea while at the same time recounting those historical figures who had enjoyed it, beginning with Emperor Shennong, whom he seems not to have considered mythical. The list includes the Duke of Zhou as well as other, similarly illustrious statesmen, including his own ancestor Lu Na. All, he said, drank tea. Shennong, as we have seen, was one of the three mythical emperors, the one whom the Chinese had worshiped since ancient times as a deity of medicine and agriculture. The others were all famed individuals from China's past.[55] By Lu Yu's own day there was hardly a household that did not take the beverage, and it had spread throughout the country from the capitals of Chang'an and Luoyang to all provinces north and south.

The types of tea in popular use took a variety of forms. There was *cucha*, which was a coarse tea made by chopping the leaves. *Sancha* was a loose leaf tea roasted over a fire, while *mocha* was roasted beside a fire and then ground in a mortar. *Bingcha* was tea that was pressed into a round cake. Finally, *ancha* was tea pressed into the bottom of a bottle into which hot water could be poured when ready to use. Sometimes people added other things to the tea, such as onion, root ginger or ginger sprouts, orange peel, or peppermint. These might be used roasted for a glossy effect or they might be boiled together with the tea, then removed and the foam skimmed and discarded. Despite their popularity, however, Lu Yu declared that such teas were fit only to be tossed into a gutter or a ditch.

Indeed, Lu Yu deplored the vulgarization of tea that had accompanied its popularity. He wrote: "In the ten thousand objects that nature nourishes, there is supreme perfection. It is only for ease and comfort that man works at things."[56] The implication was an indictment of the shallowness of human acts in which people ruined the Heaven-sent flavor of tea by adding all sorts of extraneous, old seasonings. One seems to catch a glimpse of Lu Yu's moral world view, which made him juxtapose the perfection of Heaven with the vulgarity of a humanity who lacked even a rudimentary understanding of that perfection.

To be able to attain such perfection without contrivance was not at all an easy matter. It was, in fact, extremely difficult, as he showed by listing nine problems to be overcome in dealing with tea. First, he said, one must manufacture the tea. Next one must sharpen one's powers of discrimination among tea types. Then, there were the problems of securing the correct implements, building the right kind of fire, and selecting the right water. Next one must roast the tea properly, grind it well, and brew it perfectly. Finally, one must drink the tea.[57] In other words, picking the tea on a cloudy day and drying it at night were not the right way to manufacture tea. Nibbling it or sniffing it was not the true way to appreciate its flavor. It was wrong to put the tea in a foul-smelling kettle or bowl. To roast or brew the tea over a fire made with resinous wood or old kitchen charcoal was hardly suitable. One must not draw water from a source that was either turbulent or stagnant. To roast the tea on the outside while leaving the inside wet and raw was not the right way. Grinding the tea until it was a bright blue powder was wrong. It was a mistake to brew it by rushing the stirring along. Drinking copiously in summer while abstaining in winter was a poor way to drink tea.[58]

Finally, it is noteworthy that Lu Yu wrote that one should take only three cups of tea when the brew is freshest and its flavor most outstanding. As many as five cups were permissible when the quality was somewhat less. That is, the rarer the flavor, the less one should drink in order to appreciate its quality.

In the seventh section he repeated his list of famous tea drinkers in greater detail. He also provided an extensive list of classical writings and evaluated their merits and utility.

Beginning with Emperor Shennong as the representative of the legendary age of the three emperors, Lu Yu traced the drinkers of tea era by era down to Xu Ji in his own Tang dynasty, while at the same time skillfully weaving classical references into his text. There were altogether forty-eight such items, of three general types: (1) those relating to production areas, (2) those relating to utility, and (3) those relating to myth and legend.

He related the accounts of the famous tea drinkers to one or another of his previous entries, and he was quite detailed in providing names of areas of production, terms used for tea types, as well as the benefits of tea drinking, but the most important items related to how one should partake of tea itself.[59]

First, he explained the manufacture and drinking of brick tea. The *Guangya* explained that in the area between Jing and Ba provinces, people picked tea leaves and formed them into cakes.[60] Old leaves were insufficiently sticky, so they added hot water from rice for starch to make the cakes. When they were ready to drink the tea, they roasted it until it turned red. Then they pounded and ground it before putting it into a porcelain container, adding hot water, and covering it with a lid. Moreover, they would finely chop onion, fresh ginger, or orange peel and add it to the brew. When one drank this tea, it cleared the head from the effects of wine and staved off sleep.[61] Note that this was the sort of cake tea that Lu Yu described above, whose method of manufacture he deplored as producing tea fit only to pour into a ditch.

One of the noteworthy aspects of this section is that it contains quite a few tales involving tea. From Fu Xian's *Sili Jiao* there is the story that in the south a woman from Sichuan who was in reduced circumstances was selling a kind of tea gruel in the market. The official in charge of the area, however, destroyed her utensils, so she resorted to selling cakes of tea. What did the official think the woman would do when he forbade her sales of gruel?[62] Stories like this give a sense of social conditions as they related to tea at that time.

There is also this poem on "Charming Ladies" by Zuo Si.

> In my house is a charming lady,
> Her face, the whitest of white.

So fair we call her Fine Silk.
Each feature, her mouth, her teeth, so pure.
She has an elder sister, Fragrant Grace,
With fine-carved eyes and brow, like a picture.
They fly about field and forest,
Finding fruit, ripe to pluck,
Searching for flowers in the wind and rain.
Suddenly they grow impatient and race back.
Wanting to drink tea, they quickly return.
To sit before the kettle and blow to fan the flames.[63]

The poem describes two beautiful women who love tea. When they think of it, no matter how far away they are, they hurry back to the tea room and frantically try to speed the boiling of the water.

Lu Yu also cited a legend from *Yiyuan*. There was a young widow with two young children who enjoyed tea. Each time they drank it, they first offered some at old burial mounds that were near the house. The children finally became annoyed at this practice and were about to destroy the graves. The mother, however, remonstrated with them and dissuaded them from doing so. The same night someone came to her in a dream to express thanks for the delicious tea that had been offered and then disappeared. When the mother awoke the next morning, she discovered one hundred thousand copper cash in her garden.[64]

The above three episodes allow us to perceive that, although tea was in reality nothing more than a simple beverage, it carried one to a world of fantasy far removed from the commonplace. The tea that slaked thirst and delighted the palate wafted one to a realm of suprareality that far transcended those ordinary senses. The image of beautiful women dallying merrily in a flower garden and busily preparing tea shows the same dreamlike quality. Perhaps one might view it as using tea to create such a world. The tea that the widow offered day by day at the graves outside her home brought her as thanks a gift of a hundred thousand cash, but it was not in expectation of that reward that she made her offering. The desire for tea itself produced her behavior, enacted through the spirits represented by the graves, and her reward was an inevitable result.

Now what shall we make of this next legend? It seems there was an old woman who sold tea in the marketplace, and people competed among themselves to buy from her. No matter how much she sold, however, the quantity of tea in her basket did not diminish in the least. All the money she earned, moreover, she shared with orphans and beggars in the streets. The magistrate had her arrested and confined her to prison, but to everyone's consternation she disappeared from the jail flying out on her tea container.[65]

This tale had very much the same import as the story of the young widow. Neither dealt with tea in the ordinary sense, for both were set in a fantastic world of wealth and freedom that was depicted through tea. Lu Yu had read the classics tirelessly, and through tales such as these he tried to create his own world. He wanted to give form to an ultimate realm of tea, whether it be through dreamlike expressions peculiar to the Chinese or through portraits of beautiful ladies.

Nevertheless, it was not enough for Lu Yu merely to stress such a world of fantasy. He was careful also to discuss the efficacy of tea in the world of reality. The value of *The Classic of Tea* came from his ability to weave together these two seemingly contradictory elements.

Section eight listed the areas that produced tea:

In Shannan
  Best quality: Xiazhou
  Next quality: Xiangzhou, Jingzhou
  Lowest quality: Hengzhou, Jinzhou, Liangzhou

In Huainan
  Best quality: Guangzhou
  Next quality: Yiyangjun, Suzhou
  Lowest quality: Shouzhou, Qizhou, Huangzhou

In Zhexi
  Best quality: Huzhou
  Next quality: Changzhou
  Lowest quality: Xuanzhou, Hangzhou, Muzhou, Xizhou, Runzhou, Suzhou

In Jiannan
  Best quality: Mengzhou
  Next quality: Mianzhou, Suzhou
  Third quality: Hanzhou
  Lowest quality: Yazhou, Luzhou, Meizhou, Hanzhou

In *Zhedong*
    Best quality: Yuezhou
    Next quality: Mingzhou, Wuzhou
    Lowest quality: Taizhou

In *Qianzhong*
    Production areas: Sizhou, Bozhou, Feizhou, Yizhou

In *Jiangnan*
    Production areas: Erzhou, Yuanzhou, Jizhou

In *Lingnan*
    Production areas: Fuzhou, Jianzhou, Shaozhou, Xiangzhou[66]

This list assayed in detail the areas producing tea in China. Lu Yu took up the tea from each area in turn and closely considered its taste, finally ranking each of the types. The degree of care and precision with which Lu Yu approached this task demonstrates that the matter of taste was no ordinary concern. He spared no effort even for those types from the most remote areas.

Section nine dealt with simplified and abbreviated ways of preparing tea.[67] Yet at the same time Lu Yu declared that to make tea properly required the full set of twenty-four implements. As he put it, "When in the walled city at the gate of a prince or a duke, if the Twenty-Four Implements find their number diminished by only one, then it is best to dispense with the tea."[68] Thus, even in this section on simplified forms, he reiterated the twenty-four implement tea service as the basis of proper tea preparation. Note, however, that these twenty-four were primarily tools for the manufacture of tea. He paid not one iota of attention to their artistic merit. As we saw in the section on tea bowls, the inclusion of an implement in his équipage was not at all conditioned upon its rarity or value.

The final section, ten, described a chart of tea. In this Lu Yu suggested copying each of the sections of the *Classic* on rolls of white silk so that they could be hung in the corner of the room where the seats for serving tea were. In this way they might act as a visual aid for teaching and understanding everything relating to tea.[69] However, something is amiss here. Why ever would one want to learn so much about tea, from its origins to tools for it and on to the ways to drink it, just to enjoy a cup of the beverage? Maybe knowing these details was better than not, but why was there a need for a chart at all? Lu Yu directed his readers with the force of a command to display his *Classic* in this graphic way in preference to any image of a sage that might be set in the corner where the seats were. In sum, Lu Yu wrote this *Classic* in its ten chapters, divided it into its three volumes, and gave it the name *The Classic of Tea*. But at no point to the very end of his life did he explain either his motive or his intent in writing it. It remains a mystery.

2 Tea in China after The Classic of Tea

We have seen in the previous chapter that the drinking of tea became widely popular in China after Lu Yu wrote his *Classic*. As soon as the work appeared, extraordinary reverberations burst forth. Lu Yu himself became the immortal sage of tea and was called "Doctor Tea." Tea merchants worshiped statues of him fashioned in porcelain and gave them as gifts to favored customers. Poets continued to write paeans to Lu Yu and his *Classic*. His work not only enjoyed a wide readership, but was even esteemed as the canon of tea.

This reaction was surely strange. From the most remote times the Chinese abhorred the notion of using the character *jing*, "classic," for any except the teachings of their most revered ancient sages. Even if Lu Yu had been a religious figure rather than the Confucianist he was, his unequivocal use of this character *jing* in the title of his book of tea would surely have excited the suspicions of ordinary Chinese. That notwithstanding, the *Chajing* provoked not the slightest hostile criticism. On the contrary, the public venerated it and its author, whom they termed the tea sage and the doctor of tea. Indeed, he even became a tea god, an object of devotion. It was, moreover, not merely those who sold tea or dealers in tea ceramics who venerated him. Even the literati and artists affixed his portrait to the wall when they enjoyed their tea and gave him an honored place as a companion at their tea gatherings. Xu Zhao, the famed poet from the end of the Song dynasty, described how he quietly enjoyed tea given him by a friend as he gazed up at a painting of Lu Yu hanging on his wall. He wrote:

> In Gratitude for the Gracious Gift of Tea from Xu Ji
> The tea from Jianzhou is reserved for tribute to the imperial court, and is quite impossible to obtain. Yet you have shared

some with me. I know that the gift is no mere boastful show and rejoice in the sincerity that prompted it, especially as I am so far away and could never acquire any for myself.

When I opened the container, the tea brick appeared to be a full moon, and its lively flavor when brewed in spring water was incomparable. No guests have joined me in my quiet room, so I think I shall just enjoy the tea you have given me alone with the picture of Lu Yu on my wall.[1]

It is interesting to note that the tea Xu Zhao had received was the brick tea variety that had survived from the Tang dynasty, though we are told that Song tea was normally of the powdered type.

It was common at the time to display portraits of ancient sages on one's walls, but for this man of letters enjoying his poetic sentiments and inclinations, tea was his solitary pleasure, and it was tea that enriched his poetic feelings. He was not, however, merely drinking a beverage, for just as Lu Yu had earlier set forth in his *Classic*, the tea was an essential consideration, and one needed to pay attention to the subtleties of water as well as to the way one brewed it.

Jianchashuiji by Zhang Youxin of the Tang era contains an account of the relationship between Lu Yu and the Chan priest Zhiji of Jingling, the benefactor who had rescued him in his youth. According to this story, Zhiji, who was famed as a priest at the time of the founding of the Tang dynasty, would take no tea prepared by anyone other than Lu Yu. For this reason the priest drank no tea at all during a period of four or five years while Lu Yu was away. The dynasty's founder, however, learned of Zhiji and summoned him to the court to serve there. One of the court ladies, who was most skillful at preparing the beverage, brewed a cup for him, but the priest took no more than a single sip before putting his cup down, and he drank no more. When the emperor heard, he imagined that Zhiji was putting on airs as a connoisseur, and, since Lu Yu had just at that time returned to the capital, he had him make a cup to be taken to Zhiji without telling the priest who had made it. The latter drained his drink at a gulp, and when the emperor asked why, the priest replied, "Because it tasted like Lu Yu's tea, so I drank it up." The emperor, surprised, called Lu Yu in and reunited the pair.[2]

Other anecdotes can be found in Zhang Youxin's *Jianchashuiji*. Morooka Tamotsu writes in *Rikuu to Chakyō* that Zhang Youxin obtained his academic degree in the government examinations in 814 and shortly thereafter went with a classmate to the Jianfusi Temple in Raozhou. While there he met a priest who came from the home village of Lu Yu. The latter happened to leave without taking along one of his bags, and, when they examined it, it proved to contain books, one of which was a closely written set of notes labeled at the end with a title that read, "Records of the Brewing of Tea." Morooka observes that Zhang Youxin himself had explained this set of peculiar circumstances and that his *Jianchashuiji* was presumably compiled from those notes left by the priest from Lu Yu's home.[3]

According to one of the stories in this work, the governor of the province, Li Ji, met Lu Yu from time to time and on one occasion planned to dine with him. He said, "I've heard that the water from Nanling in the middle of the Yangzi (Yangtze) is the finest in the land and that you are the foremost man of tea. This is a splendid opportunity I may never have again, and I do not want to waste it." Thereupon, he ordered an earnest aide to go to Nanling, draw a jar of water, and bring it back. Lu Yu organized his utensils as he waited, and presently the water arrived. At once he scooped some of it and tasted. "This water is from the Yangzi sure enough, but it's not from Nanling; it is like water drawn from near the bank," he averred. The aide protested, "But I rowed the boat out to draw the water, and you can believe me because over a hundred people watched me do it." Lu Yu said nothing but began to transfer the water from the jar until at last just half remained. Then he stopped, drew a scoop, and said, "From here on down is the water from Nanling, isn't it?" The aide was as chagrined as he was astonished. He replied, "The fact is, I did draw the water from Nanling, but as I approached the bank the boat began to rock terribly, and I spilled half of it. I feared there wouldn't be enough, so I refilled the jar from water near the bank. Your powers of discrimination are like a god's!" he exclaimed. The governor and his many guests were equally astounded.[4] Whether stories such as this one are true is beside the point. They may be completely unscientific, but they do illustrate the veneration of Lu Yu as the sage or doctor of tea.

Let us consider for a moment Zhang Youxin and the *Jianchashuiji*. Just as described in the book, Zhang Youxin passed the government examination and attained a scholarly degree at the first level in the year 814. He was a man of great talent who wrote both poetry and prose and was also fond of tea. *Jianchashuiji*, which he wrote in one volume, literally meant "an account of water for the brewing of tea," and it contained a listing of sources of water with evaluations of them. The work began with the anecdote that we just saw of Lu Yu's powers of discrimination with water, and then it had the governor, Li, ask Lu Yu from his experience to rank them according to source. The latter replied, "Chu [on the Yangzi] is best, and Jin [in Shanxi] is worst." Thereupon Li ordered him to dictate his list, and these were the top three:

> First is the pellucid, flowing water of Kangwang Valley in Lushan.
> Second is water from the rocky spring at the Huishan Temple in Wuxi.
> Third is the famed water of Lanxi in Qizhou.[5]

Finally the last was water from snow. Lu Yu said that very cold water was not suitable. Altogether the work ranked water of twenty different varieties. Morooka Tamotsu in *Rikuu to Chakyō* writes about this work, "Zhang Youxin, by his own determination, assigned a rank to each of the principal springs throughout China and then ascribed the ranking to Lu Yu. In other words, Zhang Youxin's ranking came to be known as Lu Yu's ranking. This was truly an extreme disservice both to Lu Yu and to the Way of Tea itself."[6] Thus, as we can see here, *The Classic of Tea* had come to be so widely read and Lu Yu's reputation so elevated that later writers sought to reinforce their own work with greater authority by falsely attributing it to him.

Lu Yu's fame gave rise to numerous poems to him and his *Classic* by artists and men of letters. Not only Shi Jiaoran, Lu Tong, and Huang Furan, but also Bai Juyi and Du Mu wrote several "Chashan Shi" (literally, tea mountain poems). There is also a poem, which Wei Yingwu composed when he was traveling to Suzhou on assignment as an official by Emperor Dezong, titled "The Joy of Growing Tea in my Garden." It contains these lines:

> Defile not its purity,
> For drinking it expunges dust and woe.
> The taste of this thing is spiritual.
> Taking it from the mountain,
> Where naturally it grew,
> I planted it in my own wild garden.
> The bushes, to my delight, flourished,
> And I could invite my wonderful friends.[7]

This thing called tea, he said, is pure and cannot be sullied. To drink it is to wash away the dust of the world's cares. Fortunately, when the poet planted this worker of miracles in his own wild garden, it flourished, so he was able to invite his refined friends to gather for tea.

It is noteworthy that the author used terms that suggest the miraculous and that liken tea to a nectar from the realm of the divine, for these imply that tea was precisely what the poet needed to transport himself from the dreary, mundane world to the realm of the immortals. The term he used for his refined friends suggests that they, too, transcended the commonplace.

Other works celebrating *The Classic of Tea* were without limit. One light-hearted piece by the late Tang poet Ji Zhong, titled "To the Venerable Qianming," expressed these thoughts:

> Although you have taken lodgings in the busy capital, you are sleeping in a temple in a bamboo grove like a sage, aloof from the affairs of men, so that you must feel that you are living at the edge of the white clouds.
>
> I had some free time, so I climbed the bell tower hill. It was a bleak daybreak in the village, and with my friend away the wind and rain were cold. Once again I tried to brew tea as the *Chajing* prescribes, and brewing it helped to comfort me. Since my youth I have been quite addicted to poetry and cannot put it down.
>
> I hear of you often and have learned that you seldom sleep on these autumn evenings. With the moon at its summit, you must be leaning against the balustrade gazing at it.[8]

It is interesting here that Ji Zhong was trying to put the theory of the *Chajing* into practice and that he contrasted his addiction to poetry to the flavor of brewing tea. One can find numerous poems that juxtapose the devil of poetry, the trials of poetry, the disease of poetry, or the amusement of poetry with the brewing of tea, the roasting of tea, and the beauty of tea. The Chinese saw tea as an extremely efficacious means of fostering spiritual interests in poetic diversions, and by drinking tea as they wrote poetry they could attain a state of spiritual creativity that spurred their artistic output.

There is an anecdote in *Taiping Guangji*, an early Song era imperial anthology that I have cited above. Unfortunately, I have not had the opportunity to examine the original text, but it concerns a government official called Xi Zhi. This man had passed the government examinations in the reign of Daizong (762–780) and had received steady promotions on into the reign of Dezong (780–805), so the anecdote appears to have originated from a time when Lu Yu was exerting his influence on the way of tea. In outline it goes like this.

Xi Zhi's appointment to office was at about the time that tea was beginning to enjoy its special esteem, and, since he had long had a taste for luxury, he had assembled a full set of rare and exquisite tea utensils. One day, just as summer was at its hottest, he invited his government colleagues to an after-dinner tea party. There were over twenty guests, with Xi Zhi himself at the head of the table on the east side, and he started the service from the west. With just two pots and not a great quantity of tea, the progress of the tea bowls around the room was extremely slow. Xi Zhi became increasingly irritated with the heat and his own thirst. Just at this point, when the perspiration was streaming down his face, a dark, fat member of his staff came in, placed an inkstone and writing brush on the table, and wanted his signature on a huge register. At the limit of his patience, the official shouted, "Take it away!" and shoved the unfortunate fellow so that he and the table both tumbled over together. The chap's face as well as the register were both covered with black ink. The assembled guests were greatly amused at this entertainment and laughed heartily.[9]

What is noteworthy here is the appearance of the term "*chahui*," literally "tea gathering" or "tea party." The characters used were the same as for the Japanese "*chakai*," which has the same meaning. From this anecdote we can see that special gatherings were being held for the purpose of enjoying tea. In this case there were over twenty guests, divided into east and west groups and slowly taking tea from two bowls. Whether all were drinking from the same bowls, as Japanese do with thick tea today, or whether each person was being served individually with tea brought into the room is unclear, though the quantity of tea must have been small. In any event, it is significant that this was a tea party, which had not existed at the time of Lu Yu, and that the service of tea conformed to rules of etiquette.

From the mid-Tang era on, as the drinking of tea became increasingly popular, there were a number of improvements in its cultivation and preparation. No matter how commanding the *Chajing* had been as a classic for its own day, a new age perceived new needs and demanded still further works on the Way of Tea, suited to those requirements. Among the works to address these was the *Chalu, The Record of Tea*, by Cai Xiang of the Song dynasty.[10]

Cai Xiang was an illustrious official of the courts of Renzong and Yingzong of the Northern Song. Born in 1012, he died in 1067, during the reign of the latter emperor. This corresponded to the era in Japan when the aristocrats of Heian were losing their grip on affairs and the military houses of the Taira and the Minamoto were just beginning to emerge as new powers that would ultimately replace them. Cai Xiang wrote *Chalu* in nineteen sections divided between two volumes. He

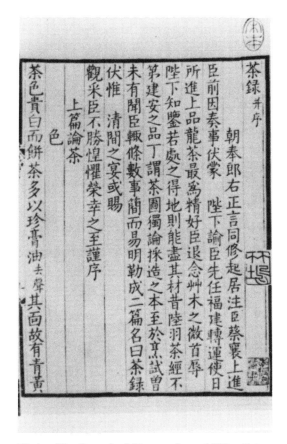

Chalu, The Record of Tea, preface. 1928 edition based on the Baichuan Xuehai version, Southern Song dynasty Hsienchun era (1265–1274) edition.

gave the date as 1064 and appended a preface dedicated to Yingzong as reigning emperor.[11]

In this introduction he explained his intent in compiling the work. He noted that he had served as an official responsible for the transport of tribute goods from Fujian. Among these tribute items was *longcha*, literally dragon tea, which was named after the mythical beast that symbolized the Chinese emperor. After leaving his post, he had researched this subject thoroughly. He had been able to secure good materials for his study and hoped to share his findings with the imperial court.

His aim was to set forth the superiority of the tea of Fujian. Cai Xiang clarified his position when he stated, "Lu Yu in the *Chajing* did not rank the tea of Jian'an, nor did Dingwei in the *Chatu* mention how to roast or steam it, though he did explain how to cultivate and pick tea. Therefore, I have compiled this study in two volumes and have titled it *Chalu*."[12] Cai Xiang's aim was to distance himself from the *Chajing*.

In the first volume, titled "On Tea," he treated the form and content of tea itself and said at the outset that in color "white is precious." Then, in a section titled "Fragrance," he wrote, "Tea has its own true fragrance, though people add flavoring agents in an effort to improve upon it. When the people of Jian'an test tea, however, they add no such agents, for they fear it will rob the tea of its true aroma. In the same way, one must absolutely never destroy the fragrance of the tea by insinuating unusual flavors into it at the time of steaming or roasting."[13]

Next there were sections on flavor, storage, steaming, and grinding, and then he continued with a section on roasting. In it he wrote: "Fragrance, color, and flavor all suffer with the passage of the years. One should, therefore, bring water to a boil in a clean vessel and place the tea in it to remove the oil. Once or twice is enough. Then one should grasp it with pincers, dry it over a low flame, and grind it. This is not necessary for new tea picked this year."[14] Note that the *Chajing* mentioned nothing about putting the tea into hot water. This was because the issue of the fragrance of the tea did not arise, since Lu Yu was dealing with brick tea. That constitutes one difference from the Song era method of preparation. We can see from the reference to grinding, moreover, that this was powdered tea like the *matcha* of Japan. As did the *Chajing*, this work also said that one should first wrap the tea in clean paper and then break it up with a hammer before carefully grinding it.

Following the section on roasting was a section on sifting the tea powder and then one on adjusting the boil of the hot water. "Getting the temperature of the water right," Cai Xiang wrote, "is one of the most difficult matters. If it is too cool, a scum will form on top, but if it is too hot, the tea will sink. In earlier days people likened this overheated condition to 'crabs' eyes.' " [15] In fact, the *Chajing* did not mention "crabs' eyes" at all, though it did refer to "fish eyes." No doubt the two terms both referred to the same condition.

Next came sections on warming the tea bowls and on preparing the tea itself. Cai Xiang said, "If the quantity of tea is too small and that of the water too great, the foam will scatter like the wisps hanging down from clouds, which we call clouds' legs. With too much tea and too little water, on the contrary, it will stick together like gruel. One should take the tea with a spoon the size of a copper coin and then mix while pouring hot water until the proportions are right and the tea is completely suffused throughout. Later add more hot water and mix again. Slap and sweep the surface. Stop when the cup is four-tenths full." [16] It is notable that the *Chajing* said no more about this way of preparing tea than it had about "crabs' eyes." This section concluded the first volume.

The second volume had the title "On Tea Utensils" and discussed various types of implements used for tea, including roasters, baskets, mortars and pestles, pincers, and grinders. Pincers, for example, were best made from green bamboo though at times also from carefully wrought iron or bronze, according to the *Chajing,* but Cai Xiang noted that they should be made from bent gold or iron. It was much the same with tea mortars. *Chajing* declared orangewood best, followed by pear, domestic mulberry, paulownia, and wild mulberry, but *Chalu* recommended silver or iron, noting that gold was too soft and other metals like bronze and natural copper were too inclined to tarnish. It said nothing about fruit woods. The entry for the tea sifter or screen was the same as in *Chajing.* Then for tea bowls *Chalu* recommended wares from Jian'an, though *Chajing* omitted any reference to them at all. Finally, it concluded with sections on scoops and hot water containers. [17] *Chajing* had said that for kettles, iron was customary but silver was good for long-term use. Cai Xiang, by contrast, asserted the superiority of gold. It seems clear that the latter author bore his predecessor's work in mind as he wrote and made an effort to improve upon it.

The Song poet Su Shi (1036–1101) had the following to say about brewing tea in his poem "Shiyin Jiancha."

Crab eyes are past, and fish eyes have started.
The wind whispers through the pines.
Tiny pearls fall polished from the rough pile.
Dizzily, flying snow swirls about the edges.
Then boiling water from the silver kettle.
People of old hardly knew the spirit of boiling water.[18]

Thus, for him the boiling of water fell into two stages, first small bubbles and then larger ones, which he likened first to crab eyes and then to fish eyes. The boiling process was further along in the latter stage. Nowadays in Japan we call the sound of water boiling "*matsukaze*," the wind in the pines, and Su Shi, indeed, used precisely that term in his poem for the hissing sound of water boiling. He likened the tea as it came from the grinder to fine pearls and the foam to driven snow. He went on to say that his only desire was to be able to take a cup of tea after he had enjoyed ample sleep and the sun was high in the sky.

No doubt Su Shi was alluding to Lu Tong's "Song of Tea." The earlier poet had said that three cups of tea made him want to consume five thousand volumes of literature, while for Su Shi even one cup would actually take the place of five thousand volumes.

There is yet one other work on tea from the late Song era that ranks with *Chalu* in its influence on later ages. That is *Daguan Chalun* (Japanese, *Daikan Charon*), attributed to Emperor Huizong. "Daguan" was an era name from his reign, dating from 1107 to 1110. Saeki Futoshi, however, has expressed reservations about the conventionally supposed authorship. He writes:

It is extremely doubtful that *Chalun* came from the brush of the refined Emperor Huizong. Neither the tone nor the structure of the introductory material, which we may take to be the preface . . . conveys a sense of imperial authorship. No matter that he reigned at a time of dynastic decline, an imperial work is after all an imperial work. The sentences lack a sense of grandeur, and officials about the throne seem to make light of the emperor, so he would hardly allow it to be published as his own work. I believe, therefore, that some later tea aficionado attributed his own words to this cultivated emperor to give them more authority. However, judging by their reference to brick tea, there can be no doubt that the twenty sections beginning with "Production" are of quite ancient provenience. . . . We must concede, moreover, that it is especially valuable, for we know of no other work to give a comparably detailed account of the method of preparation of brick tea.[19]

Let us consider some of the points he raises. The *Daguan Chalun* consists of twenty sections in one volume, and its preface contains the following statement: "Since the inception of this [Song] dynasty, Jian'an has been made to present brick tea as tribute to the throne, and the land has enjoyed tranquillity down to the present day. Not only the Son of Heaven and his ministers, but gentlemen and those without office as well have grown accustomed to luxury, familiar with virtue and great refinement, and so have come to drink tea. The excellence with which tea is picked, processed, and graded as well as the exquisiteness with which it is roasted and prepared have achieved great heights."[20] If the emperor had written this himself, he would have attributed the flourishing of tea to the excellence of his own rule.

The first section had the heading "Production," which referred to the cultivation of the plant. It differed from the *Chajing*, for example, in recommending that tea be grown in a place that had a balance between sun and shade, for that would produce the best flavor.[21]

The second section, which was on weather, explained how to provide the best climatic conditions for the plant, and the next, how to select the most suitable leaves for picking. *Chajing* had recommended that tea be collected in the morning, and this work had the same advice. It also said: "Pick at dawn, and stop when you see the sun." *Chalun*, however, had somewhat more detailed instructions. It also said: "Pinch the buds with the nails and not with the ball of the finger. Perspiration will spoil the fragrance, so the pickers should keep freshly drawn water with them and toss the picked leaves into it from time to time." *Chajing*, by contrast, had instructed the pickers to place the newly plucked leaves into steamer baskets and after steaming to pound them in a mortar, heat until dry, and then store them in tea jars. At this time tea tasting competitions seem to have been in vogue, and *Chalun* advised: "Picked buds the size of a sparrow's tongue make the best tea for contests. One stem with one leaf is best; one stem with two is next; the rest cannot compete."[22]

The following section explained how to steam and press the tea into bricks, and the fifth, titled "Processing," how to prepare to powder it. The sixth part was about distinguishing types of tea and the seventh about so-called white tea, which was considered the very finest. Subsequent sections dealt with mortars, bowls, whisks, jars, and scoops.[23] Its section on bowls was different from both *Chajing* and *Chalun*.

The whisk seems to be a new implement here. *Chajing* had explained the use of bamboo scrubbers, but *Chalun* advised making "tea whisks from mature bamboo with pronounced vertical striping." The term "tea whisk" here used the same characters as *chasen*, the current Japanese term for that tool, and bamboo was the material used to make it, just as it is today. *Chalun* continued with several other categories, including sections on water, preparation, flavor, fragrance, color, and the like.[24]

All of the above works from the Song era dealt with the practical aspects of tea, from the manufacturing process to the tools needed for it. Now, in the concluding pages of this chapter, I propose to take up the ceremonial usage of tea in the Chan (Zen) temples of China. The first item that one should examine in this context is no doubt the *Baizhang Qinggui* (in Japanese, *Ekai Shingi*), promulgated by Baizhang Huaihai (724–814).

Baizhang Huaihai, a disciple of Mazu Daoyi, was a preeminent prelate of Chan Buddhism in China. He was born in Changle, Fuzhou, and took the canonical name Huaihai. His other name derived from his long residence at the monastery on Mount Baizhang. The *Qinggui*, literally "Pure Rules," were a discipline for Chan monasteries in China. Previously the Chan discipline had necessarily been based on that of the Hinayana form of Buddhism, but with this formulation Baizhang was able to meet the needs of changed circumstances found in China. The version we have today, however, has been further adapted, according to Fukushima Shun'ō. He claims that the original was scattered and lost, and what we have today is a reconstruction from the Yuan era by Dongyang Dehui, who was the eighteenth-generation disciple of Baizhang. Since he acted at the behest of Emperor Shunzong, the resulting discipline might be more properly termed an "Imperially Sanctioned Discipline" or the "Imperial Discipline of Baizhang."[25] As we shall see later, this was a basis for the *Eihei Shingi*, which Dōgen provided as a discipline for the Sōtō sect of Zen in Japan.

In this collection, there are many items that involved the use of tea on ceremonial occasions. The appointment or departure of prelates, seasonal assemblies, and the arrival and departure of monks all called for celebrations with a formal partaking of tea. The appointment of a new abbot, to select an example, called for a service whose preparations and order of progression were specified. Details of precisely how the monks conducted each stage were not necessarily spelled out, but there can be no doubt that tea played an integral role on these occasions.[26]

Those who took tea, however, whether monks or literati, may have drunk it simply as a beverage. Yet there was more to it than just the physical, physiological refreshment that they received from tea. It was also a means of spiritual refreshment, of moving into a realm of spiritual conviviality. Reports about the physiological or medicinal effects of tea circulate widely nowadays, but significant even in that connection is the desire that individuals have, by drinking tea, to disencumber themselves, to rise above the vexations of the mundane, and to cross over into another dimension where they can enjoy freedom from the world's cares.

In other words, for its drinkers tea becomes the occasion for creating an abstract life apart even before they realize it. It is this effect that has brought tea its esteem. To couch the point somewhat differently, the desire of Chinese to construct a distinctive world view, an abstract realm apart, may at times have taken form through the medium of tea as a beverage.

PART 2

The Arrival of Tea in Japan

3 Tea in the Heian Era

No one has been able to determine precisely when the practice of drinking tea came into Japan, but so far as I have been able to ascertain, the earliest reference we have to tea in this country dates back at least to 814 to *Kūkai Hōken Hyō* (*Shōryōshū*, volume 4) in a passage dated the twenty-eighth day of the intercalary seventh month. The great Shingon monk Kūkai had traveled to Tang China in 804 and had returned two years later laden with an enormous quantity of books, paintings, and Buddhist statutes. The passage explains how Kūkai presented ten of these volumes to Emperor Saga and requested him to view them, and then it says, as he studied, he drank *"chanoyu,"* which we believe to be hot water with tea. The Heian era was a sinophilic age, and Chinese thought continued to permeate the country as it had before. Japan dispatched students and monks to China in great numbers, including the famous prelates Saichō and Kūkai. Such students were precisely those with the greatest intellectual appetites, and the tea drinking practices that they found in China impressed them greatly. I shall attempt to survey in the following pages as many Heian era documents relating to tea as possible.

We have already seen the theory that the drinking of tea in Japan began with Kūkai. It is clear that ancient Japanese culture was based on the relationship with China, and from the beginning of the association with Tang, starting with the dispatch of Inugami no Mitasuki under Emperor Jomei in 630, to the abandonment of the official relationship in 894, there were fifteen embassies altogether. It is far from certain that tea seeds first came with Saichō and Kūkai during this time. The *Kūkai Hōken Hyō* is simply the first historical record of tea that we have found.

The *Chakyō Shōsetsu*, for example, says, "In 729 Emperor Shōmu called one hundred priests for a reading of the Hannya [Sutra]; on the second day, tea was served."[2] Based on this passage one might conclude that tea had come from China much earlier than the time of Kūkai. The source leaves room for doubt, however, because it is not founded upon reliable contemporaneous documentary evidence. In the same vein, Ichijō Kanera, explaining the seasonal reading of the sutras in *Kuji Kongen,* wrote in 1422: "On the eighth day of the second month, there is a reading of the Great Hannya Sutra at the Court. This lasts four days and, on the second day, there is a ceremony called Incha, which is a service of tea to the priests. This [practice] began on the eighth day of the fourth month of 729 and is said to have been conducted each season during the Jōgan era [859–876]."[3] Presumably he had some documentary source for this statement. In any event, though we have no concrete evidence about tea at that time, it would not require too great a stretch of the imagination to conclude that at least one segment of the populace drank tea during the Nara period.[4]

Only shortly after that era we do have credible information about tea drinking. It appears in *Ruijū Kokushi,* in its record of the reign of Emperor Saga dated the fourth month of 815, the year following *Kūkai Hōken Hyō.* It says: "Emperor Saga went to Shiga Karasaki in Ōmi province and proceeded past the Sūfukuji. The Abbot Eichū led numerous priests out the gate to greet the emperor, who alighted from his palanquin and entered the hall to worship the Buddha. His Majesty then progressed to the Bonshakuji, stopped his palanquin, and composed a poem to which the heir apparent and the imperial retainers responded. Thereupon, the Abbot Eichū prepared tea with his own hands and served the emperor, who gave him a garment."[5] The source does not make it clear what type of tea it was, whether it was conventional green tea or brick tea, but this may be taken as one of our first authentically documented glimpses of the drinking of tea in Japan.

Since tea was quite widespread in China, many poets wrote about the beverage there, and in Japan as well poems mentioning tea were not uncommon. There was first of all a collection of verses about Kūkai in "Chūsu Kankō Shi Jo" in the third volume of *Shōryōshū.* In this collection the term "*chanoyu*" appeared, and there were in addition numerous poems that enable us to learn something of the lives of the Buddhists of that day. When they found the leisure, they sipped tea as they sampled the pleasures of Chinese poetry and letters and even made their way through books from India. Such a life was not confined to the Bud-

Emperor Saga (r. 809–823). Heian period. Not only does Emperor Saga appear in one of the earliest authentically documented references to the drinking of tea in Japan, but he also left a number of poems that make mention of tea. Property of the Imperial Household Agency.

dhist clergy but was probably also characteristic of the cultivated members of the highest classes in society at large who enjoyed a knowledge of letters.

Thus, tea had already come to occupy a special place among cultured circles as a means by which they could transcend the mundane. Shi Jiaoran, the poet whom we encountered in the previous chapter, made it clear that wine had come to be enjoyed long before, but people looked down on it as a vulgar pleasure. Tea by contrast achieved a higher and qualitatively superior dimension, so that the Chinese were able to emphasize its significance as a device for avoiding or rising above the vulgar. This peculiarly Chinese understanding of the world of tea and the consequent attitudes that flowed from it thus appear to have made their way intact directly to Japan. Just as tea enabled Chinese poets and literati to achieve their desire to escape from the depravity of the world, the corruption of public affairs, and the anxieties of life, and to soar up to an ideal world of freedom where they might do as they wished and enjoy their poetry, so it also provided the Japanese a similar means of reaching those same ends. For the Japanese upper classes tea was a unique and supreme device for abandoning the desires of reality and for building a world of freedom that transcended that reality. Tea at that time no doubt had about it an exotic flavor, and its rarity and its having come over from China greatly influenced attitudes toward it.

One can graphically appreciate the place that tea held in the Heian court as a result of its association with the recitation of poetry from China or the reading of books from India, which the nobility respected as having come from advanced cultures. The *Ryōunshū*, compiled by Ono no Minemori, for example, contained the following poem in which Emperor Saga recorded his impressions of a visit at a pondside pavilion with his younger brother, later Emperor Junna.

> Rice harvested, fields as still as Xuanpu of the sages,
> From the pond pavilion we gaze in peace at the autumn sky
> Surprised by the cries of wild geese on wing.
> The last cicadas sing in the growing cold.
> Willows on the bank make me long for China's River of
>   Willows.
> I yearn to see the lotuses there.
> I regard the scene in tranquillity
> The sky behind filled with the smoke of roasting tea.[6]

The rich poetic imagery here was a dream of tea by which the poet might attain a realm apart. In much the same way, Emperor Saga in the summer of 814 called at the villa of the Great General of the Left, Fujiwara no Fuyutsugu (775–826), and wrote these lines:

> To escape the heat I've come to the palace retreat.
> Fishing poles bundled by the pavilion's pond.
> About the banks the willows' green turns black in the fading
>   light.

The whisper of the pines cools the day's heat.
One never tires of writing poetry or the pleasing fragrance of
    pounding tea.
Someone agreeably entertains us with a lute.
The clear waters of the pond cleanse our cares.
The evening tranquillity brings joy.[7]

It seems that he did not weary of composing Chinese verses or of pounding tea. One should enjoy oneself and earnestly listen to the lute. The imagery of abandoning cares, plucking the lute, and forgetting the passage of time in poetry calls to mind the painting "Listening to the Lute" by Chou Ying,[8] which supposedly was a copy of the no longer extant "Women Roasting Tea" by the foremost Tang beauty and artist, Zhang Xuan. One finds two beautiful ladies seated at a table listening raptly to the strains of a lute. An attendant has appeared with a tea bowl on a stand raised in her hands. The joy of plucking the lute and savoring tea was the highest pleasure of that day, but the reason was that tea carried one to that world of illusion for which we all yearn.

The same collection that told about Emperor Saga and tea, *Ryōunshū*, had another verse dedicated to Kūkai by Nakao Ō that contained this line, "A child washes a basin at a rocky spring, a girl prepares tea at a hearth." The phrase "prepares tea" used the same characters that we use today for green tea.[9] Similarly, a poem in *Keikokushū* that Emperor Saga dedicated to Kūkai celebrated partaking of tea upon the latter's return to the cloud-enshrouded remoteness of Mount Kōya. It splendidly depicted the poignance he felt at the parting in these words:

Long years have passed; yours in the Way, mine in worldly life.
I am fortunate to speak with you this autumn.
Drinking fragrant tea until late,
Painful though the parting be, I bow to you as I see you off to
    the distant clouds.[10]

Another verse from the same collection dedicated to Kūkai by a courtier named Ono no Minemori had a line that evoked the image of the holy man relishing his solitude at a temple deep in the mountains "intoxicated by tea, savoring to the full the fragrant herb."[11]

Another of Emperor Saga's poems, found in *Bunka Shūreishū* compiled by Fujiwara no Fuyutsugu, was dedicated to the priest Saichō in response to an earlier verse from the priest.

> You transmit the Way from the distant southern mountain
> Of Tiantai, where you have grown old.
> Monk's staff in hand, you crossed the broad sea.
> You entered the mountains to call at Penglai, home of sages.[12]

The poem continues, tracing the monk's arduous career and evoking his image, living in a hermitage deep in the mountains on an early spring day, passing his time offering bowls of tea. Another verse, by Kinhiko, calls to mind a scene of early spring with a scholar in the deep mountains absorbed in his study of Buddhist texts, exchanging tea with an intimate.

> Temple in the mountain fastness,
> The High Priest will not return to the secular.
> Flourishing his staff sounding his priestly bells, he goes.
> With plain surplice he sits in peace.
> In the cold, snow still clings to the bamboo leaves;
> Spring herbs sprout in the ancient mountains.
> Talking together, we dip the beautiful green tea,
> While smoke and fire arise amid the evening snow.[13]

The reign of Emperor Saga, as one can see from his imperial sponsorship of collections of Chinese poetry, was the very summit of Japan's yearning for Tang culture, and as we peruse several of these verses, we see the key role that tea played in creating the poetic climate of the era.[14]

Finally, let us take up the poem that provides us the fullest view of the drinking of tea in the Heian era. That is a poem from the *Keikokushū* by Koreuji, called "Song of Tea for the Governor of Izumo."

> Early spring, the branches of the tea plants sprout buds.
> We pluck them to make tea.
> An old man near the temple loves it as a treasure.
> Alone he faces the golden flames and roasts his gems.
> Beneath a wood of bare branches limpid waters flow.
> He strains it into his silvery vessel.
> With finest charcoal the fire soon glows.
> The kettle boils in flowery waves.
> Like Pan of ancient Shang in China
> Blending in the best salt to bring out the flavor,

In essence it is mysterious and pure,
Nothing could excel it.
After roasting the fragrance lingers.
To drink is to be in white clouds, cares vanished.
Like a Taoist mystic one is pure and brisk.[15]

The poem depicts the tea plants in the mountains, the gathering of the fresh buds that have appeared in the early spring, and the preparing of tea, but the overall sense is one of withdrawal from the world as one drinks it. It is a picture of the hermit secluded among the white clouds. We also see that in the Heian era people added salt to the tea, as we saw in *Chajing*. Indeed, it seems significant that what we find here is the spirit of *Chajing* itself. The poem treats the act of drinking tea as one of seclusion, presenting a realm of boundless freedom and eternal joy like that of a Taoist recluse among the clouds far from the dust and cares of the world.

In the past in China one of the chief attributes of a ruler was his enjoyment of the arts. This was not simply because the world of the arts was isolated from reality and was the product of idle fancy. Rather, the arts represented a kind of ultrareality that impinged upon reality with a force greater than that of the actual world. For that reason the arts bolstered reality from beneath and gave it underpinnings. The realm attained through tea played a similar role making the real possible.

Various other Heian era sources also mentioned the taking of tea. One of these was *Honchō Monzui*, which contained a palindrome titled "Inscription on a Dipper" by Miyako no Yoshika. This was a verse that made sense and followed correct meter and rhyme whether one read it forward or backward, and it was, as its title indicated, a phrase inscribed on a dipper.

Roasting tea copiously, how shall I feel upon drinking it?
It will harmonize my body and scatter my cares and ills.[16]

The inscription used two different characters for tea, and perhaps these were tea picked early and tea picked late, the distinction made by Guo Pu. In any event, it meant something like this: "When one prepares and drinks ample tea, one will be able to achieve balance within the body, remove cares, and avoid disease." Clearly, the writer valued his tea for its medicinal effect.

Another was a piece by Yoshishige no Yasutane, written as he passed the temple in Mikawa called Yakuōji.

> Hekikai county in Mikawa province
> Has a Hall of the Way called Yakuōji.
> The bodhisattva Gyōki founded it long ago.
> Though his works are ancient,
> The aura there stays fresh.
> Before it is water of lapis lazuli;
> Behind, a wood of autumnal tints.
> It has a rustic hall, a hut of miscanthus,
> A sutra treasury, bell tower, gardens for tea and medicine.[17]

Yakuōji was established by Gyōki, the famed Buddhist missionary, and had, as the poem recounts, in addition to a hermitage, sutra depository and bell tower, a tea garden and a medicinal garden.

In the *Kanke Bunsō*, an anthology compiled by Sugawara no Michizane, we find phrases like these: "So fine is the fragrance of the hot tea, one forgets drinking wine" or "When troubled, I drink a cup of tea."[18] Another, later Sugawara family collection, *Kanke Kōshū*,[19] said of Michizane during his famed exile in Tsukushi in Kyushu, "He had only a cup of tea to ease the grief of his barren days."

In other words, as we can see from the above, there were two quite contrasting styles. For priests, tea rites had about them an element of sacerdotal gravity, while for men of letters and leisure, tea drinking was an elegant and escapist pastime redolent of the reclusive features of Taoism. In some respects this contrast foreshadowed a division into the dual aspects of powdered tea and infused green tea that we find later in Japanese tea history.[20]

Engishiki contained a list of utensils to be used for the Great Thanksgiving Festival, which followed an emperor's enthronement. Several of these were types of ceramics that would later be favored by practitioners of *chanoyu,* including Seto ware from Owari and Bizen ware. The section on Civil Affairs in volume 23 contained detailed measurements of miscellaneous utensils, including tea bowls, and it also listed ceramics from Owari as well as those from Hagi in Nagato and Korean ware.[21] The reason *Engishiki* had such detailed lists of ceramics was that they were essential for the use of tea in ceremonies in the court and at temples.

Twice each year during the spring and fall, there were readings at the court of the Hannya Sutra by assembled priests, and they employed tea on those occasions as well. *Saikyūki*, a diary by Minamoto no Takaaki, had this passage on the sutra reading in the ninth month: "[The emperor] called Kyokuyaku Kōboku and had him prepare gifts of tea (*incha*)." The section on interim readings of the sutras said, "During the summer there were distributions of gifts of tea (*incha*)." Those of the fifth and sixth ranks particularly received them.[22] The term "*incha*," which appeared in the above passages, was used later, sometimes with the meaning of "powdered tea." Murai Yasuhiko, however, has shown that the meaning at this time was "tea received as a gift or souvenir," and the priests received it as a part of their allowance and used it as a sort of tonic. The official who prepared the gifts was the one responsible for medicines. The kind of tea that they used at that time was brick tea, as in Tang China.[23]

In summary, there are several conclusions that one might draw about tea in the Heian era. Inasmuch as the introduction of tea into Japan had been the work of the ambassadors, students, and monks who had traveled to China in search of Chinese culture, the opportunity to drink the beverage and to become intoxicated by its fragrance was a special privilege limited to those who stood at the leading edge of that cultural movement. Though botanists have a theory that the tea plant may be indigenous to Japan, nonetheless, it was Lu Yu and the other Chinese poets and literati who truly made tea known to the Japanese. It was these Chinese who were the first to drink it and to discover its extraordinary value as a beverage. They were the ones, moreover, who found in it more than a beverage, for they were the first to see it as an indispensable ingredient in creating an ideal world of human freedom, and they taught the Japanese to find supreme joy as human beings in attaining such a world through tea. In other words, they taught the Japanese the superlative value of tea as a beverage together with the philosophy of tea. The ambassadors who crossed over to Tang became the heirs of this lofty philosophy and thought, which Lu Yu first drew together.

It is perhaps a subsidiary issue, but there is no doubt that an exotic Chinese flavor permeated the cultured circles of the day, and those who longed for this Chinese flavor wished to absorb in a physical way the world view of the Chinese. There was a tendency for tea, since it had also come from China, to share that exoticism with other aspects of culture. Accordingly, among the upper classes the interest in tea, abetted by its rarity, grew extraordinarily intense. As a result, we must consider that the conventions for enjoying tea, as we saw in the previously cited sources, involved the importation intact of the philosophy of tea of the Chinese Lu Yu. During an age when culture at large was overwhelmed by the imitation of things Chinese and people were impatient to attain the level of China by means of such imitation, tea was an integral part of that picture and could hardly escape the prevailing tendencies.

The dreams of the Chinese literati inspired by tea and the world they depicted thus moved into Japan unchanged. These dreams constituted a peculiarly Chinese view of the world. The passive sense of the Taoist immortals, which we saw in poetry, the transcendent world reached through tea, the attempt to wash away worldly cares and to attain a realm apart are all elements of this view. The effort to fly away from constraint, confinement, and constriction into an existence of freedom unrestricted by deeds was a deeply rooted tendency in Chinese culture. Theirs was not simply an idle fancy. Predominant in the Chinese intellectual tradition was not so much the attempt to create a real world in which one attained one's desires through one's own efforts, but the attempt to create within the real world a spiritual realm in which the actualization of one's own personal desires mattered as little as possible.

4 The Ethos of the *Kissa Yōjōki*

In the previous chapter I referred to the poetry of the Heian era and observed that the way of thinking about tea that the aristocratic and priestly classes depicted in their writing was a direct importation from China. This was, no doubt, a consequence of Japan's position in the East Asian cultural sphere. The flow of culture from China was unidirectional, as if Tang were at the summit of a mountain and all the streams ran down into Korea and Japan. The attitude toward tea found in the poetry of Heian seemed to move in an unbroken line from the poetic tradition that began with Lu Yu. With respect to broader culture as well, it was an age of imitation of China and the Tang dynasty.

Toward the middle of the Heian era, however, the borrowing came to an end. What had previously been a blind craving for things Chinese slowed, partly as a result of a disruption of relations with Tang, and that allowed the Japanese to digest what they had already consumed. What resulted was an independent cultural style that the Japanese had created for themselves. It was quite natural that Japan should have passed Chinese culture through a distinctly Japanese filter, and it is that process that brings me to the heart of this monograph. Even though the Tang embassies had introduced tea drinking to Japan, it seems likely that the practice was restricted to a small segment of the aristocracy and the priesthood. Thereafter until the Kamakura era, few records involving tea come to hand, and it seems quite possible that tea fell quietly into disuse. Meanwhile, in China, the Tang dynasty fell in 907 to be replaced by the Song in 960, and the founding of the latter dynasty led to an active trade with Japan.

In Japan the work that headed up the renewal of writing on tea during this era was the *Kissa Yōjōki* by Eisai (also called Yōsai). Whereas

Myōan Eisai (also read Yōsai; 1141–1215), founder of the Rinzai sect of Zen Buddhism in Japan, and author of the *Kissa Yōjōki* (Drinking Tea for Health). Kamakura period, 13th century. Property of Kenninji Temple, Kyoto.

the references to tea in the Heian period were all scattered ones in poetry, this book was devoted primarily to tea, and its title might be rendered as "Drinking Tea for Health." The first point about Eisai that one must bear in mind is that it was he, together with Shunjōbō Chōgen of Tōdaiji,[1] who revived the cultural exchange between China and Japan after it had fallen into abeyance during the middle of the Heian era. Second, it was Eisai who brought Zen Buddhism to Japan from China, where it had flourished as Chan, and who established the Rinzai sect of Zen in Japan. Third among his achievements was that he popularized Chinese-style tea drinking among the Japanese.

Eisai was born in 1141 in Kibitsu in Bitchū province (modern Okayama prefecture) and died in his seventy-fifth year in 1215. He began his career by exploring the esoteric teachings of Tendai Buddhism and was called Yōjō Shōnin, Saint Yōjō, for his espousal of the Tendai teachings. In 1168 at age twenty-seven he ventured to Song China, there met Chōgen, who had gone before, and together they proceeded up to Mount Tiantai, the institutional center of his sect. Though he returned to Japan within the year, later, in 1187, Eisai crossed over to

China a second time and remained for an additional four years. During this second sojourn he abandoned his original intention, which was to travel on to India, and studied instead at the Wenniansi on Mount Tiantai with Xu'an Huaibi, from whom he received formal certification of his enlightenment. Once again in 1191, by now fifty years old, he departed Song China for Hirado in Kyushu.

When he returned to Japan, he brought with him the precepts of Zen, of course, and was determined to propagate that sect's teachings. But he had also closely followed the customs and uses of the drinking of tea and brought back seeds of the tea plant. These he would also propagate, for he had learned how to cultivate the plant during his years in China. The experience and knowledge that Eisai had accumulated there were to become the basis for *Kissa Yōjōki*. Tradition tells us that Eisai planted his tea seeds in the garden of the Ishigamibō at Seburiyama in Hizen.

From his use of tea to treat the ailing Shogun Sanetomo and from his writing of the *Kissa Yōjōki*, we can guess how enthusiastically Eisai promoted his discovery. The record of his treatment of Sanetomo can be found in *Azuma Kagami*, particularly the entries for the second month of 1214. On the third day of that month, the entry of this official record of the shogunate said that the shogun had returned from a pilgrimage to Izu and had attended an entertainment given by Adachi Kagemori. The entry for the fourth day said:

> The shogun was taken a bit ill, and various attendants attempted to treat him. This was not so serious but was from overindulgence in wine the previous evening. The priest Yōjō, who had come to perform incantations and learned the situation, brought a bowl of tea from his temple, saying it was good medicine. He also asked the attendants to give the shogun a scroll of writings about the virtues of tea, and the shogun was said to have been greatly pleased. Priest Yōjō indicated he had written it recently during his breaks from meditation.[2]

This well-known source demonstrates Eisai's attitude toward tea and his interest in it, how he regarded the drinking of tea in China, and why he wrote the *Kissa Yōjōki* to promote its spread. That is, he was primarily concerned with the medicinal effects of tea and viewed it in quite a practical light. There was virtually no mention of how tea was to be served or of matters of mental preparation for the taking of tea.

Those of us who are interested in the development of "tea" into an art find works like *Kissa Yōjōki* to be extremely valuable for our researches. That is to say, though there are major differences from the way we think about tea today, the differences themselves may have historical utility for our understanding of tea.

In the last section of the second volume of *Kissa Yōjōki* Eisai noted the following:

> When Eisai [that is, I] was in China and was traveling from Mount Tiantai to Mingzhou, it was the tenth day of the sixth month and so extremely hot that people were fainting. Just at that point the proprietor of a shop produced a container eight parts full of clove and then filled it with water. This decoction he heated well for some time. Why he did this, I do not know. After he had finished heating it he poured a generous amount into a tea cup, brought it to Eisai, and had him drink it. The man said: "Priest, when the weather is hot and you have walked a long way and perspired freely, you will certainly feel bad. So that is why I had you drink this."
>
> To make this brew one needs one measure of clove and a measure and a half of water. Heat these together until it boils down to two cups. After drinking, one will feel cool and refreshed in spirit. [Everyone in China] knows that this makes one feel cool in hot weather and warm when it is very cold.[3]

The decoction described in this passage was not tea at all but clove, a spice, and the entry, near the end of a volume on tea, raises questions about its inclusion. Yet, it is precisely a passage such as this that shows us what Eisai was trying to do in *Kissa Yōjōki*. Moreover, he explained, "Spice decoctions have the same effectiveness as tea, so one may take them [as well]."[4] Clearly, Eisai considered tea to be a medicine, and it is for that reason that he wrote *Kissa Yōjōki*.

Also near the end of the volume, Eisai wrote: "I have written this book on health in this latter, degenerate age, with the aid of the Buddha. One will find here only correct information that I have brought over from China and not merely something that I have written as I pleased. With it one can cure all manner of diseases."[5] He then went on to assert with great confidence at the very end of the volume that there was a basis for everything he had written and that these practices continued in China at present. He said that those who doubted were free to travel there to find out for themselves.[6]

Let us now examine *Kissa Yōjōki* more closely, to see its structure and content in detail as well as Eisai's purpose in compiling it. First of all, there are several variants of the text, the two main strains of which are distinguished by the dates of the inscriptions in them. The first set of variants have the date "First day, first month of the fifth year of the Jōgen era [1211]" inscribed at the beginning and, at the end, "Brushed by my own hand after the season of silence, the third day of the first month of the fifth year of the Jōgen era."[7] Eisai would have seen his seventieth birthday in that year. Two copies from this textual line have been discovered, the Jufukuji and the Tawa Bunko versions.[8]

The latter line of textual variants contains a prefatory date three years later, that is, the first month of the second year of Kenpō (1214). There are several known copies, including the Shiryō Hensanjo, Kenninji, and *Gunsho Ruijū* texts. Both main variants contain two volumes, but there are some disparities between them. The version that I have chosen to consult here is the earlier of the two.

The work comprises two main sections, the first of which is titled, "The Harmonizing of the Five Organs" and the second, "Avoiding the Evil Spirits." The former was a physiological study of ways to maintain balance among the body's internal organs, while the latter was a pathological treatise on exorcising the external demons that were thought to invade the body and cause disease. Moreover, the former advocated the use of tea, while the latter relied on mulberry for medicinal effect. For this reason an alternate title is *Chasōkyō, The Classic of Tea and Mulberry*. *Shoken Nichiroku*, a diary by Kikō Daishuku, has an entry dated 1486/3/15 that mentions that a certain Honkyoshi had come to borrow a book on mulberry and that the volume dated from the founding of the Kenninji.[9] Since Eisai had founded the Kenninji in 1202, Daishuku must have been referring to the second volume of this work.

The preface had this statement that delivered exactly what the title promised:

> In this latter age, tea is a marvelous elixir of health that has the capacity to prolong human life. It grows in mountains and valleys, the sort of land where the spirits of gods dwell. We humans

take it and extend our lives. India and China both esteem this drink. In olden days in Japan as well, people loved to use it. Thus, from ancient times to the present, both here and abroad, tea has served us well. There is certainly no reason we should stop using it now. Indeed, it is a splendid medicine for this latter, degenerate age, and there is no need to stint in its use. The human body was formerly as strong as that of a god, containing, as it does, the four elements of earth [flesh and bone], water [blood], fire [body heat], and wind [energy and movement]. In this latter age, however, flesh and bone have withered like wood that has gone rotten. Acupuncture and moxabustion are painful, while mineral baths offer no effective relief, so that people who use these treatments grow weaker and finally expire. One can but dread this result.[10]

Eisai was extraordinarily conscious of the Buddhist concept of the Latter Day of the Law, which was a time of degeneracy and decline, and seemed convinced that his was precisely such an age. He was concerned with ways that people could survive the trials of this difficult era. Thus it was that he stressed how admirably tea was suited to this purpose and described it as "a marvelous elixir of health with the capacity to prolong life." Since tea grew in land inhabited by gods, one's health could only improve by imbibing its divine qualities.

It is clear that the Buddhist concept of the Ages of the Law was a major factor in Eisai's thinking. There were three such ages of the Law or the Dharma: the age of the correct law, that of semblance law, and that of the latter law. There were a variety of theories in Japan regarding the length of each era, but two predominated. One held that the correct law would last for one thousand years after the Buddha's death, semblance law for five hundred more, and the latter law for another ten thousand years. The other maintained that each of the first two ages would last for one thousand years and the third stage for ten thousand years. This thinking derived from the parts of the Buddhist canon, the Tripitaka, which comprised three types of law. The first was the Buddha's teachings, the second, his discipline, and the third, the theological or philosophical proofs of his thought. During the first age of the correct law, all three of these would be abroad in the world. In the second, however, though believers would continue to have the capacity to follow the forms embodied in the first two parts, those who understood the philosophical rationale would disappear, leaving only the semblance of Buddhism embodied in the first two. In the final stage of the law, the teachings would remain, but discipline would also vanish, making this an era of strife, upheaval, and natural calamity. In Japan it was widely accepted that this third stage would arrive in the seventh year of the Eijō era, 1052, during the reign of Emperor Go-Reizei. *Fusō Ryakki,* a historical compilation by a priest from Mount Hiei, contained an entry for the twenty-sixth day of the first month of that year that said, "This year saw the onset of the Latter Day of the Law."[11] In Japan the theologian Genshin has been most closely identified with the Latter Law concept. He wrote *Ōjōyōshū,* Elements Essential for Salvation, perhaps in 985, which would have been less than a century before the supposed date of entry into the Latter Day of the Law.

Eisai's life spanned the late twelfth and early thirteenth centuries, and a glimpse at his era reveals why it was that he and others believed that Japan had entered just such an age of conflict and disorder as the Latter Day theologians had predicted. It was during his lifetime that Japan passed from the Heian era into the Kamakura, a transition that was attended by bloodshed. The samurai of the Taira house contended against the Minamoto, and each sought support among the civil aristocrats of the capital. The Hōgen Disturbance of 1156 was soon followed by the Heiji, three years later, and these proved only the prelude to the epoch-making Genpei War of 1180 to 1185, which drew its name from the Chinese-style pronunciations of the characters for Minamoto and Taira, respectively, the two chief warrior adversaries in it. That war reached its denouement at the Battle of Dannoura in 1185, with the destruction of the Taira forces and the death of the boy emperor whose cause they claimed to serve.

As often as not, fractious monks from the principal temples in the capital region armed themselves and participated freely in the melee. Sometimes, as in 1169 or 1177, armed monks from Mount Hiei bullied the court. At other times, the aristocrats recruited warriors to fend off threats in response to rumors of monkish extortion. The religious orders reserved their most vicious attacks for competing temples, and there were regular battles between the monks from the top of Mount Hiei and those at its foot. Pagodas and temple buildings literally went up in smoke, torched by hostile clerics. Squabbles within a single temple were as likely as pitched battles between temples. Eisai was not alone in his dismay at this turbulence; anyone might conclude that the order the Buddha had prescribed for the brotherhood of monks had vanished. One of Eisai's contemporaries, the monk Jien, son of Fujiwara Tadamichi, regent for the emperor, felt the upheavals of the era, with its warring monks, no less keenly. Jien served on four occasions as a Tendai sect abbot at Mount Hiei, with his first appointment in 1192. He lamented:

> Painful to contemplate, the waters of the Law
> Grow shallow in this Latter Day. Wild temple of Hiei.
>
> Already the Law is vanishing, its lamp extinguished.
> Fearsome indeed is the darkness.
>
> Yet we are powerless to arrest the ebbing of the light,
> Lamp of the vanishing Law.[12]

Jien's most famous work was *Gukanshō*, a history that he wrote in about 1220. In it he sought to interpret the age of the Latter Day of the Law by applying the principle of *dōri*, reason. He explained the circumstances that impelled him to write by saying that since the Hōgen era (1156–1159) there had been nothing but turbulence. People had avoided writing about it because they preferred to deal with better times, but "I have begun to write, hoping that this will bring peace to a mind that has been mulling over matters of [conflict and confusion]."[13]

Jien was attempting to discover the underlying reasons behind the instability and chaos of his own Age of the Latter Law, and his approach in doing so was to take up the issue of the true Dharma of Buddhism. My purpose here is not to examine the thinking behind the concept of the Latter Day of the Law, but to consider further the social conditions of that day. A useful source for that is *Gyokuyō*, the diary of the Kanpaku Kujō Kanezane, Jien's elder brother. Several references in the journal refer to meetings with Saint Hōnen (1133–1212), the founder of the Pure Land Sect of Buddhism. The entry for 1189/8/1, for example, said, "I asked the sage of Hōnen Hall to explain to me the Dharma and rebirth." Other entries refer to having Hōnen perform the ceremony of Jukai, which admits the believer to the discipline of the Buddha, and the intoning of the Nenbutsu, the praise of the Buddha Amida. The entry for 1200/9/30 noted: "A great event occurred in the women's quarters, and so we called Hōnen to perform the Jukai.

It was effective; we should be extremely grateful."[14] Kanezane did many favors for his younger brother, Jien. During the latter's first term as abbot, he established a temple at Mudōji and completed a great temple complex on his own initiative, while Jien cooperated with that effort. Yet even as he performed these acts on behalf of the Tendai sect, he himself was a devout follower of the Pure Land teachings of Hōnen and had converted in hopes of receiving the quotidian benefits that Hōnen promised. Kanezane found scant comfort in the strained logic of his younger brother and the efforts to escape the Latter Day of the Law. He preferred the faith in the Buddha Amida that Hōnen expounded.[15]

After 1052, when the world was thought to have entered the Latter Day of the Law, some buried their bodies in the earth, trusting to the bodhisattva Miroku; others copied sutras or found faith in the Buddha Amida; and some simply despaired. This is the context in which Eisai took up his interest in tea, hoping to survive the end of the Law. It is for this reason that we find expressions such as "[Tea] is a good medicine for preserving one's health in this Latter Day."[16] Eisai may have considered tea drinking to be a way to cope with the challenges of his era.

Eisai explained the significance of the human body from the beginning of the world when he wrote, "If one considers matters fully, he will see that when Heaven created all things it gave the closest attention to the creation of humankind. The most prudent course, therefore, is to preserve our health and carefully to protect the life that Heaven has given us."[17] His reasoning rests essentially on a Confucian view of the world and of humanity, which maintains that since Heaven is the creator of all things, our physical bodies have been entrusted to us by Heaven. It is, therefore, incumbent upon us to maximize the span of our years. At the very least we ought to avoid unhealthy habits that will cause damage. This is clear from the Confucian belief that holds, for example, that it is an act of filial piety to avoid harm to oneself, inasmuch as the body is a gift from one's parents. No doubt Taoist notions of immortality also played a role in his thinking.

It was a distinctly Chinese concept that maintained because life is the "gift of Heaven," one should do as Heaven dictated and obey the Decree of Heaven. Alas, however, the Latter Day of the Law had made it impossible to achieve this end. With disharmony within the body, one would die an untimely death. People took medicine and freely applied acupuncture and moxabustion, but these served only to weaken the body further and achieved no useful purpose. This, asserted Eisai, was a lamentable state. The reason, he said, was that people, lacking fundamental knowledge about disease itself, did not know how to maintain their health based upon such knowledge. He continued:

> The way to preserve one's health is to pacify the five organs [liver, lungs, heart, spleen, kidneys]. Among these five the heart is sovereign, and the drinking of tea is a superior way to promote its strength. To ignore the heart invites weakness in all the organs, and that in turn endangers not only the organs but life itself. It has been over two thousand years since the illustrious healer, Jīva, passed away in India, and in these latter degenerate days there is none who correctly understands the pulsing of the heart. It has been over three thousand years since Shennong, the discoverer of Chinese medicine, disappeared, and today we no longer understand the use of medicine. Accordingly, with no one to turn to for treatment, people suffer needlessly until they die. Even if they learn methods of treatment but use them incorrectly, as with useless moxabustion, for example, great damage to the body can result. I have heard that the use of medicine today often harms the heart because the medicines are inappropriate. Since moxabustion, for example, can conflict with the pulse, the patient may die from its use. Consequently, I wish to set forth modern methods of treatment such as those I have investigated in China. There are in general two approaches suitable for the diseases in this latter degenerate age, and I have explained them in hopes they will be helpful to others in future.[18]

Thus, Eisai explained, in accordance with the Decree of Heaven, one should maintain the well-being of the body's five principal internal organs, of which the heart was the most important. The way to do that best, he said, was to drink tea. The healers of the classical age in India and China, Jīva and Shennong, had been gone for thousands of years and the knowledge they had was lost, so that proper treatments were no longer available in the latter day. Misunderstanding the proper methods, alas, caused pain and death. That was why he wrote: to explain for the benefit of later ages the two main types of treatments available, first, the harmonizing of the five internal organs to preserve health, and second, defense of the body against external diseases. In these ways, he said, one could deal with the diseases common in the age of degeneracy.

When Eisai wrote, "Tea is a marvelous medicine for preserving people's health in this Latter Age," he was spelling out his intent in writing the treatise. His intent was to explain the health secrets and the proper practice of medicine that had been passed on to him during his studies in China. These secrets would allow people to live out the naturally allotted span of their years in robust health. We can assume that Eisai's aim was to propagate approaches to tea drinking that were current in China while he was there. Since he was interested primarily in its medicinal properties and its uses for prolonging life, one will discover here no trace of the spiritual attitudes or high, poetic realm that Lu Yu and the Chinese literati found in tea. Eisai's interests were extremely utilitarian.

Following the preface came the two main parts of the text. Eisai began with a discourse on the fundamental principles that governed the health of the human body, the section on the harmonizing of the five organs. The second part dealt with the defense of the body from external diseases. The former, therefore, took up physiological issues, while the latter dealt with pathological ones. Eisai explained disease first as it related to the body's constitution, and then he examined the causes of disease, which he attributed to one's attitude toward life.

In the first part, "Harmonizing of the Five Organs," Eisai quoted an esoteric scripture called the Conquest of Hell to the effect that the liver likes acid tastes; the lung, pungent tastes; the heart, bitter ones; the spleen, sweet; and the kidneys, salty flavors. These in turn were related to the five elements of Chinese science as shown below:

Organ	Direction	Season	Element	Color	Spirit	Sense Organ
liver	east	spring	wood	blue	soul (of spirit)	eyes
lungs	west	autumn	metal	white	soul (of flesh)	nose
heart	south	summer	fire	red	deity	tongue
spleen	center	ends of seasons	earth	yellow	will	mouth
kidneys	north	winter	water	black	imagination	spine and ears

Eisai explained that when the organs were out of balance, the body immediately suffered. The heart, which was central among them, played a key part, and any weakness there would derange the whole and so shorten life.

> Each of the five organs prefers a different taste, and if one organ enjoys too much of the taste it prefers, it will grow too strong and overpower the other organs near it, producing disease. The four flavors of pungent, acid, sweet, and salty we eat in abundance, but the bitter taste [preferred by the heart] is lacking. This means that the other four organs are strong while the heart remains weak, and disease results. (In Japanese we call this illness *shinjo*.) When the heart is diseased, all of the tastes change. Thus, we vomit what we eat or stop eating altogether. If we drink tea, however, we will restore the heart and banish disease.[19]

He thereupon explained how the five organs related to the other sets of fives that Chinese science had determined to be important in understanding the physical world. In particular, each organ had a special flavor that it preferred. When one took an excessive amount of a single flavor, the corresponding organ would grow strong at the expense of the others. The Japanese diet, he said, provided ample quantities of pungent, acid, sweet, and salty flavors but not the bitter taste. For this reason Japanese suffered excessively from diseases of the heart, which depended on such bitter flavors. Indeed, the weakness of the heart affected all the organs adversely. For this reason he prescribed the drinking of tea as the way to develop the heart's strength and so eradicate disease. Tea, he asserted, supplied this one essential ingredient that the heart required for its well-being.

The basis of this thinking, which identified the five organs as key anatomical components, lay in the Chinese concept of *wuxing*, the five first principles. No doubt, Indian ideas of five great elements also played a role. The scientists of traditional Asia had analyzed all phenomena in the world in terms of these five fundamental units, which were the building blocks for the universe. In China the five were wood, fire, earth, metal, and water, while in India they were earth, water, fire, wind, and the sky or the void. In anatomy they had cleverly aligned the major internal organs with one or another of these elements. The principal flavors similarly fell into the five categories. Therefore, just as the heart was the central organ, the bitter taste that the heart preferred was the principal flavor. Tea, of course, was a source of that bitter taste.

For Eisai, this method of analysis, aligning the five elements with the five organs and the five flavors, was associated with the secret lore of esoteric Buddhism, particularly the Shingon sect. Today one can no longer find such Shingon teachings, which Eisai cited as his authority, but they provided the unifying principles behind his physiological analysis. As we have seen, however, Eisai was an adherent of Zen, which professed a belief in the transmission of truth outside the scriptures. It is unclear, therefore, how he came to employ Shingon esotericism as the basis for his arguments. It is not enough simply to dismiss Eisai as an eclectic. Perhaps he used them because they were among the most widely understood teachings of his day. In any event, as one reads the *Kissa Yōjōki*, one is impressed with his erudition and the dexterity with which he constructed his analysis.

Eisai concluded his general statement by writing, "The heart is sovereign among the organs; tea is the chief source of its preferred taste; and bitter is chief among the flavors." He then continued with his main point, "Drink lots of tea, for it will restore your energy and spirits to full strength."

After having explained the *wuxing* with its five organs and five flavors and having told his readers how tea benefits the heart, Eisai next turned his attention to tea itself, drawing from the Chinese classics including Lu Yu's *Chajing* to explain what sort of plant and beverage it was. First he took up the issue of the name "tea." He recounted the various Chinese names for it that we have encountered earlier in this volume. He cited *Erya*, for example, as well as gazetteers from south China to provide information on variant ways of writing the Chinese characters for its different names. Next, in the second section of part 1 he turned to the appearance of the tea plant and its flower. *Erya* called it "a shrub like a gardenia" as did other works, including *Chajing* itself. The latter also indicated that it had a white flower, which Lu Yu described as similar to a rose.[20]

The third section, "Clarifying Effects," dealt with tea's medicinal efficacy, no doubt the most significant topic for Eisai. He began by explaining how priceless it was, citing *Wuxingji* to indicate that tea was a valued product grown as tribute paid to the sovereign. *Songlu* described its taste as like nectar, the dew of the gods.[21]

He then moved into the heart of the topic, quoting sources that showed how it could be used. *Guangya*, for example, said that tea suppressed drunkenness and banished drowsiness. It also said that sleep causes disease and that one who avoids sleep will not fall ill. Another work, *Bowuzhi*, said that sleep dulls intellectual function and that tea will prevent that problem by reducing the need for rest. *Bencao*, a work on botany, noted that tea had a sweet, bitter, cool taste and was not poison. Drinking it healed pox. It was also a diuretic, a stimulant, and an aid to digestion whose regular use prevented disease.[22]

A further train of Chinese authorities was evoked to add weight to the argument, including one that asserted that regular tea drinking would cause one to sprout wings and become a sage, though eating leeks at the same time would counteract that effect and make the body heavy. An account of Mount Tiantai corroborated that regular tea usage would cause wings to develop and enable the drinker to fly. Eisai himself testified that it contributed to sagelike qualities. In a more practical vein, *Xinlu* indicated that it not only made the body lighter but also alleviated symptoms that modern scholars have interpreted as those of beriberi. Eisai called it a marvelous medicine to counteract that deficiency.[23]

He also recorded that the people in the islands off Guangzhou prized tea highly for its prophylactic properties. Miasmal fevers were endemic in that area of southern China, so that officials posted there from the capital often fell ill, and most died before being able to return north. Eisai explained that was because the food in the area, though delicious, was quite indigestible. For that reason the local people chewed betel nut and drank tea. If they ate too much of the wonderful cuisine without drinking tea, it wrought havoc on the body. The cause was the continual presence of the miasmal vapors there. Japan had no such worries, since it lay in a more northerly climate. So highly esteemed was tea in this part of China that it was a tribute product to be supplied to the court and not for the use of the lower orders in society.[24]

Finally, the third section of part 1 concluded with notes to the poems of Bai Letian, which mentioned tea drinking. One said that by drinking the beverage one could stay awake all night without hardship and another that drinking wine made the drinker thirsty but tea slaked that thirst. If instead of tea one took plain hot water, however, a variety of illnesses would ensue.[25]

The fourth section had the title "Explanation of the Season to Pick Tea." Eisai first cited the *Chajing* and *Chalu* in this connection. The former had said, "One picks tea in the second, third and fourth months." The latter referred to an imperial ordinance that decreed that new tea for imperial tribute should be picked following the onset of spring (February 4 by the modern calendar). That provided an opportunity for peasants to rest during the winter. Following the decree, therefore, that had become the season for harvesting tribute tea. Eisai noted that taking tea early in the year for imperial tribute first began in the Tang era, according to a history of that dynasty. The Song court also had it harvested at the same time. It was their practice to assemble the laborers during the first three days of the new year and to send them out into tea fields behind the palace. The first day they would walk about and inspect the fields. The second day they would pick just about two-tenths of an inch of the newest shoots. The tea produced in this manner was extremely rare and valuable, costing a thousand strings of cash for one spoonful.[26]

The following section explained how to pick tea and relied on the *Chajing,* which advised not picking, roasting, or steaming tea on days when it rained or even when it was cloudy. The reason was that the essence of the product would be weak and inferior in quality.[27]

The processing of tea was Eisai's next topic. All the previous sections had relied primarily on citations to classical sources, but this sixth section alone did not. In fact, Mori Shikazō has discovered that Eisai employed some twenty-two types of citations and that all appeared in one compilation called *Taiping Yulan.*[28] Here, however, Eisai began with the line "As I have seen in Song China," suggesting that he based this section on what he had actually seen and heard while on the continent. He wrote, "One picks the tea in the morning and immediately steams and then roasts it." With no chance to rest between, he said, this was no work for sluggards. Then he described the processing:

> One spreads paper on a roasting shelf and heats it just so that the paper will not burn. This needs ingenuity and should be neither too slow nor too fast. Roast it through the night without sleeping, and roast that night all the tea that has been picked. Finally, put it into a container of high quality and seal it tightly with bamboo leaves. If one does so, the tea will keep for years without going bad.[29]

He concluded that it was most important to complete all preparations in advance when one intended to pick tea. It is of interest that the processing of tea described here is completely different from that in *Chajing*. One sealed the roasted tea leaves in a storage jar directly without further processing. This demonstrates that Eisai was describing not brick-tea but leaf-tea production.

Finally, in the first volume, Eisai explained his greatest motive for writing in this fashion: "The way to preserve health in this Latter Day is as I have documented. In general, those who practice medicine in our country do not know how to produce tea and so do not use it as a remedy. Not only that, but they even speak ill of it and claim that it is not a medicine. This is because they do not know the virtue of tea."[30] Eisai hoped to rectify this state of affairs.

He continued that while on the continent he had observed how highly the Chinese esteemed tea. They had written so often about it that it was not feasible to cite all of the references to it. But in China, now as in the past, when an emperor has a loyal minister, he will always reward him with tea. To a priest who can explain the Dharma, he will likewise supply the beverage. Eisai went on to put his case even more pointedly, for he said that if one does not drink tea, the heart will grow weak and taking medicine will be of no avail. He hoped, therefore, that all persons in the Latter Day, regardless of social station, would be aware of its importance.[31] Perhaps what is most distinct about *Kissa Yōjōki* as opposed to *Chajing* or other works is not so much its desire to propagate the use of tea as its adoption of the Latter Day world view as a means to do so. The structure of this first volume, paradoxically, may be described as a rational, inductive explanation of tea. To sum up his intent in writing *Kissa Yōjōki*, we can conclude the following: First, Eisai was interested only in the physiological properties of tea. Second, he attached no significance to the act of drinking tea and had scant interest in any intellectual concerns incidental to that act.

For Eisai tea was a beverage. His concern was with its medicinal and botanical properties only. When from time to time he cited Chinese authorities such as Lu Yu, he did so only for the purpose of clarifying these effects of tea. In no way did this approach resemble the world view of Lu Yu.

In the second volume, "Avoiding the Evil Spirits," Eisai reinforced his message of medical succor for the Latter Day of the Law. He began by quoting the secret teachings of Ātavaka, which said: "In the Latter Day the human life span will be one hundred years. Even those who follow the austerities and who should strive to follow the Way of the Buddha will transgress dignity. When that occurs, the land will descend into chaos and the people will lament. In such an age evil spirits and ghosts will assault the land, vex the populace, and cause manifold ills for which there will be no remedy."[32] Eisai averred that "in recent years such ills have in fact befallen us"; the Latter Day had arrived. There were five types of ailments that would prevail: diseases of thirst, stroke in which the limbs do not obey the will, diseases of appetite, those of the skin, and finally beriberi. Eisai explained the symptoms and treatments for each. However, the best way to treat these, he said, was to use mulberry, because it was a tree "sacred to those who have striven to become buddhas in past ages" and thus can be used to heal all five of these conditions. Altogether he listed eight types of treatments using the leaves, wood, and fruit of the mulberry in infusion, in gruel, and even as a pillow. As additional treatments he listed also "tea drinking" and "the five-fragrance decoction."[33]

The "tea drinking" he prescribed was the method he had learned in Song China and for which he had brought tea seeds back to Japan. He wrote that the tea should be drunk extremely hot, and the amount of tea should be two or three spoons about the size of a copper coin. One may use more or less and vary the amount of water according to taste. Since he used the expression "two or three spoons the size of a copper coin," clearly he was referring to powdered tea. After mentioning its effects, he continued, "The gods have a taste for tea, so when making an offering to them, one should present it; if one does not present tea, the offering will be wanting." He concluded his adulation of tea, saying it "is a treasure and may be found among the gods in the realm above as well as below as a nourishment to save those whose bodies have been violated." "Most medicines treat only a single ailment, but tea is a panacea for all ills."[34]

The final section covered his "five-fragrance decoction." The treatment involved drinking an infusion of five different sorts of aromatic substances: laurel, aloe, clove, benzoin, and musk. One should grind these and take one *monme* (ca. 3.75 grams) per day. To infuse and drink them without powdering them would reduce their effectiveness. Perhaps this was also the reason for powdering tea rather than simply infusing that as well. Eisai asserted that the five-fragrance decoction and tea both had the same effect.[35]

Such a quotidian interpretation as found in *Kissa Yōjōki* may seem surprising from a devotee of Zen, but it may be characteristic of the thought of Eisai himself. We are told that the proximate motive be-hind the writing of the book was the treatment of the indisposition of Sanetomo, but the reason Eisai took the approach he did in the book may have had less to do with that immediate goal than with the fact that Eisai was really interested in tea only from such a rational, practi-cal standpoint. It hardly mattered to Eisai whether tea came from China or not; for him it was simply a beverage. It was perhaps quite natural for him to view it in that extremely pragmatic light.

5 Tea in the Temples of the Medieval Era

Tradition has it that it was in 1214 that Eisai wrote his *Kissa Yōjōki*.[1] Thereafter, up until the end of the Kamakura era, priests especially, as well as many warriors and aristocrats, enjoyed drinking tea. As we have seen in the previous chapter, Eisai returned to Japan from his second sojourn in China in 1191 carrying tea seeds, which he then planted at Seburiyama in Hizen province. This was called Ishigami tea. The traditional account continues that Eisai presented some of his tea seeds to Saint Myōe at Toganoo in Kyoto and that they were in a persimmon-shaped tea container, which had been brought over from China and is still preserved at the nearby temple Kōzanji. Myōe planted his seeds there and they flourished, eventually spreading to other areas.

One can surmise the contemporary view of tea from the *Isei Teikin Ōrai*, which said, "In our country tea comes originally from Toganoo. For the founder of the temple there, the devil of sleep was an obstacle to Zen practice, so as a means to overcome it, he planted tea to be a food for the concentration of the mind."[2] This then was the initial reason for the cultivation of tea. The postscript on a copy of a sutra dated 1321 and preserved in the well-known medieval library the Kanazawa Bunko asserted, "After seven cups of tea I have conquered the devil of sleep and burned nine wicks in my lamp to accomplish the copying [of this sutra]."[3] Thus, as late as the end of the Kamakura era, for priests, tea was nothing more than a means "to conquer the devil of sleep."

Saint Myōe, who planted the tea at Toganoo, is regarded today as among the patrons of the Way of Tea. He had an Ashiya-type kettle on which he had had cast an inscription listing the ten virtues of its effects:

The *Ayanokakiheta chaire*, persimmon-shaped tea container, which tradition says Eisai used to present tea seeds to Myōe. The ivory lid dates from a later era. Southern Song dynasty. Height, 4.5 cm; diameter of mouth, 6.2 cm; diameter of base, 2.8 cm. Property of Kōzanji Temple, Kyoto.

1. Divine protection of the buddhas
2. Harmonizing of the five organs
3. Filial piety
4. Expunging desire
5. Prolonging life
6. Banishing sleep
7. Freedom from morbidity
8. No ill effects from regular use
9. Divine protection of the [Shinto] gods
10. Equanimity in the face of death[4]

The second of these, the harmonizing of the five organs, had come from the *Chajing* through Eisai. Others, such as prolonging life, banishing sleep, freedom from morbidity, or no ill effects from regular use, were no doubt ideas that Myōe had taken up from Eisai's *Kissa Yōjōki*. The remaining ones, the protection of the gods and buddhas or the belief in nirvana and equanimity in the face of death, may have been virtues of

Detail of a painting of Myōe (1173–1232) in meditation. Kamakura period, 13th century. National Treasure. Myōe, a Buddhist monk of the Kegon sect, played an important role in propagating tea in Japan by planting tea seeds, which he had received from Eisai, nearby his temple, Kōzanji, at Toganoo in Kyoto. Property of Kōzanji Temple, Kyoto.

tea that he had conceived as useful in preaching to the people about its benefits.

We have thus far devoted our attention primarily to materials on tea relating to Eisai, the founder of the Rinzai sect in Japan. The growth of tea drinking from the Kamakura era on has enjoyed a close connection to that variety of Zen. The taste for tea, however, was by no means confined to priests of the Rinzai sect. A second major figure who employed tea in connection with Zen meditation and at temple meals was Dōgen, who traveled to Song China somewhat later than Eisai and returned with the teachings of the Sōtō sect, which he preached at his temple, the Eiheiji.

Dōgen was born in 1200 the scion of an aristocratic lineage. His father was Kuga Michichika, the Great Minister of the Center, and his mother was the daughter of Fujiwara Motofusa, the prime minister. At the age of twelve he took the tonsure to study with the Tendai abbot Kōen, and in 1214 he visited Eisai at the Kenninji to seek the Way. Later, in 1223, he traveled to China with Myōzen and remained until 1227, when he returned to Japan full of zeal to save his countrymen. At age forty-three he betook his monk's staff to the mountains of Echizen province and founded there the monastery Eiheiji. Finally, in 1253 he entrusted the temple's affairs to his successor, Gikai, and with his companion Kaisō returned to Kyoto, where he died in the eighth month. Dōgen's thinking is a splendid example of religious philosophy. His keen logic and profound theory have given him a leading place in Japanese thought. The special character of his religious ideas can be found in his detailed discipline, which he expounded in *Eihei Shingi*. Dōgen displayed a noble heart and lived simply. He spurned worldly fame and wealth, making no effort to align himself with the political powers of his day.[5]

Eihei Shingi comprises two sections, the greater discipline and the lesser discipline. The former, in a section titled "Preaching the Way," explained the daily routine and etiquette for entering and leaving the meditation hall. It made provision for the drinking of tea, as we can see from the line "After meals, return to the assembly hall to drink tea or hot water."[6] Another passage, explaining twelve charts of the assembly area, indicated that this was the place where the monks could read and take tea after meals, warm themselves with heated stones in their clothing, or conduct special tea functions. The lesser discipline, in the section for the New Year, similarly noted, "The leader will sound the gong two times before the hall, and the lay brothers will serve tea bowls first to the chief priest and any special guests who are to be entertained and then to the general assembly. Later after a break, when they are bidden, the company will drink the tea."[7] From this it appears that the practice in this case was first to carry tea bowls to everyone and after that to make the tea. The bowls were distributed with tea already in them, and the individual who was to make the tea would then go from person to person to add hot water and whisk it up. This was a ceremony for New Year's Day.

Entries in the *Eihei Shingi* that mention tea in a formal, ceremonial context are not uncommon. Whether following meals or during rituals, tea was a regular feature of temple life. During the first three days of the New Year, for example, the assembly of monks as well as special dignitaries would take tea after they had eaten. The discipline instructed the temple's steward to serve the monks on other days throughout the year as well. Following a ritual held on the twelfth day of the fourth month, the monks would receive food and tea and would be joined in this by the chief monk. When an itinerant monk first joined the brotherhood for a brief stay, the other monks would prepare tea as a part of their ritual of welcome. What was noteworthy about these entries was the ceremonial, systematic nature of the use of tea on these occasions. *Eihei Shingi* specified quite detailed actions, as during the New Year service when the monks were to bow once after clearing away their dishes. Again on the twenty-fifth day of the eighth month, those serving tea and sweets were enjoined "to withdraw, bowing three times."[8] Such careful regulation of tea service in Zen temples was never characteristic of China, by contrast. The following will give an idea of the degree of specificity the discipline contained:

> First, the individual responsible for tea will strike the sounding board before the monks' quarters. When he does, the assembly will place their hands palms together, bow once in thanks, and take their seats. The one who is to prepare the tea will proceed to the center brazier and light incense. There should not be more than nine people assembled at this time. When the small sounding board inside the monks' quarters is struck, there will be a bow and the tea bowls, distributed. Thereupon, the server will move around the room preparing the tea. The assembly will then raise their bowls in presentation and drink the tea. When finished they will bow and collect the tea bowls. Finally, the chief of the monks' quarters will express thanks to the person who prepared the tea.[9]

Though Dōgen had based his discipline on earlier Chinese models, including Baizhang Huaihai's *Baizhang Qinggui* from the Tang period and Songyi's *Chanyuan Qinggui* from Song, his *Eihei Shingi* is the oldest source to deal with rituals involving tea in a Zen context. At the stage when Eisai had brought his seeds over from China, there were as yet absolutely no rituals for the use of tea, but in *Eihei Shingi* they appear fully developed. To learn of these early tea rituals as they survive in Zen temples today one can see the memorial service held for Eisai at Kenninji in Kyoto each year in April. Kyoto's Myōshinji has similar ceremonies. These preserve the primitive forms found in Dōgen's discipline.

Though it is difficult to determine precisely when the tea rituals at Kenninji and Myōshinji began, it is virtually certain that they date from the late Kamakura or Nanbokuchō era, that is, the fourteenth century. Two sources provide some support for this view. One is a copybook, *Kissa Ōrai*, which deals with tea rituals and is said to have been written by the priest Gen'e in the late Kamakura era. Since I intend to treat that work in some detail later, I shall set it aside for the moment. The second source is the *Taiheiki*, the famed war tale set in the turbulence of the fourteenth century, which describes a tea party of the parvenu daimyo Sasaki Dōyo: "Assembling priceless treasures from both Japan and abroad, he adorned a great hall. He spread the skins of leopards and tigers over all the chairs, lavished damask and brocade to his liking and formed four files of seats. When one saw how they were all lined up like glorious manifestations of the Buddha, it looked no different from the haloes of a thousand deities emanating from the lines of seats."[10] The description of the guests as seated in four files, a practice still found in Zen tea rituals, leaves little doubt that Dōyo had imitated the Zen monks in his own gorgeous tea affair.

Thus far we have examined tea rituals primarily in Zen institutions. Tea in the Zen context served chiefly a medicinal, physiological function as a means of preventing the drowsiness that hindered the sect's meditative practices. Other sects, however, took much the same interest in tea for its stimulating effect.

Let us look first of all at Eison, who began the Ōchamori ritual, with its huge servings of tea, which the Saidaiji in Nara still celebrates today. Eison, who was also known as Shien, took the tonsure at a young age at Gongōōin and immersed himself in esoteric Buddhism at such temples as Kōyasan, Daigoji, and Tōdaiji. At the last of these, in particular, he studied Ritsu sect practices with Kakusei, and finally in 1235, at age thirty-four, he took up residence at the Saidaiji. At that time the temple was in an advanced state of disrepair, so he sought ways to restore it to its earlier glory, building a priests' hall in 1247 and a main Buddha Hall in 1249.

The origin of the Ōchamori ceremony dates back to 1281, when the Mongols invaded Japan. At that time Eison prayed for deliverance from the foreign threat, and on the first New Year following the destruction of the enemy fleet, he held a special celebration. First he worshiped the Shinto patron god of war, Hachiman, at his shrine within the temple's precincts and conducted a tea service there for the shrine priests. Finally, he served tea to the assembled guests. This is thought to be the earliest tradition of tea service to the public at large.[11] It was, nonetheless, merely a matter of serving the public as guests and not a ceremony in which the general populace had any pivotal role. No doubt, moreover, the people who drank the tea on those occasions left with the feeling that they had taken a dose of medicine.

Another temple practice is that of Ōbukucha at the New Year, in which participants take tea brewed with dried plum or kelp. Professor Murai Yasuhiko has said that this ceremony, like the Ōchamori rite, can be traced to offerings to the Buddha. In a text of 854 dedicated to the great prelates Ennin and Saichō, he found a mention of "an offering of

Monk preparing tea at the Ōchamori event at Saidaiji Temple, Nara. This unique ceremony, in which the general public shares in drinking huge servings of tea, dates back to 1281 and represents the earliest tradition of tea service to the public at large. Photo courtesy of Murai Yasuhiko.

cakes and tea medicine."[12] In 954 the Tendai priest Zenki made a statue of his late mother and, after offering tea and cakes, he himself partook of these offerings. It was the custom first to place the tea on the altar as an offering to the Buddha and then to remove it and drink it oneself, as Japanese continue to do today. The Ōbukucha tradition is said to have begun about the time of Emperor Murakami (r. 946–967), when the emperor recovered from an illness following an offering of tea by the monk Kūya, revered as the saint of the marketplace. Legend has it that Kūya earned his living thereafter by selling tea whisks that he made.[13]

Let us turn next to the matter of the *tenshin* food that temples, especially Zen temples, served with tea. The classical medieval copybook *Teikin Ōrai* contains quite a lengthy list of foods and utensils that one could use in serving tea. These included soups, cakes, noodles and the like for a light meal, as well as confections to follow the meal.[14] A similar source, *Yūgaku Ōrai*, contains a letter that Ōkura Hōkyō, a prelate of the temple Kajūji, wrote in reply to another divine. His letter explained how to prepare for a tea ritual at a temple. It is clear from his description that the order of the ceremony involved serving first hot water, next tea, and finally a *tenshin* meal. He also listed various sorts of fruits, noodles, dumplings, and the like that one could serve to one's guests.[15]

It is significant that one can find in all these sources taken together many of the elements that exist in a modern, formal service of tea. Today, when one has been invited on such an occasion, one finds that once all the guests have arrived, their presence is made known to the host by striking a hanging sounding board as many times as there are persons in attendance. At a Zen temple they would strike the board before the hall only once, a difference to be sure, but relatively minor. This accomplished, the host will then direct his guests by saying, "Please enjoy the hot water, and then move to the seating area by the garden." At a Zen temple one would have the hot water and drink the tea within the temple hall, whereas in *chanoyu* the guests first finish drinking the hot water, which may be lightly flavored, in the waiting area. Today the guests also walk through the tea garden, and then they enter the tea room through a low "crawling in entrance." These were absent from Zen rites, so I shall not take them up here.

Once the guests enter the room, they proceed to the alcove to appreciate the hanging scroll, and if there is a flower display, the flowers and vase as well. In the case of a modern tea service, it is customary to display only the scroll without flowers during the first half of the gathering. After a greeting from the host comes the lighting of the charcoal, followed immediately by the serving of a *kaiseki* meal. When the simple meal is complete, the host finally serves a tea confection, whereupon the guests leave the tea room for a brief break. During the recess the host rearranges the room, taking the scroll down and replacing it with a flower display. He will also lay out a water supply jar, tea container, and the like. When his preparations are complete, he will signal his guests by striking a small gong. They reenter the room, where the host carries in a tea bowl to perform the thick tea service. By the time the guests have taken the tea and appreciated the utensils, while the host remains in the preparation area, the fire will have died down and will need to be rekindled. The host will, therefore, replenish the charcoal and then move to the final stage, the preparation of the thin tea. Much the same process can be found in the tea rituals of Zen temples as well as in *Kissa Ōrai*, which we shall presently examine. It seems safe to conclude that the ceremonial style of the Japanese tea service was something new and was not to be found in China.

So far we have examined tea service in religious institutions, but these temple practices gradually diffused to society more generally. Since the temples kept them as closely guarded secrets, many points did not readily spread to the world outside the gates. Nonetheless, certain institutions, such as Saidaiji or Kūyadō, took up the task of popularizing tea drinking as a result of their introduction of so-called *furumai* entertainments. One such case is the practice of the temple in Fushimi south of Kyoto known as Kōdaiji, which Murai Yasuhiko discusses in his *Chanoyu no Rekishi*.[16] The monks had a ceremony there that involved the drinking of outsized servings of tea, also called Ōchamori. There is a record of it in *Kanmon Gyoki*, the diary of Fushimi no Miya Sadanari for 1423/7/14–15:

7/14 Bon ceremonies as usual. Seating areas were set up before the gate of Kōdaiji, and tea was served. Great crowds gathered.

7/15 Tea entertainment in the evening at Kōdaiji. I went incognito to see. The young official, the prime minister, and others kept me company. Tea rooms: seating areas were set up and decorated with lanterns and the like. The effect was quite unusual and elegant. I was

astonished. I hurried home since there was such a
throng of people.[17]

According to this record, it was the time of the Bon festival for
the dead in summer, and tea rooms had been set up outside the Kōdaiji
with lanterns around them. Prince Sadanari and the other nobles must
have been quite impressed. Though we refer to such occasions as *furumai*, which suggests entertainment, it seems likely that the guests paid
to attend. It was not the temple itself that ran the entertainment. From
the middle of the Muromachi era on, outsiders set up stalls near the
temples to sell tea on the occasion of festivals at the temple. It became
common to offer "a cup for a copper." Such tea service can also be considered a sort of *furumai*. What had originally begun as a religious offering of tea to the Buddha at temples, therefore, had developed into
the sale of the beverage by the middle of the Muromachi period.

Hayashiya Tatsusaburō has found the earliest clear evidence
of this practice of "a cup for a copper" in a document from the fourth
month of 1403 relating to tea sales outside the south gate at Tōji in
Kyoto.[18] On the twenty-first of each month at the time of ceremonies
in honor of Kōbō Daishi, merchants would come into the temple
grounds at Tōji to sell their wares. This practice often greatly annoyed
the temple, and from time to time the priests would restrict it. The
document of 1403 was a set of regulations that the temple expected
operators of tea stalls outside the main south gate to observe. First, as
a basic principle, they were not to set up living quarters along the
south bank of the river, nor were they to set up their tea stalls on
the stone steps at the gate for even so much as a fraction of an hour.
The priests enjoined them not to leave their tea implements at the temple's tutelary shrine or to ask the people there to watch them even for
a short while. Furthermore, they were not to light their fires from the
sacred flame at the shrine or any of the various temple halls, and they
were not to draw water from the temple's sacred well, which was its
source of holy water.

Somewhat later in the same century, the *Daijōin Jisha Zōjiki*, a diary kept by the priestly Daijōin lineage of Nara, contained a number of
references to tea. One of its entries, dated 1492/3/14, reproduced a li-
cense granted by the Kōfukuji in Nara to a guild governing the selling
of tea in temple precincts.[19] This entry reveals how common the selling of tea had become by that time.

Tea Tasting (*Hincha-zu*). From the Song dynasty, outdoor tea-tasting parties were a popular pastime among the literati in China. Painting attributed to Qian Shunju (Jp., Sen Shunkyo) of the late Yuan dynasty. Ink and light colors on silk. Property of the Osaka Municipal Museum of Art.

Jian'an ware Tenmoku teabowl. A typical example, both in the quality of its glaze and its clay. Song dynasty. Height, 7.5 cm; diameter of mouth, 12.9 cm; diameter of foot, 3.8 cm. The accompanying carved red lacquer dais on which it rests is of a later period. Property of the Hayashibara Museum of Art, Okayama.

Scene of the *Gosai-e*, a week-long series of Buddhist rites annually observed at the Imperial Palace during the Heian period. At the seasonal sutra readings at the court, which were of a similar nature to this, the priests were presented with gifts of tea. Tanaka Collection set of the *Nenjū Gyōji Emaki* (Picture Scrolls of Annual Functions); seventh scroll, section 1, central portion. The Tanaka Collection scroll set, owned by the Tanaka family in Tokyo, is a mid-17th century hand-painted copy of the original *Nenjū Gyōji Emaki* painted in the 12th century. Photo from Kadokawa Shoten, Tokyo.

Teabowl named "*Haran*," of the type known as "Jukō celadon" because Murata Jukō owned a teabowl of this kind and is believed to have been particularly fond of it. Height, 7.0 cm; diameter of mouth, 16.0 cm; diameter of foot, 5.0 cm. Unlike the refined Chinese ceramics that were highly prized, this celadon ware, which was produced at folk kilns in Zhejiang province during the Southern Song and Yuan eras (12th–13th c.), has a notably rustic quality. Property of the Mitsui Bunko, Tokyo.

White Tenmoku teabowl once owned by Takeno Jōō. Important Cultural Property. This teabowl, in the "V" shape which characterizes teabowls referred to generally as Tenmoku in Japan, is a Muromachi-period (15th–16th c.) product of a domestic Japanese kiln, though whether Seto or Mino remains uncertain. Height, 6.4 cm; diameter of mouth, 12.1 cm; diameter of foot, 4.2 cm. Property of the Tokugawa Art Museum, Nagoya.

Black Raku teabowl named "*Shikorohiki*," once owned by Sen Rikyū. This teabowl, the work of the first generation in the Raku line, Chōjirō, has Rikyū's cipher (not visible in this photograph) near the foot. Height, 8.8 cm; diameter of mouth, 11.4 cm; diameter of foot, 5.1 cm. Property of Urasenke Konnichian, Kyoto.

Sen Rikyū (1522–1591), who brought the Way of Tea to fruition. Painting attributed to Hasegawa Tōhaku (1539–1610); inscription, by the 111th abbot of Daitokuji temple, Shun'oku Sōen (1529–1611), and copied onto the scroll by the 198th abbot of Daitokuji, Kan'ei Sōtan (1611–1672). Ink and colors on paper. Property of Urasenke Konnichian, Kyoto.

As the demand for tea increased, the volume available for consumption also grew. In this circumstance some temples kept their own gardens, but others had regular connections outside the temple for dealing in the product. The *Daijōin Jisha Zōjiki* contains numerous entries that show that the temple received frequent deliveries of tea from fixed suppliers. Entries for 1457, for example, show deliveries of freshly processed tea from a temple called the Ishinji in the third, fourth, eighth, and twelfth months. The following year the same supplier provided another four deliveries on approximately the same dates. A few years later, in 1479 and 1480, the Ishinji was still providing tea, suggesting that these deliveries had become a customary practice. The dates of the deliveries coincided with the picking of the new tea in the spring and the opening of tea storage jars in the autumn after the heat of summer had passed.[20]

The Daijōin also had other suppliers apart from the Ishinji. If we examine entries for the same years of 1457 and 1458, we find gifts or deliveries of tea mentioned in the third, fourth, and eighth months of the first year. The gifts in the fourth month included barrels of sake, noodles, and baskets, but the tea was specifically mentioned as being old, that is the previous year's. On the first day of the eighth month alone, some four suppliers provided seventy bags of tea. (Translator's note: each bag may have contained about sixty grams.) In the second year, eighteen entries recorded supplies of tea, with most being new tea in the third and fourth months. One of the suppliers, Gokurakubō, sent tea four times on different dates. Shinjōdoji was another temple mentioned by name, though only once. Beginning in the following year, however, the latter name appeared more frequently, and by 1480 the temple clearly had become a regular contributor of tea to the Daijōin. Some of the entries mentioned the phrase "customary delivery" of tea, showing that it was a part of an expected pattern of supply. Overall, the number of suppliers as well as the volume of tea had increased by 1480.[21]

Indeed, the quantity of tea that the Daijōin consumed had become astonishing, though the priests did not necessarily drink all of it. For example, the diarist, Jinson, mentioned a New Year's visit he made on the fourth day of 1458 to An'iji wearing a blue surplice, traveling in a palanquin, and accompanied by pages. Among the gifts he took were ten bags of tea. He also mentioned that the visit began with a service of tea "as usual."[22]

Shinto shrines as well as temples were consumers of tea. One of the earliest collections of shrine documents, the *Gion Shugyō Nikki,* contained records of both donations and purchases. The entry for 1350/3/17, for example, said: "Purchased fresh Yamashina tea leaves; prepared them at the shrine. This was the first tea preparation of the year."[23] Another entry in the same month two years later also mentioned the year's first preparation of tea and said, "Dried two catties of leaves in two dryers and made a total of twenty bags." One catty is thought to have been about 600 grams. The following day they processed thirty *ryō* in one dryer to make somewhat less.[24] The term used for tea in the last two entries suggests that it came from gardens cultivated at the shrine itself.

Tea was also a frequent gift during the Muromachi era. The *Rokuon Nichiroku,* a journal kept by Zen prelates at Kyoto's Shōkokuji, mentions tea often as gifts to the temple and occasionally from the priests to others as well. For the single year 1537, for example, no fewer than fifteen entries contain references to tea in this way. Most were lots of ten to twenty bags with some as large as thirty.[25]

Members of the warrior class as well have left us records of their involvement with tea. The *Kanazawa Bunko Komonjo* from the Kanazawa Bunko in modern Yokohama has a letter from Kanazawa Sadaaki addressed to the Shōmyōji. In it he indicated that he had wanted some tea from Kyoto but the servant he sent got lost on the way back. He would be sending some money to the capital with Gyōbu Gon Dayū in the next few days. He said that new tea was important to him. He had received some but had promptly drunk it all up. He wrote that he would be delighted to be able to get a little of the first new tea of the year grown at the temple, as he was expecting some people who liked tea and wanted to have some on hand. He concluded that he was happy to say that the priest Kensuke and the children were recovering nicely. Thus we find Sadaaki either asking for a gift of tea from the temple or offering to pay.[26]

In another letter, mostly concerned with the health of family members, he thanked the temple for their prayers for someone named Sadamasa and indicated that he had begun to recover from his illness. Doctors had been treating him and said that it was nothing serious. He suggested that the priests not bother to visit in view of rain that would make the journey inconvenient and because of the improved condition of the patient. The letter concluded by thanking the priests for grinding tea leaves. In other words, the letter was a note of thanks for having sent tea. Not only does this document show a gift of tea; it also demonstrates that the tea in question was powdered tea, in which the leaves had been ground in a mortar. It is apparent that this was the type of tea they drank at the time.[27]

These Muromachi era documents not only tell about tea rituals and the quantities of tea consumed, they also show the tea contests that we shall examine in the next chapter. Interestingly, however, they further indicate that as late as the middle of the period people still thought of tea as a medicine. Kikō Daishuku, writing in *Shoken Nichiroku* on 1485/10/4, said: "Sometime after the middle of the night I felt quite uncomfortable, so I lit the lamp, heated water, and drank tea. By daybreak I felt a bit better."[28]

This trend has survived in temples down to the present and can be seen in the widespread practice of taking Ōbukucha at the New Year. Ōbukucha is tea that celebrants drink as a wish for health and safety in the year ahead. One can see very much the same custom in the *Rokuon Nichiroku* with *umecha*, plum tea. Its entry for the New Year in 1540 noted that all the monks received "three cups of *umecha* at midnight." The first day of the following year similarly noted the arrival of a gift of tea. In 1543 the monks awoke at midnight for plum tea and then received a whole series of gifts, including kelp, dried chestnuts, sake, yam gruel, and the like plus a meal and medicinal herbs in wine as well as bundles of paper and one hundred copper cash. The entry for 1549 simply noted, "Plum tea and so on as usual," suggesting that the practice had become a regular custom of the New Year.[29]

The spirit of the tea rituals at temples in Japan seems far different from that of Lu Yu and Lu Tong in China, but one cannot say that there was absolutely no concern with Tang and Song ways. Priests at the Gozan temples in Japan have left us poems that reflect Chinese patterns, as we can see in the following examples. One is a piece in *Saihokushū* by the Zen priest Kokan (1278–1346):

> The sun, Lord of the East, grinds the fragrant dust of tea.
> Bejeweled nectar on the teeth, revives me.
> A pure wind envelopes my body.
> The whole world seen in a single cup.[30]

Kokan must have been thinking of Lu Tong's "Song of Tea" when he wrote these lines. In writing of the wind enveloping the body as he drank the ground tea, he would have been recalling the one cup, then two cups, and finally seven cups that made the poet conscious only of the blowing of the breeze. Similar sentiments can be seen in *Kūkashū* by Gidō Shūshin (1325–1388). He wrote:

> I received a small brick of tea,
> And sipping it, felt cool; I can do with the wind as I will.
> Why should I need paradise?
> My whole body is floating amid the white clouds.[31]

Once again the image suggests Lu Tong's "Song of Tea," in which the sixth cup transports the poet to the realm of the gods and makes him a Taoist immortal sweeping away the dust of the world. Lu Tong is the inspiration for Gidō Shūshin.

Finally, there is a poem in *Kūkashū* that the book's preface tells us the poet was inspired to write after eating his meal once early in the eighth month, autumn by the old calendar. He had gone into the priests' hall to sit and meditate but fell asleep, only to be startled awake by a tea seller outside.

> Outside the window a voice selling tea.
> Inside, the monk startled from his slumber.
> Lamps all abloom,
> Striking high noon in Higashiyama.[32]

For Gidō tea could also be just a way to avoid the drowsiness that hindered his Zen contemplation.

The tea rites at Zen temples and the customary events associated with them had an air of great solemnity. Yet there was more to tea than that. The next chapter will show that tea could also provide a form of entertainment and that the tea room could be a companionable gathering place for priests as well as the civil nobles and higher-ranking samurai of the day.

6 The Vogue of Tea Contests

The previous chapter focused particularly upon the drinking of tea among priests during the Kamakura era, and we have seen that they used it primarily as a medicine to treat physiological complaints. The cultivation of tea, in the meantime, appears to have spread ever more widely to various parts of the country. The *Isei Teikin Ōrai*, dating from the early Muromachi era, contains a list of tea-producing areas that shows the state of tea cultivation in Japan at that time: "The most famous temple [where tea is grown] is first of all at Toganoo. Other, secondary places include Ninnaji, Daigo, Uji, Hamuro, Hannyaji, and Jinnoji. Besides these there are Takarao in Yamato, Hattori in Iga, Kawai in Ise, Kiyomi in Suruga, and Kawagoe in Musashi. All are to be indicated as areas for tea."[1] Toganoo produced the premier tea in Japan, while the other places occupied a lesser status, though later Toganoo was to diminish in importance, putting Uji tea in first position. Since the other areas mentioned in the quotation ranged from Nara in western Japan to the Kanto Plain, one can see that tea production had spread over virtually the whole country.

Since ancient times the upper classes, both civil and military, as well as priests had enjoyed the pastime of *monoawase*, games or contests for the comparison of various objects. Examples would include contests for paintings, insects, flowers, fans, seashells, prose, poetry, and the like. Dog and cock fights were also part of this same type of entertainment. Finally, beginning in the fourteenth century, tea contests joined these ranks. Evidently, in some of these tea contests there was competition to judge the quality of the water used, but the more normal practice in Japan was to have the competitors taste several drinks made from powdered tea to have them distinguish between so-called

The Toganoo tea plantation, begun near the beginning of the 13th century with tea seeds brought from China by Eisai and given to Myōe. Through the late-Kamakura and early Muromachi periods, tea produced here was considered the premier tea in Japan. It was the "real tea" that contestants at the popular tea-tasting contests of the day were to distinguish from the "non teas" of other areas. Photo by Fujii Kinji.

honcha and *hicha*. (Literally, this meant "real tea" and "not tea" or right tea and wrong tea.) The former at that time referred to that grown at Toganoo and later would mean tea from Uji. Tea grown elsewhere fell into the latter category.

Since tea contests involved drinking tea to ascertain whether it was *honcha* or *hicha*, the purpose was to determine its place of production. *Shunsō Rōwa*, a collection of miscellany, observed that *honcha* referred to tea from Toganoo, while tea from Uji and elsewhere was *hicha*. Though it cited a source that mistakenly indicated that Saint Myōe had brought tea from China, it quoted works that listed a number of types of tea produced over the whole country and, like the previously cited *Isei Teikin Ōrai*, clearly showed the national scale of tea cultivation. One of the sources it cited, *Sekiso Ōrai*, even stated that Uji tea had assumed first place in enjoyment while the popularity of tea from Toganoo had declined.[2] Already by the time of the compilation of this copybook in the middle of the Muromachi era, therefore, we find that Uji had eclipsed Toganoo as the leading tea producer.

The basic practice was to take ten drinks of four different types of tea. Later the number of types would increase to ten and twenty and even up to one hundred different sorts of tea to be tasted. *Gion Shugyō Nikki*, as we shall see later, contained numerous examples of entertainments involving one hundred tea types. Of these parties the grandest in scale is probably to be found in the *Taiheiki*, which describes the tea affair of the nouveau arrivé daimyo Sasaki Dōyo, which we encountered briefly earlier.

> The civilian aristocrats were thus impoverished, passing through a dark vale, unable to find their way. The military houses, by contrast, daily increased their affluence a hundred-fold. For clothing they wore brocades, and as food they enjoyed no end of rare delicacies. . . . [Moreover,] there were in the capital daimyo, most prominently the lay priest Sasaki Dōyo, magistrate of Sado. These men had gathered together and had begun to hold parties for tea. They met each day and spared no expense [in their entertainment].[3]

The tale went on to depict a tea contest that was a gorgeous affair employing every luxury its organizers could conceive. They had amassed rare objects from both Japan and abroad to embellish the venue. The chief guests, "lined up as they pleased in their chairs on which lay the skins of tigers and leopards, were not unlike rows of golden and bronze buddhas" surrounded by an aura of haloes. As stakes for wagers and prizes for winners there were lengths of cloth and brocade as well as the navels of musk deer used as incense, all of which required the expenditure of huge quantities of gold—which in the imagination of the medieval author could be heaped in countless piles. There were tiger-skin bags containing flints, and swords embellished with gold foil. Since over sixty persons had whatever they fancied, one can only imagine how sumptuous it all was.[4] This occasion demonstrated the emergence of the nouveau arrivé military lords, the *shugo daimyō*, such as Sasaki Dōyo. The type of tea ritual they practiced, however, was an exact copy of the rituals of Zen temples.

After the description of the luxury of the tea party, the writer of the *Taiheiki* condemned such tea contests: "All of the riches went to the idlers they brought with them or to actors from *dengaku* or *sarugaku* and courtesans and beautiful women who had gathered to watch. The daimyo themselves returned empty-handed. Thus, they gave no help to the poor and isolated; they offered nothing to the Buddha or the priests. It was as if they had simply flung their gold into the mud, their jewels into a bottomless pool."[5] After the tea parties, the author continued, they would "gamble and disport themselves." They would bet five or ten thousand copper cash at a time, so that in an evening they might lose five or six million cash, but no one would win so much as one hundred thousand. This was because they had wasted everything on the actors of the *dengaku* and *sarugaku* dramatic forms and on the courtesans and beautiful women. We cannot accept the description as literal, historical fact; the writer no doubt indulged in hyperbole for dramatic effect. Yet at least in broad outline I suspect that there was a semblance of reality in his description. It was always the practice after samurai tea parties at that time to engage in gambling. Later the *Taiheiki* described another elaborate entertainment. The new shogun had suggested a poetry contest at the mansion of the governor of Sagami. He had proposed some seven hundred rounds of competition and tempted ten contestants to participate with an epicurean repast. Unfortunately for the governor, however, Dōyo intervened, providing a spectacle that could scarcely be outdone.

> At his own mansion [to compete with the governor] Dōyo said he would decorate seven chambers, prepare seven types of food, heap up seven hundred sorts of prizes, and hold seventy rounds of tea contests with *honcha* and *hicha*. When he invited the new shogun, the latter thought he could probably attend a poetry contest some other time, but the tea contest with its sets of sevens promised to be amusing, so he broke his earlier engagement and went instead to Dōyo's party. The governor of Sagami had made all his preparations in vain, and the [would-be] poets returned home disappointed.[6]

Tea parties such as this one in the fourteenth century demonstrate the use of tea merely as a vehicle for amusement. This element of entertainment distinguishes the tea of this period from both that of Lu Yu and that of the Zen temples in Japan.

Let us now consider the venues for tea contests, the tea rooms themselves. The *Taiheiki* has already shown us how splendid they could be with their chairs draped with the skins of tigers and leopards or with seven chambers lavishly decorated. There is, however, an earlier source, the *Kissa Ōrai*, attributed to the priest Gen'e of the late Kamakura era, that provides an even fuller view. Furthermore, the protocol for tea service had become generally accepted by his time, and the latter-day aphorism to the effect that "Zen and tea are one" can probably first be seen in his work. It contains a lengthy description of one such tea room. "The mansion where the party was held looked truly extraordinary. The guest chamber was hung with lovely blinds and before it lay a large garden attractively covered with pebbles. A valance hung all about the eaves, and silken curtains, in the windows. The guests slowly assembled, and when everyone was finally present, the party began."[7]

The term the author used for the tea venue was *kaisho*, literally, "meeting place," and was adapted from a similar term used for poetry and linked verse parties.[8] The site comprised two separate parts, one a guest chamber and the other a pavilion for drinking the tea. The former, as the quotation indicates, had blinds and a pebble-covered garden outside with valanced eaves and silk curtains at the windows. There, after the guests assembled, they partook of three cups of sake, noodles, tea, and a meal with delicacies from the mountains and the sea, according to the account. It served primarily as a reception area, and it can be thought of as having had the function of preparing the guests to receive the tea. Later, the author said, the guests went out into the garden and there some took shelter from the heat in the shade of the trees about a miniature hill in the garden that they had seen from the window on the north side earlier. Others repaired to the verandah to gaze at a waterfall to the south and there opened their collars to admit the cooling breeze.

It is at this point that we discover the pavilion for tea. This was a separate structure and quite splendid. Yet we can find in it the origin of the modern tea room as it developed from the *shoin* study, such as that in the Tōgudō at the temple of the Silver Pavilion in Kyoto. One interesting feature of this tea pavilion was that it was an extraordinarily bright room compared to the tea rooms of later ages. The author suggests that, with its verandah high up on the second storey and its view in all directions, it was meant as a place for viewing the moon and in that respect calls to mind a kind of two-storey Tōgudō. Inside the room, there was quite a pronounced flavor of Buddhism. There was Zhang Sigong's polychrome of the Buddha on the left, Muxi's monochrome of Kannon on the right with the two bodhisattvas Fugen and Monju on either side, and hanging in front, a Hanshan Shide work. Since the Hanshan Shide piece came from Chinese Zen, its placement with conventional Buddhist works represented a considerable admixture of Zen and classical Buddhist elements. Compared to the single ink monochrome hanging in the alcoves of tea rooms in later ages, this art was strikingly different. There were also a brocade-covered table with a bronze flower vase and a desk with a brass incense tool and fire chopsticks, never to be seen at any tea gathering today. The *Kissa Ōrai* account continued:

> Leopard skin covered the bench provided for the guests while the seat of the chief guest was in a place that faced the sparkling stones in the garden. On the paper panels about the room there were Chinese paintings of several types. There were the four ancients who had secluded themselves from the world under the moon at Mount Shang, the seven sages of the bamboo grove submerged in clouds, a dragon ascending a waterfall to heaven, a tiger sleeping in the wilderness, white egrets fluttering among water peppers, and mandarin ducks enjoying themselves amid willow branches. Every single painting was from China and not a one from Japan![9]

The covering of the seats for the guests with leopard skin is exactly like what we have already encountered in the *Taiheiki*. Though we cannot be sure what sort of place this tea room was, it was every bit as sumptuous as that of Sasaki Dōyo. Going into the pavilion where the tea was served, we have the illusion of having entered an especially gorgeous Zen temple. The paintings with their classically Chinese motifs of sages, animals, birds, and flowers were luxurious appointments and all, as the author was at pains to point out, imported from the continent. He went on to describe incense containers of carved lacquer and tea jars with teas from Toganoo and Takao. There was a shelf by the west window piled with rare fruits, screens on the north wall with the prizes in front, and a kettle surrounded by cups covered with napkins. All were elaborate, gorgeous trappings. One can only imagine how much it all cost. Contrast this with the tea room of later days: In the corner stands a brazier or perhaps a sunken hearth with water boiling. Before it is a simple, low screen called a *furosaki*. In the alcove hangs a single ink drawing with a modest arrangement of flowers. If there is any furnishing at all, it is confined to a simple shelf. By taking note of such modern arrangements, one can see to what expense the medieval host went.

Kissa Ōrai continues with a description of the serving of the tea itself. After the guests had all assembled and taken their places the son of the host presented tea sweets. A young man provided each guest with a tea bowl, and then he went around with a kettle of hot water in his left hand and a tea whisk in his right, from the chief guest on down in order to the last, and prepared tea for each person in his place. They probably used shallow Tenmoku cups from China. The author observed, "This was all done in proper sequence, and without being bidden they observed the etiquette of serving the successive cups of tea." They also served sake in turn, but "no one drank a drop of it."

> Then it became more amusing as first we had a contest with ten drinks of four types of tea and then judged whether each was from the capital or from the countryside, whether each was good or bad, and so on. I have never had a more enjoyable time in my life. Lu Tong said, "If the amount of tea is small in proportion to the water, the foam will soon disperse, while too much tea for the water will cause the foam to be too thick on the surface." Truly it was such a fascinating party that everyone must have had a splendid time.[10]

In the expression "observed the etiquette of serving the . . . tea," we can find the precedent for Murata Jukō's (also Shukō) "Kin Kei Sei Jaku" (Humility, Respect, Purity, and Tranquillity) and Sen Rikyū's "Wa Kei Sei Jaku" (Harmony, Respect, Purity, and Tranquillity). In the tea of Lu Yu this element of etiquette was not to be found. Up to this point tea affairs had valued a quiet etiquette, but from here on that was to change. The contest with its ten drinks of four types of tea and its discrimination between tea from the capital and from the countryside and between good and bad tea added an aspect of entertainment.

As the day drew to a close, they finished the tea party and removed the utensils. To the accompaniment of a fine meal the guests exchanged cups of sake. They then began merrymaking with singing, dancing, and musical instruments. In this way at tea contests the host amused his guests with decorations that were as lavish as possible and with rare fruits, and it was the custom to end with a drinking party.

If we compare this sort of tea entertainment with the tea rituals in Zen temples that we saw in the previous chapter, the similarities between them are apparent. Such features as the tokonoma alcove were still not present in this era. On the main wall there hung a painting of the Buddha with a sutra table before it containing a censer, a flower vase, and candelabra. One could as well perform Zen meditation there as hold a tea ritual. It seems clear that the tea ceremonies in both the *Taiheiki* and the *Kissa Ōrai* followed the style of ornamentation as well as the rituals employed at Zen temples. The method of preparing tea depicted in the *Kissa Ōrai* was the same as that performed today at such temples in Kyoto as the Myōshinji or Kenninji. The appointments in the tea room, moreover, were also the same as those in a Zen temple.

A style of furnishing similar to that in the *Taiheiki* and the *Kissa Ōrai* is also found in the *Kanmon Gyoki*, a Muromachi era court diary. Its entries for 1416/12/24 and 1417/11/18 both itemize the furnishings in a Zen temple. The list includes a screen and, as the principal object of worship, a painting of the Buddha, with an image of Amida Buddha on the west side. Before these was a single large desk spread with Chinese fabric on which rested a memorial tablet as well as a flower container, censer, and candle stand. There were in addition an image of the thousand-armed Kannon and a Buddhist shrine (Butsudan). In the recesses of the room where the Buddha image was, there stood screens at the sides in the four bays at the north of the room. On the east hung a painting of Fudō, the God of Fire, while the four bays on the south were hung with blinds. More blinds hung from the west eaves, the area where listeners sat.[11] There was no difference between the setting described here and that for a tea party. Tea rituals conducted in such an atmosphere shared points in common with other sorts of ceremonies and were closely associated with meetings for linked verse in particular. In fact, the appointments for linked verse parties were quite the same as those for tea gatherings. The elaborate style of these decorations can also be seen in the *Kanmon Gyoki* entry for 1433/7/7, which described the decorations for Tanabata, the Festival of the Weaver. The room held screens as well as twenty-five paintings and sixty-five flower vases, so many that it was difficult to find flowers for all of them, with the result that some held different sorts of objects. Most celebrations shared the same general type of decorating style.[12]

To this point we have directed our inquiry primarily toward the appointments of the venues where tea contests took place. Yet the tea enjoyed there had become completely different from before. Whereas it had earlier been a medicine essential for physiological uses, here it served purely as an object of entertainment. In fact, tea had attracted so much attention that everyone was talking about it. A graffiti writer, quoted in "Nijō Kawara Rakugaki," was moved to proclaim:

> Kyoto and Kamakura are all jumbled together. Fake linked verse parties that come up short; bumpkins' poetry contests where everyone's a judge. Conventions ignored, it's a world where anyone can do exactly as he pleases. Though they said the inept *dengaku* plays of the East would die out, they're as popular as ever. Parties with ten batches of tea or incense. Kamakura is trying to upstage the capital, but after all, the action's still in Kyoto.[13]

The graffiti writer was lamenting that linked verse and *waka* poetry contests were so popular that there was no one left who was not a judge. Kamakura still could not compete with the capital, Kyoto. The word translated as "batch" here is a character that suggests burning, which would be more suitable to incense than to tea, but its pronunciation "shu" makes it a homonym of "type," and that is probably what he wanted to suggest.[14] We shall see later that "ten types" could also mean "ten times," so perhaps he avoided using "types" to disambiguate the latter meaning. In any event, if the tea parties were like those we saw in *Taiheiki* and *Kissa Ōrai*, they would stand out as being disruptive of social order. The second article of the *Kenmu Shikimoku*, a fourteenth-century law code, titled "The Necessity of Limitation of Drinking and Debauchery," addressed this matter. It stated: "Penalties for violating these provisions are especially severe, but even more so for those who indulge in sexually immoral behavior or gambling. Furthermore, there are those who wager huge sums on the pretext of holding tea gatherings or linked verse meetings. It is difficult to calculate how much is spent in such pursuits."[15] Gambling huge sums at these *chayoriai*,[16] literally, tea gatherings, is precisely what we have seen at the affairs given by hosts such as Sasaki Dōyo. No doubt, the inclusion of *chayoriai* among prohibited activities had little effect. Legal proscription notwithstanding, they would be difficult to stop.

Let us look now at the way they conducted these tea contests. The *Isei Teikin Ōrai* has this to say about tea production areas: "The tea from such famous places as Ninnaji, Yamato, and Iga compared to that from elsewhere is like agate compared to rubble, while the tea of Toganoo compared to Ninnaji or Daigo tea is like gold compared to lead or iron." It goes on to say that these differences in flavor are what make it possible to have various kinds of contests, of which it lists six: the ten types, six colors, ten drinks of four types, four drinks of two types, three types, and seasonal teas.[17]

As for the method of play, it says there were seven types of contests. However, there was one basic type, despite the many different varieties of competition that had evolved by the late fourteenth century. The most common was the one called "*yonshu juppuku*" (literally, "four types, ten drinks"). There were other names as well. "*Yonshu juppen*" ("four types, ten times") was used for the same game, and for a time in the mid-Muromachi some groups used the term *kaicha* (tea by turns). Examples of this last term can be found in *Kanmon Gyoki*. The entry for 1416/1/27 notes that the night had been one during which calendrical divination required everyone to go without sleep. To pass the time the courtiers played *sugoroku*, a type of backgammon, as well as *kaicha*. In the following month, 1416/2/26, the diarist said that it had been his turn to prepare for *kaicha* and to have the stakes ready. He said he arranged some amusing activities, as he had been instructed.[18]

A lexicon from the Muromachi era called *Ainōshō* defined the word *kaicha*. "We find the term *kaicha* in records referring to contests with ten drinks of tea. The first character, *kai*, meaning round, is used perhaps because the contestants sit in a circle and drink by turns. It is correctly written only with this particular character and not with others also pronounced *kai*. It can also be called *kōcha* (tribute tea)."[19] It continues that there were two variations of the basic type of contest involving ten drinks of four types of tea. In the first there were twelve packets with four each of three types, and the rules allowed the contestants to taste one of each of the different types before the contest began. Then a new tea type, called the guest, was added to the nine packs that were left. These ten were then brewed up, and the team that identified the most varieties won. The three packets that they tasted before the contest were the *kokoromi*, the sample. Since the contest used four types of tea with a total of ten drinks, a number of terms were used, variously suggesting four types with ten drinks or ten times and the like.

In the second style, the contestants took the same number of drinks in the same four types but without sampling beforehand. Either of these two variations, with or without the prior tasting, might be called *kaicha* and constituted the basic format of contest. The lexicographer explained, "The reason for using the particular character *kai* is that it was the [Japanese pronunciation of the] second character of the name of Confucius' most intelligent disciple, Yan Hui, of whom it was said, 'Hearing one, he knew ten.' "[20]

Tea competitions appear in several different records. There is no way of ascertaining precisely when such contests began, but the graffiti referring to "ten batches of tea" in the "Nijō Kawara Rakugaki" and the prohibition of "tea gatherings" in the *Kenmu Shikimoku* demonstrate that the practice must have been fairly widespread. The earliest reference to tea in the diary of a courtier may be that dated 1339/7/22 in *Moromoriki*, the diary of Nakahara Moromori. It detailed the visit of the entourage of the Acting Lesser Exterior Secretary Morochika carrying an imperial edict to the priests at Kenninji, who provided him with a light meal, tea, and the like. Though there was nothing specific about tea contests, an entry for the following month, 1339/8/27, noted, "Tea party all day; there was nothing that was not interesting." A third entry, dated 1340/1/25, spelled out unequivocally, "ten types of *hon*[*cha*] and *hi*[*cha*] with wagers." Priests and courtiers had attended, and Moromori pronounced it a great success. Three more times in as many months Moromori noted his pleasure over wagers with "ten drinks of tea" or "ten types of *hon*[*cha*] and *hi*[*cha*]."[21] As noted above, "types" can be construed to mean times or portions of tea.

Similar references also appear in *Gion Shugyō Nikki*, which dates from about the same era and contains the fullest documentation for tea contests at this time. I should like to select a limited number of references concerning "*jusshucha*" (ten tea types) for consideration here. For example, in 1343, sometime after Moromori wrote, we find three occasions when the author enjoyed tea contests. One (9/24) indicated he had gone to the home of the Great Councilor on Nishiōji Street and won the contest, having correctly guessed nine of the ten types. He mentioned two other occasions in the next two months (10/13 and 11/3).[22]

Chart on the back of the *Gion Shugyō Nikki* entry for 1343/12/4, illustrating a tea-tasting contest involving ten types of *honcha* (right tea) and *hicha* (wrong tea). The *Gion Shugyō Nikki* is in the archives of Yasaka Shrine, Kyoto.

The same source also recorded how the contestants conducted the matches. On the back of the sheet that contains the entry for 1343/12/4, there is a chart illustrating a contest with ten types of *honcha* and *hicha* (see Chart 1). This is an extremely valuable source, for it dates from the same era as *Moromoriki* and therefore provides a clear view of tea contests at their earliest recorded period. The chart shows across the top single characters that appear to be abbreviations for the names of nine competitors. Beneath each name is a line containing the characters for *hon* and *hi*, as abbreviations for *honcha* and *hicha*, that is, recording the contestant's guess as to whether the drink was one or the other. There were a total of ten of these. A slash mark in vermilion ink designated correct judgments, and a number at the bottom of the line was the total of correct tries. In this case, two individuals tied for first place with eight right answers. In this contest there were five rounds of *honcha* and five of *hicha* all in random order.

It was customary for the contestants to provide the tea for the match themselves, and this case was no exception. On the right edge

CHART 1:   A Ten-Round Contest of *Honcha* and *Hicha*

B	Su	Y	To	N	Sa	M	D	Ta	
O/	X	O/	X	O/	O/	X	X	X	**To**
X/	X/	X/	O	X/	X/	O	O	X/	**To**
X/	O	X/	X/	O	X/	X/	X/	X/	**Sa**
X	O/	X	O/	O/	O/	O/	O/	X	**Su**
O/	O/	O/	X	X	X	O/	X	O/	**M**
X	X	O/	O/	O/	O/	O/	O/	O/	**N**
X/	X/	X/	X/	O	X/	X/	X/	O	**D**
O/	O/	O/	X	X	X	O/	X	X	**D**
X/	X/	X/	O	X/	O	O	O	O	**Su**
X/	X/	O	O	X/	X/	X/	O	X/	**N**
8	7	8	4	6	7	7	4	5	TOTAL CORRECT

Note: O = *honcha*; X = *hicha*; / = correct judgment

of the chart written in small characters beside each round was the abbreviated name of the person who had supplied the tea for the round. Evidently it was the practice for each guest to bring one set of both *honcha* and *hicha*, and four persons appear here as having supplied a set of both types.

One cannot tell from this chart whether or not the guests had had the opportunity to sample the tea beforehand, but we can see that the first round was *hon*, the second, *hi*, the third, *hi*, the fourth, *hon*, the fifth *hon*, and so on. In the tea contests of this earliest period the participants simply made these judgments between the two types for ten rounds, hence the name *jusshucha* or *juppukucha*, ten types or drinks of tea. However, by responding in one of these two ways, the guests had a 50 percent probability of a correct answer, and no doubt they quickly tired of such a simple method of play. For this reason they soon devised other varieties of contests, such as those alluded to in *Isei Teikin Ōrai*.

The section of the *Taiheiki* titled "The Betrayal of Kiyouji [governor of Sagami]" stated, as we saw above, "[Dōyo] would decorate seven chambers, prepare seven types of food, heap up seven hundred sorts of prizes, and hold seventy rounds of tea contests with *honcha* and *hicha*." The same tale in a later chapter has this to say: "[Dōyo] burned a whole catty of precious incense all at one time, and the winds carried the aroma in all directions, causing all to feel as if they were in the Buddhist

Paradise of Floating Fragrance. In the shadow of the smoke, they cur-
tained off an area, filled it with lines of chairs, prepared trays of delicacies, drank a hundred rounds of *honcha* and *hicha*, and piled up prizes as
high as mountains."[23] Another useful collection from a later era is
Hakudō Zuihitsu, which observes that at the time of the Hōjō Regency
at the end of the Kamakura period, one frequently encountered parties
with seventy or one hundred servings of tea, and these became even more
common during the time of Ashikaga Yoshimasa in the late fifteenth
century. The essayist says that tea functions were different in those days.
They distinguished between what they called *honcha* and *hicha*, and prepared anywhere from ten to one hundred servings of tea, whose quality
they competed to critique.[24] What was the meaning of such large numbers of servings of tea as we see here? Let us defer the answer to that and
explain how they played their tea games later. For now let us examine
some of the contests that we find in such sources as diaries.

References to tea affairs are ubiquitous in the previously cited
Gion Shugyō Nikki. In the half year from the middle of the seventh
month to year's end in 1343, for example, one can find more than fifty
appearances of tea functions.[25] For the era before Rikyū, this is one of
the most valuable sources for understanding the tea entertainments of
the civil aristocrats and clerics of a particular period as well as the nature of tea itself as an amusement. For that reason I should like to devote close attention to it.

During these six months of 1343, the diarist regularly visited the
homes of acquaintances, where he drank multiple rounds of tea, often
thirty, at times ten or twenty, and sometimes more. Occasionally, as on
8/10, when there were too few for a proper contest, the guests would enjoy a more relaxed evening and at times provide wine (9/6). One can
also find formal contests with results recorded, as on 9/9. Each guest
brought wine and noodles, perhaps as stakes for wagers. Then they
drank one hundred rounds. Eleven scores duly appear, ranging from a
high of eighty-four down to a low of seventy-three. A twelfth guest was
listed with three rounds, six types each. Then just six days later on 9/15
there was another hundred-round contest. Each guest brought a prize as
well as a set of *honcha* and *hicha*, and they started at the hour of the dog,
about eight o'clock in the evening, continuing until dawn. Of thirteen
players three, including the writer, tied for first place with sixty-nine
each. Two tied at the bottom with fifty. Thereafter, every few days the
diarist attended still more parties. These were regularly scheduled

events, with the same names appearing as guests. On 10/6, for example, he noted, "Today was number two in the schedule of rounds," and on 10/20, "Monthly tea party at the Dainagon's residence on Nishiōji." On the latter occasion there were thirty in attendance and several sorts of prizes, including bundles of paper, a Chinese utensil, a knife blade, straw matting, a fan, footgear, fire chopsticks, a Buddhist adamant, and even a chicken coop. Three men had collaborated as hosts.[26]

These occasions displayed considerable variety in the numbers of drinks and showed the guests enjoying food and wine as well as tea. One interesting permutation, however, was that of the guest identified with the abbreviation "To," perhaps Tōbō, a regular participant, who had "three rounds, six types each" at the party on 9/9. The entry suggests that he correctly identified six types in each of three rounds. This was evidently a different style of play, and to understand it we will refer to the later method of drinking ten rounds with four varieties of tea, illustrated in Chart 2. At the end of that chart there is a line that says, "Note, Ten Ten Ten Type Contest." Another line also shows that this had been a "ten-type contest" with eleven competitors, so that one can easily ascertain what the format was. The phrase "Note, Ten Ten Ten Type Contest," therefore, unquestionably meant three rounds with ten portions of tea each.

In other words, what was meant by a tea party of one hundred rounds of tea was simply ten rounds of ten types of tea each. The seventy portions of tea in the *Taiheiki* thus meant seven rounds of ten types of tea. The twenty, thirty, fifty portions we find in *Gion Shugyō Nikki*, likewise, were two, three, or five rounds of ten portions.

We might note parenthetically that it is not at all clear whether the ten servings of tea mentioned in this context were in any way similar to the service of tea in modern *chanoyu*. There are many unresolved points in trying to ascertain how attendees drank the tea or whether the amounts of tea and hot water might be the same as today. Neither are we sure how they could so easily drink one hundred portions of tea. Indeed, the entry for 9/15 indicates that they started at the hour of the dog, about 8:00 P.M., and ended at dawn, a span of approximately ten hours. There is no doubt about it: to drink one hundred servings of tea as it is served today would be an incredible feat given that length of time, even considering that it was night or that they may have been consuming it with medicinal intent. Perhaps the quantities consumed had something to do with why the success rate on 9/15 was so much lower than it had been on 9/9. The best score was just sixty-one and the lowest was only fifty, with a 50 percent chance of guessing correctly. Also on that occasion the entry tells us that each guest had brought one set of tea types.

We need to look at this phenomenon of "one hundred types of tea" somewhat more closely. Though the diary's entries for 1343 show people taking one hundred portions of tea in a day or in a span of several hours, entries for 1350 indicate this:

> 3/5   Went to Nanbō. Had tea there.
> 3/7   One hundred servings of tea at Tōbō. Junjun served as host. Yoshi got eighty-eight (first place); Suke got eighty-five (second place).
> 3/9   Tea at Nanbu; fifty-five types.[26]

As these indicate, the diarist's friends were holding parties every other day and on the middle one took one hundred servings. Just two days later they had fifty-five more. That was rather hard labor even if it was for recreation. Then again on 6/21 an entry mentioned, "Regular monthly meeting at Nishiōji; one hundred types." The fact that parties for drinking one hundred portions of tea were regularly held every month shows how enthusiastic the participants were for tea contests. Again on 8/12 the diary recorded one hundred servings of tea with wagers and listed the guests and their results with seventy-eight as the winning score. The writer himself tied for second with seventy-four. On 9/6 a similar party met at the diarist's own place, and once again he listed guests and their scores. Each of these events took place on a single day.[27]

Presently, however, a series of entries appeared depicting a function unlike the usual ones. In the middle of the ninth month of 1350, there was a party that took place over several days:

> 9/12   Came to Nakanobō. Two sets tea. (Beginning of one-hundred-round contest.)
> 9/13   Came to Nakanobō. Three sets tea. (Part of one-hundred-round contest.)
> 9/16   Came to Shinbō. Three sets tea. (Part of one-hundred-round contest.)
> 9/18   Came to Nakanobō. Three sets tea. (Completion of one-hundred-round contest.)[29]

If this were a contest with one hundred types of incense, it might not be so difficult to tell them apart, but to compete in a contest drinking one hundred types of tea would require a considerable effort, would it not? Our focus so far has been on tea contests with one hundred rounds, but of course, other types also appeared in the diaries of the day. As we saw with the entries for 1343, tea parties of several different types occurred, including some we cannot fully interpret. On 1343/11/12, for example, the writer and two others had a regular monthly party. The entry mentioned seven contests and forty-five rounds, and indicated that he won eleven "*hiki,*" perhaps eleven strings of ten copper cash each. Again the entry for 1350/3/9, which we encountered above, mentioned fifty-five rounds, and there were twenty-five rounds at a regular monthly party on 1350/9/21. Since ten rounds seems to have been the basic pattern, it is difficult to reconcile the entries that have numbers of rounds like forty-five or fifty-five that are not divisible by ten. We shall have to rely on future research to explain this phenomenon.

Let us return to the ten-round format and examine next the type of event in which contestants sampled four types of tea in sets of ten portions. This was an outgrowth of the contests with ten servings of *honcha* and *hicha* and developed along the same lines as incense contests that also had ten rounds. We have already seen reference to this pattern in the lexicon *Ainōshō,* which was introduced above as an explanation of entries from *Kanmon Gyoki*. Chart 2 shows a record of this type of contest. Its date of 1491 means that it is a relatively early record, but it clearly shows the basic pattern of *yonshu juppuku* (four types, ten portions).[30]

The contest that it records had eleven participants, and they had the opportunity to sample the tea beforehand. As the name implies, they used four varieties of tea, identified in Chart 2 as types 1, 2, 3, and "U." This last designation was actually the "guest" and was an abbreviation using just the top portion of the character meaning "guest." The figures on the extreme right indicate what the correct answer was while those at the bottom show the number of correct identifications each guest achieved, for most contestants just three, four, or five. Only a single individual, the one designated "Yama" (Y), attained a perfect score of ten. Contests of this sort went by a number of names, all suggesting ten portions of tea or four types in ten rounds or servings.

It is clear that tea had become simply an object of entertainment. Let us turn, therefore, to contemporary sources that make reference to

CHART 2:   A Contest of Ten Rounds and Four Types

K	Y	Ka	Ta	M	S	U	Ts	Kz	To	H	
2/	2/	2/	U	2/	2/	2/	U	3	2/	2/	2
1/	1/	U	2	1/	1/	1/	2	2	1/	3	1
3	2/	3	3	U	3	3	3	U	3	U	2
3/	3/	2	1	1	U	3/	3/	3/	3/	2	3
3/	3/	3/	2	3/	2	U	2	3/	U	3/	3
U	3/	1	3/	3/	1	2	1	1	2	1	3
1	2/	3	1	1	3	1	2/	3	1	1	2
1/	1/	1/	2	2	2	1/	1/	2	1/	2	1
2	1/	1/	1/	1/	1/	3	1/	1/	2	1/	1
2	U/	2	2	2	3	2	3	3	3	3	U
5	10	4	2	5	3	4	4	3	4	3	TOTAL CORRECT

Note: 1 = type 1; 2 = type 2; 3 = type 3; U = guest; / = correct answer

tea competitions during this era, beginning with those of priests from religious institutions, which we touched upon briefly in the previous chapter. One such cleric, the abbot Jinson, who wrote *Daijōin Jisha Zōjiki,* was inordinately fond of tea contests. We have already noted his references to gifts of tea in the 1450s, but there were also numerous other entries related to contests.

Suddenly in 1458, numerous references to tea contests appear in his diary, with five in the first month alone. They seem to have been a new trend that appeared at this point. Four specifically mentioned "*jusshucha*" (ten rounds of tea) of the sort we have just discussed. Indeed, over the next several years tea contests appear to have become a regular New Year's practice at the temple, for there were almost annual references to them. Often Jinson mentioned wagers (1459/1/4, for example) or listed prizes such as a bundle of paper, a fan, and a pair of fire chopsticks (1460/1/4) or cloth, a round mirror, a bundle of paper, and a fan (1462/1/4). The same date in 1463 and 1465 contained similar lists of almost identical prizes. The venues were various, his own temple or others nearby, and the dates ranged from the fourth to the tenth with occasional parties later in the first month. They continued with annual entries from 1470 to 1475. Jinson was certain to have a tea contest at some point during the New Year celebrations.[31] Though *Gion Shugyō Nikki* reflects no seasonal pattern of contests, this diary clearly does, and people no doubt eagerly anticipated tea competitions as a part of their New Year celebrations. As time passed, moreover, the rage for tea contests grew in intensity, as reflected in greater numbers of entries. By 1480, for example, there were eight contests from the fourth through the twenty-sixth of the New Year. The first of these entries states that they provided prizes "as customary."

Those who enjoyed the tea contests included not only warriors like Sasaki Dōyo, Buddhist clerics like Jinson, or Shinto priests like those from Yasaka Shrine in Gion. Persons of many classes joined in. Higher-ranking aristocrats from the imperial court were no exception, as seen in some of their diaries, which we have already sampled.

As we have already seen, tea had begun to lose its reputation as a medicinal herb by the fourteenth century, and by the Muromachi era that reputation disappeared completely, so that tea was just as much a vehicle of entertainment as the backgammon game called *sugoroku*. Competitions like those of the *Daijōin Jisha Zōjiki* regularly took place on the fourth, sixth, or seventh days of each New Year. Monthly parties joined the list of auspicious events that the people of the day routinely celebrated. Additionally, there came to be a fixed group of participants, each of whom served his turn as host for the contests. Tea, in short, settled into a kind of regimen.

Moromoriki provided an early example of this sort of fixed round of tea contests. The entry for 1340/4/11 is the first, noting: "A course of tea affairs began today. Since I drew the number one lot, I was the first host. There was nothing that was not interesting." We cannot tell who took part, but eight subsequent entries, running from the next day until 4/28, identified each host in turn, with Moromori recording his great pleasure as the contests took place.[32] *Gion Shugyō Nikki* also mentioned such rounds, as in its entry for 1343/9/5, "Rounds of tea preparation began at the suggestion of Ryō." A month later on 10/6 there was a record of the second in the series "at the suggestion of Taishin" plus a note that the writer and other participants had decided to meet again on the ninth for a party of one hundred servings.[33] The phrase that he used on both dates meant literally "to prepare tea in turns" and clearly suggests the same sort of regularly recurring party as Moromori had enjoyed. Very likely they drew lots to determine who would serve as host each time. In *Moromoriki*, once they had drawn lots on 4/11 for the position of host, they had nine tea meetings within the month. In *Gion Shugyō Nikki,* however, the parties took place a month apart, first "at the suggestion of Ryō," and next "at the suggestion of Taishin." Then on 11/5 the third entry noted, "Fixed turns [to serve as host] began. We had a contest of thirty rounds."³⁴ The previously cited *Gion Shugyō Nikki* entry for 1343/10/20 recorded a monthly contest at the Dainagon's home on Nishiōji. Three men had collaborated as hosts and probably provided the prizes. There had been thirty rounds of tea with eleven in attendance.³⁵ The prizes would hardly bear comparison with those of Sasaki Dōyo, no doubt because the meetings did occur once a month.

A number of other entries shed light on these so-called monthly parties. *Gion Shugyō Nikki* has these:

11/10　Went to the home of Wada Kōshū. Today was a monthly gathering with thirty rounds of tea. I placed first [and won] thirty-seven *hiki* (strings of cash).

11/12　Went to the home of Aiba Inaba. Today was a monthly gathering. I joined for the first time. Seven contests. Forty-five rounds. I won ten *hiki*.

11/21　Went to the home of the Dainagon on Nishiōji for a monthly gathering. Sono no Kami Chūjō Mototaka was host, so I went. Twenty rounds of tea.

　12/2　Went to the home of Aiba Inaba. Today was a monthly gathering. Seven contests. Fifty rounds. I won forty *hiki*. Also I collected the eleven *hiki* I won at the gathering on 9/12.³⁶

Judging from these, what the diarist called "monthly gatherings" were regularly held contests that met at the homes of different people. The meeting at Wada Kōshū's residence may have been an exception, but that on 11/21 at the home of the Dainagon on Nishiōji followed a similar function at the same place on 10/20, and that at Aiba Inaba's, which he attended for the first time on 11/12, was a mate for the second meeting on 12/2. From these entries one can conclude that "monthly gatherings" met regularly at the private residences of several different civil aristocrats, and those who attended did so as they pleased. In this way these rounds of tea gatherings had gradually become a routine feature of the social calendar.

Moving into the mid-Muromachi era, we find this same phenomenon of regularly occurring tea functions with provision for wagers or prizes.³⁷ As tea contests increased in frequency and settled into a routine pattern, however, wagers came to be less simply objects for gambling than vehicles for demonstrating one's aesthetic sensibilities. One begins to find references to *fūryū*, meaning artistic taste or nuance, in contemporary diaries. *Kanmon Gyoki*, for example, after remarking on one round of a set of tea contests on 1416/2/26, comments on the objects offered as wagers:

> We were told that we ought to bring as prizes things that would be amusing, so, true to form, we presented ones that had an elegant flair. The things that I brought were one prize in the shape of a bamboo branch with a flute (made of the sort of paper used for love notes), a musical instrument (made from tea), a willow-branch comb, [a miniature scene of] an island of rock and moss with waves (these last two had a poetical sense of long hair blowing in a refreshing breeze) . . . a flower basket . . . decorated with toy dogs of pasted paper (as well as flowers), a branch of flowers with a wind chime (made of paper), and several dapple-gray horses on a flower branch. Naginata Ason brought flower branches (with five different sorts of flowers), and Yukimitsu made flower branches with little dog-shaped boxes of pasted paper.[38]

Each contestant, therefore, was supposed to provide his own prizes for the tea contest, and this was true not only of tea functions but also of linked verse parties and contests involving other amusements. The story of the cat monster from *Tsurezuregusa*, for example, tells about going home with prizes like this.

When *Kanmon Gyoki* wrote of *fūryū*, it meant prizes with a special elegance or perhaps some literary allusion, as for example one described on 1416/3/1, a toy boat carrying a lady formally attired and having a fan at the prow. Inside it were gold dust and the *Book of Zhang Liang* together with a box of tea cups and other Chinese utensils. The scene recalls *Tales of the Heike*, in which Nasu no Yoichi hit the fan at the prow with one shot from his bow. Another prize mentioned on the same date was one in the shape of a hammer called Uchide no Kozuchi, dropped by a demon after Issunbōshi, the fairy-tale character, attacked him.[39] Guests at tea contests, in fact, began to pay more attention to displaying their originality in bringing prizes than to anything else. Both for those who brought the prizes and for those who took them home, elegance seemed to matter more than extravagance. Though these prizes were fairly luxurious, we have already noted that *Gion Shugyō Nikki* mentioned just simple noodles as possible wagers.

One might imagine that everyone was much taken with these tea contests, but such was not necessarily the case. Moving back in time just a bit, there was the well-known Musō Kokushi (1275–1351), who lived in the period covered by *Gion Shugyō Nikki* and *Kanmon Gyoki*. He left us a famous work, *Muchū Mondō,* and he was renowned as one who truly made the Zen sect a Japanese institution. Among the accomplishments that made his name was garden design at Zen temples, including the garden at Saihōji in Kyoto, the Hōjō garden at Tenryūji, as well as that at Tōjiin. As Musō also expressed himself on the subject of tea drinking, let us take a look at his opinions.

What he said was partly in answer to a query by Ashikaga Tadayoshi, younger brother of the shogun Takauji, who asked, "Why is it, if you make no distinction between the material and the spiritual, that Buddhist teachings and Zen priests so often recommend study and advise people to abandon the material and to renounce the concerns of the world?" Musō answered by referring to landscapes. "One cannot say that deciding that one likes a natural scene is a bad thing, but it is hard to call it a good thing either. The merit or demerit is not in the scene itself. Rather, that is in the mind of the person [viewing it]." He continued: "It is the custom among the people of China for everyone to enjoy tea. This is because . . . [of its medicinal value], but if one takes too much [medicine], it will be harmful. So it is with tea. Medical books advise against excessive use of it." Musō then explained that Lu Yu and Lu Tong drank it to help continue their studies, while Eisai and Myōe took it as an aid to Buddhist austerities, but he lamented:

> When we see the scandalous vogue of tea that is abroad in the world today, it is clear that it serves no useful purpose for health. Indeed, no one conceives of drinking it for the sake of scholarship or for the Buddhist Way. Worse yet, they are squandering their resources, thereby impairing the Dharma. All of the above individuals are alike in their enjoyment of tea, but what makes it advantageous or disadvantageous to them is what is in their hearts. . . . Accordingly, this is why Buddhist teachings and Zen priests urge that one should concentrate on the spiritual rather than the material. There are also times when they preach that one should even abandon material things in favor of the spiritual. There is nothing strange about it at all.[40]

In this way Musō explained the original utility of tea for the sake of health before criticizing its current excessive use as a means of entertainment. He said that tea had the potential to aid scholarship or Buddhist practices, but he condemned the "scandalous vogue" of tea entertainments of his own time and lamented that no one seemed to use it any more for its original purposes. Nagashima Fukutarō has said that Musō's influence on later ages was great and that the rules of etiquette for tea came into being as people vied with one another to contrive controls on tea in the midst of the immoderation of tea contests. The drinking of tea has always contained the mutually contradictory elements of crassness and refinement.[41]

Certainly the age in which Musō Kokushi lived was still one of great popularity of tea contests. Yet during the same era in Zen temples there had emerged a formal set of manners for tea service. This was the single connection to the Way of Tea in later ages. But it was not only the civil aristocrats, priests, and upper ranks of warriors who indulged in tea contests; we must also investigate the drinking of tea by common people, for that was the most decisive element in the development of tea as it moved into later ages.

Despite the role of priests, aristocrats, and samurai in the history of tea, in order for the simple drinking of the beverage to develop into the Way of Tea, it was essential that the practice penetrate into the ranks of ordinary people. Had tea remained merely a plaything for persons of high social station, it would never have attained the sort of fruition that it did in later ages with the incorporation of elements of aesthetic consciousness, notably the adoption of the principle of "*wabi*" as a sort of spiritual aesthetic. Instead, it might have suffered the same fate as other aristocratic pastimes such as fan or seashell contests, *kemari* kickball, or falconry, bare relics confined to a limited segment of the population. That it did not was thanks to its transfer into the hands of common people. Examples of the drinking of tea by commoners began with the Ōchamori celebrations, which we encountered at the end of the Kamakura period but by the time the era of Ashikaga Yoshimitsu came to an end, one can see that tea had begun to permeate the mass of the people at large and not only the priests and upper classes.

Kanmon Gyoki in particular has several such examples. The entry for 1416/3/1 recorded: "First, before the tea we had a drink of sake. Next there was a tea contest (seven places). . . . Some did not drink, though the men and women all took it." Some days later, on 3/7, it said:

"Regular tea round. . . . Elegant though it was, it was unspeakably outrageous and shocking to the eye. Men and women flocked to the garden to see. First there was sake, then a tea contest (seven places)."[42] It is unclear what sort of people these "men and women" were, but it may be that they were retainers of the aristocrats who had organized the affairs. On the seventh particularly, since we find them in the garden, it is likely that they were lower-ranking persons who would not have been allowed inside. Such people would not have gathered there so much to drink tea themselves as to peer at the grand function inside and to admire the elegance of the prizes. Sources like this leave us with the feeling that it may still have been impossible for commoners to be active participants. Besides the contests of the distinguished members of the civil and military aristocracy, however, ones that persons of somewhat lower status organized also began to appear about this time. These were so-called *unkyaku* tea rounds, which we first encounter also in *Kanmon Gyoki*, in 1416/6/27 with the phrase "*unkyaku* tea round in the palace."[43] Thereafter, several references appeared.

> 1417/intercalary 5/14
>> We began a set of *unkyaku* tea parties in the kitchen. Ladies serving at the court and men of lower rank joined in from time to time. This is to be a round. It is an annual event.
>
> 1417/6/5
>> Early in the morning something amusing happened. I played seven Korean flute melodies. Then, as people were tired of having tea parties in the kitchen, Juzōzu, as host [did something different]. He prepared a venue by the riverside in the valley with several splendid things there. Afterwards we bathed. It was a wild affair. . . .
>
> 1420/7/10
>> There was a palace tea party, which the men were obliged to attend. Today we finished a regular cycle of tea parties. There were gifts each time. We got sake [from the emperor]. The ladies also participated as did samurai and men of lower rank from time to time.

1425/intercalary 6/1

> We started an *unkyaku* tea cycle and drew lots to deter-
> mine the order [of serving as host]. The elder [priest]
> served today with the prime minister and others in at-
> tendance so Hōsen had tea.[44]

Such "rounds of *unkyaku* tea" appeared even more frequently as time passed. By the Eikyō era (1429–1441) most of the entries referring to tea specified rounds of *unkyaku* tea, and those in the sixth month particularly were of this sort. It is safe to conclude that it had spread widely so as to include the commoner class as well. Organizers held these *unkyaku* tea parties, moreover, in the kitchen or in the quarters of the court ladies, indeed, taking pains to hold them even outdoors by the riverside. They made them enjoyable affairs, serving wine and playing the game of go as well. It is worth noting specially that on such occasions the social classes mixed. The highest levels of courtiers joined in the festivities with those whose inferior status prevented their entry into formal halls. As before, these affairs continued to be links in a series of parties, with participants drawing to determine the role of host.

Unkyaku tea, however, represented a new phenomenon. *Kagakushū*, a lexicon dating from about 1444, defines it thus: "This is a name for bad tea and is so-called because its foam dissipates as quickly as the tendrils of clouds floating in the sky."[45] The name literally means "legs of clouds" and refers to the wisps that seem to hang down from clouds. Hence this was powdered tea of an inferior grade so that it would have been natural to serve it informally in the kitchen or the quarters of the court ladies. The modern scholar Horinouchi Tajirō writes in "Murata Jukō to Chakai no Dentō" that *unkyaku* tea parties played a pioneering role because of their tendency to involve commoners.[46] They allowed ladies and men of lower rank in large numbers to join the aristocratic men who had hitherto dominated tea affairs. The old-fashioned tea contests to distinguish between *honcha* and *hicha*, therefore, had already withdrawn from center stage. Tea parties became occasions to enjoy wine, and they shed much of their ponderous solemnity from the early Muromachi period. Tea, now liberated, was moving forward into a new era. Horinouchi's remarks, therefore, identify *unkyaku* tea as an underlying cause of the decline of tea contests, but there was a more proximate cause as well. That was the appearance of

Furuichi Harima Chōin, said to have been the recipient of the secret teachings of Murata Jukō, the founder of the grass hut tea tradition. Furuichi Harima was a powerful adherent of the Kōfukuji in Nara and frequently appeared in Jinson's *Daijōin Jisha Zōjiki*. We also find him in *Kyōkaku Shiyōshō*, the diary of the abbot Kyōkaku, also of Kōfukuji. Its entry for 1469/5/23 relates an occasion when the abbot accepted an invitation to the Furuichi bath.

> Today I had a bath of a new sort. [My] servants, the Furuichi family, and their young retainers all joined in at the behest of Furuichi to heat the water. We had *chanoyu* in the bath with two kinds of tea. (One was from Uji, and the other was lower quality.) There were two tubs of white muskmelon, a tray of wild peaches [myrica fruit], and noodles with lotus leaves as a garnish. . . . After the bath I had a cup of sake. Later as many as one hundred fifty people took a bath, including the Furuichi family, the young retainers, Nagai, Yokoi, and Gengen. After the men the Furuichi women also bathed.[47]

The diary's term for bath, ironically "lonely perspiration," appears in *Kagakushū* with the definition "summer bath."[48] The scene we find here of relaxing after bathing and enjoying fruit and noodles is not one in which tea had great significance. It was little more than an adjunct to the bath itself, just a refreshing beverage. Moreover, the fact that they served two kinds of tea, Uji tea and an inferior one,[49] did not mean that they held a tea contest. It was simply that the higher-ranking guests drank the better grade, leaving the lesser one for the rest. Horinouchi says that what is of interest about this party is that it was not a formal ten-round tea contest but an extremely candid and open expression of commoner taste. People drank tea, enjoyed food and wine, and then to these frenzied commoner pleasures they added the element of the bath.

I have just suggested that the remote cause of the decline of tea contests was to be found in the advent of *unkyaku* tea or bathing tea, and I believe it is not far wrong to see the beginnings of commoner tea particularly in the former. Also, as we have seen, by the late medieval era tea drinking was a well-established practice. As the *Isei Teikin Ōrai* illustrates, tea cultivation had reached a nationwide scale by the early Muromachi era, and though initially it was Zen priests who cultivated it in temple gardens, finally ordinary farmers took it up. It is hard to imagine that the cultivators would not drink it themselves. On the contrary, for all we know they may have scrambled to drink it as a medicine. Such a phenomenon was evident in the Ōchamori ritual of the Saidaiji as well as other temple tea gatherings. The great extent of tea gatherings can be surmised from their prohibition in the *Kenmu Shikimoku,* and though to be sure the framers of the law did not have the mass of people in mind, its enactment did nevertheless reflect the widespread diffusion of such tea entertainments.

Hayashiya Tatsusaburō in *Chūsei Bunka no Kichō* has pointed out that progress in agricultural productivity in the villages of Japan during the late Kamakura period resulted in a surplus that enabled farmers to embark upon the cultivation of tea as a sideline. In the home provinces especially, the village became a significant social and governmental unit, replacing the estate system. Peasants there banded together to protect their own interests and to resist proprietors and oppressive officials.[50] One imagines that village tea gatherings played a role in that process. The same economic developments also encouraged the appearance of tea peddlers, whose activities became especially evident in the middle of the Muromachi era, from the 1390s into the 1430s. Nōami, one of the forerunners who began the process of transforming *chanoyu* into a Way of Tea, was at that time one of the Dōbōshū, Companions, of the shogun Ashikaga Yoshinori. The appearance of Nōami marked the first step in this process of converting tea entertainment into tea ritual.

PART 3

The Creation of a
Way of Tea

7 Murata Jukō and the Birth of the Way of Tea

As each age progressed, cultural leadership shifted greatly from one social class to another. And there was a corresponding, qualitative change in the nature of culture itself because of the differing spiritual climates and intellectual forms among those who bore the cultural burden. In the age of massive borrowing from China, for example, the monks and students who had returned from the continent and were in the vanguard of cultural importation uncritically accepted Chinese customs and life-styles. For this reason, as the culture of tea amply illustrates, they swallowed Lu Yu's world view whole and intact. Accordingly, Japanese culture had to await a new age when more nearly Japanese forms would appear and when Japanese thinking about such issues would also shift.

The content of Heian era collections such as *Bunka Shūreishū* and *Keikokushū*, cited earlier, displays a style that evinces direct importation into Japan of a Chinese world view and is innocent of any transformation or refraction by a Japanese prism. With the shift from the Kamakura to the Muromachi era, however, Japanese cultural understanding became more immediate and lost its insubstantial character. Eisai's attraction to tea as a mystical medicine to nourish health meant that he esteemed it as an object that he sought to incorporate into Japanese life. So long as the cultural leaders of Japan attempted to recreate in their own country a Chinese cultural sense, the Chinese style of tea drinking remained unchanged, but changing cultural leadership as the ages progressed brought new forms to the fore.

The cultural elite of Heian, whose first thought was of pedigree and refinement, lived lives of assured economic well-being, political authority, and social status. For them, therefore, culture meant refinement and that in turn implied the creation of an international life-style that necessarily conformed to Chinese patterns, which were merely formal and conceptual. By contrast, the new cultural leaders who ascended the stage at Kamakura were the products of a completely different background. Pedigree hardly mattered. Economically insecure, they sought only to eke out an existence in lands far from the traditional centers of culture. Refinement was a frill, and ceremonial formality held no meaning for them. Compared to the courtiers of Heian who enjoyed lives of intellectual, conceptual refinement, these were warriors whose style was passionate and physical. They lived in an age of revolutionary upheaval, one in which lineage and cultivation had lost all import. Strength was all that counted, and only those who had it prevailed. That strength was not something that had come down from divine ancestors through an ancient pedigree. It had to be seized through the spilling of blood. And by the spilling of blood they eroded the archaic authority of Heian. Theirs was a strength that had to be won through their own physical prowess and at the expense of those who lacked it.

Accordingly, when these newly arisen warriors took up the culture of Heian, they did not adopt the sinified forms of the gentlemen there. Their approach to the drinking of tea was fundamentally different from that of the men of class and breeding, the scholars and learned monks, who had taken to it as one element of the Chinese life-style. Though cultural transmission generally involves some copying, their new culture differed from the imitation of China by the Heian courtiers. For the new classes following the Kamakura era, the ultimate import and value of cultural adoption had changed completely, and we find a qualitative shift in the nature of culture from that time on.

Even though at first glance the new classes seemed to be imitating the tea-drinking practices of the Heian elite, further examination reveals a sharp distinction in content. First, there was the desire to display the power that they had won. Having seized authority they wanted to show it off lavishly. Indeed, they had to do so, for by imitating the life-styles of the previously established political powers, they demonstrated their own newly achieved authority not only to those who are governed but also to the established powers themselves. Second, tea had previously been esteemed because initially it was in short supply and therefore expensive, but it had ceased to be rare and had become merely a beverage enjoyed for its pleasant taste. The new elite made no effort to appreciate the poetic aura that came from rarity.

Rather, their approach was the purely physical perception that tea tasted good whether it was rare or not and that when they had built up their power, they could enjoy as much as they liked even if it was rare. They had, moreover, a rationalism that permitted the expansion of tea production after the masses of people discovered what a delicious drink it was. This process can easily be seen in the Muromachi era with the spread of tea cultivation throughout the country that came with the increase in demand. These two factors meant that there was an actual, qualitative dissimilarity in tea-drinking practices in the two eras despite apparent imitation.

For the men of culture in Heian, tea drinking was a way to emphasize their commonality with the Chinese world. Whether tea tasted good was not their first concern, for it carried an aura of romanticism that came from its association with a foreign, not to say advanced, civilization. There can be no doubt that the act of taking tea itself represented a yearning for an exotic realm just as it had for Lu Yu when he enjoyed tea in his world apart. The joy, the exaltation of spirit that came from drinking tea, which we found in poetry, reflected this yearning, and that overshadowed the significance of tea as a beverage. Initially offered to the Buddha or merely taken for medicinal effect, it would not become a beverage for daily use or a pleasant but simple luxury until after the emergence of the new warrior class. Their lives allowed of no considerations that were not immediate, practical, and physical. The ideal, spiritual style of life in which one gazed dreamily into a bowl of tea to perceive dimly some poetic emotion was hardly a part of their existence. For them the primary concern was that tea tasted good and had a beneficial effect. Scarcity value was not an issue. What was foremost in their minds was that tea was delicious and brought them delight. No scarcity value could stand before their steadily burgeoning authority, and because of that authority they turned tea into just another item of daily consumption rather than the pompously ceremonial object of esteem that it had been in the hands of the early Heian intellectuals. It was entirely natural that they should have valued it, together with gambling and wine, as a means for enjoying life. For these reasons there appeared a sharp devaluation in prevailing attitudes toward tea after the Kamakura era and especially after the dynastic disputes of the fourteenth century. Such a turn was an absolutely indispensable condition for the formation of the practice we know as *chanoyu*.

In the background of the doctrine of *chanoyu* according to Rikyū lay all of these vicissitudes, beginning in the remote past of Tang dynasty China and continuing until we find the formation of a comprehensive cultural system. For a fuller understanding of the lineage of tea we require a more complete exposition; particularly we need to analyze the beginnings of *chanoyu* in the Muromachi era. The major elements in the formation of this system can be represented as follows:

Conceptual illusion of a realm apart
Lu Yu–style elements → Heian · · · · · → literature

Concern for quotidian effect
Eisai-style elements → Muromachi · · · · · → artistic
　　　　　　　　　　　　　　　　　　　　　　accomplishment

The Heian interest in tea, confined to the aristocracy, was to be found in a Chinese-style notion of a world apart. Accordingly, it took expression in literature and evoked a sympathy of feeling. There were no presentiments of the later elements of entertainment such as we saw in the tea contests. In the Kamakura era, however, the focus moved to tea's medicinal effect and the interest in it became quotidian and rational. With its capacity for the exhilaration of body and mind, it was natural for it to spread to the world of entertainment.

It would appear at first glance these two were quite separate strands in the history of tea, and when we examine each in its own historical setting it appears that a great change had taken place in attitudes toward tea. In reality, however, already in the age of Lu Yu we find quotidian factors in his thinking about tea. It was precisely because he was aware of its medicinal effects that Lu Yu wrote his *Classic of Tea* and turned to the fantasy of a world apart. The difference between the two strands is merely a function of how we frame our argument and place our emphasis. The elements were all in place in the background of tea prior to its taking shape as a comprehensive cultural system.

How then did these two strands come to be woven together to create a complete cultural entity? It was not a question of one having negated the other. Rather the negation of each consisted of the two combining together, and in order for this union to occur an entirely new factor needed to be put into play. This new factor at once comprehended the literary notion of a world apart and promoted the quotidian interest in tea. It was a unifying theory that served to bring the two together on a higher dimension.

The factor in question was the religious and aesthetic thought that steadily emerged with tea at its center beginning in the Muromachi era. This was a somewhat abstract mode of expression, but in the late fifteenth century, when culture focused on the Eastern Hills section of Kyoto, called Higashiyama, tea itself was swept up in a tide of fascination with rare Chinese objects and was drawn into a world of aestheticism. In the pages that follow, I will trace these events in detail, looking first at Jukō and Jōō and then at the formative era in the early modern Way of Tea.

What made this aesthetic awakening possible was the creation in the realm of tea of a religious world view, a development that constituted an extraordinary revolution. This unification of the culture of tea following religious principles served to raise it to a higher dimension while distilling the essence of its previously limited concern with quotidian effect and the entertainment value based upon it. The men of tea used this religious awakening into the world of aesthetics in an effort to achieve a qualitative leap up into a plane that could reconcile both Lu Yu's otherworldly thinking and the quotidian concerns of Eisai. In the succeeding Higashiyama era, for example, they realized just how pointless the earlier tea contests had been with their gross excesses, the splendid ponds and gardens, which manipulated the landscape in any way one wished, the surfeit of famous paintings and treasures. Instead, they turned to the true ideal of tea. *Yamanoue Sōji Ki* said, "Because *chanoyu* comes from the Zen sect, it is chiefly the work of priests; Jukō and Jōō were both Zen [adherents]."[1] These often cited words reveal the unity of tea and religious thinking, especially that of Zen. Zen transformed and advanced tea mightily. The *chanoyu* that we saw in the previous chapter involved gambling with great sums of money or valuable prizes. Its ceremonial content was minimal and its spiritual content, nil. It is now time for us to consider the question of when the spiritual elevation of *chanoyu* developed.

At the end of the preceding chapter, I mentioned Nōami, one of the Dōbōshū of Yoshimasa (1435–1490), the shogun who built the Silver Pavilion in Kyoto's Higashiyama and lived there as a recluse. Yamanoue Sōji's statement "Nōami was famed among the Dōbōshū and the one who wrote the titles for the shogun's paintings" suggests his importance to Yoshimasa.[2] He was instrumental in making the Zen reading room called a *shoin* a venue for tea, for he was the first to devise the so-called *shoin kazari* style of layout, suitable to the serving of tea there in contrast to the layout that had been used for tea contests. It was also he who originated the *daisu kazari* style, which employed the *daisu* shelf in making tea. His son Geiami and his grandson Sōami continued his practices, and together they founded the style of tea service known as the Higashiyama School. He is said to have written *Kundaikan Sōchōki*,[3] a catalog of Yoshimasa's treasures, and Sōami, to have written a companion volume, *Okazarisho*.[4] The former had two main sections, one devoted to paintings and the other to utensils. The painting section listed famous Chinese artists through the ages with brief biographical entries and titles of their works, while the section on utensils described the correct use of trays, incense containers, candle stands, censers, vases, tea bowls, leaf tea storage containers, tea caddies, and other, miscellaneous items. One can easily see how great an artistic influence Nōami exerted upon the shogun.

In creating a venue for tea in a *shoin* using treasured Chinese utensils and making tea using a *daisu*, Nōami, though still following rules for tea service, created norms that were different from those we saw in the tea contests of the *Kissa Ōrai*, in which the host's son brought out tea while a young man followed with hot water to make the brew. As Kuwata Tadachika, writing in *Nihon Chadōshi* has said, this was neither the obscene luxury of the tea contests of the upper class samurai nor the austere tea rite of a plain Zen temple. It was a tea gathering that had the splendid adornments of the *shoin* as a backdrop and employed the most excellent of utensils in a discerning manner and arranged following the most formal style of the *daisu*. It was tea clad in rigorously proper attire and adhering to the most orthodox patterns. It was a clear amalgam of the tea entertainments of the military aristocracy and the tea rituals of Buddhism.[5] In this way, the Higashiyama era of the mid-Muromachi period witnessed an epoch-making change in the path of *chanoyu* through the innovations of the distinguished artist Nōami.

Another figure who appeared at about the time these great changes were occurring was Murata Jukō of the Shōmyōji in Nara. *Chōandōki* by the early Edo tea man Kubo Gondayū identifies the Higashiyama era as the beginning of *chanoyu* and says this about Jukō:

Murata Jukō (also pronounced Shukō; ca. 1423–1502), early proponent of the "cold and withered" sensibility in the practice of tea, and the first to create a style of tea based on the concept of *wabi*. Property of Shōmyōji Temple, Nara.

The origins of *suki,* the tea ritual, are unknown. Though I have asked people who are familiar with the Way, I cannot get a clear answer. However, it appears to have emerged at the time of Higashiyama-dono. By this name I refer to the shogun Lord Yoshimasa of the Jishōin [the Silver Pavilion]. It seems that he abdicated his office in favor of his son and retired to Higashiyama, where he devoted himself for many years to pleasure. It is said that Jukō was a man of this same age, the Bunmei era [1469–1487], a time of many famous men such as Ikkyū [Sōjun] and Higashi no Yasu.[6]

Another early modern work, *Wakan Chashi,* says that Jukō was a priest of the Bunmei era and lived in the Shōmyōji in Nara. It continues:

He cut miscanthus and used it to make a thatched hut, which he called a *sukiya,* and hung a scroll on its wall. He sought to follow the path [of those who had gone before] in order to find truth. In the dead of winter just before the New Year he looked for plum blossoms, and he tried to find chrysanthemums before it had become autumn. In a space as confined as the inside of a bottle, he was as tranquil as if he were in a broad hall. The society of others did not make him coarse, and his tea utensils were always out and ready, whether or not guests had arrived.[7]

Thus, Jukō, in his thatched *sukiya,* hung a scroll on the wall and tried to enter into the world it portrayed. He always wanted flowers before they were in season but lived a life of ease alone with his tea utensils.

Another more extended description of Jukō's life comes from *Chajidan* by Nanshūjo, writing in 1760. She provides some clues to his family background as well as his personality:

> Long ago in a place called Nakanomikado in Nara, Yamato province, there was a person named Murata Mokuichi Kengyō. (Note: Mokuichi Kengyō, according to *Shokugen Daizen,* was a Buddhist title, together with Nagon and Sangi, which was given to a layman who trained carpenters. Murata may have been the chief of the carpenters at the Tōdaiji.) He had one son whose childhood name was Mokichi. At the age of ten the son left his home to enter the Shōmyōji [in Nara] . . . and took the Buddhist name Jukō. At age seventeen he moved to the Hōrin'an in the same temple. (Note: There is today in the back of the Shōmyōji a well and the remains of the Hōrin'an. People call this Jukō's Well, but I have not been able to confirm the association. There is also a chart from Jakushōji that shows Jukō's Well [and other sites].) At about age twenty he tired of the priest's life and preferred secular activities, so he neglected his priestly duties. His teacher reproached him to no avail. At last the teacher remonstrated with his parents, and Jukō left Hōrin'an to become a vagabond. (Note: Shōmyōji was a separate branch of Jison'in, which was affiliated with Kōfukuji and jointly associated with four sects. The teacher at the time was Karyōkai, the eleventh-generation head of the temple.) Thereafter, at about age thirty, Jukō became a Zen priest in Shinjūan of Daitokuji in Murasakino, Kyoto. (Note: There is said to be a memorial tablet to him at Shinjūan, but I have not yet confirmed that.)[8]

The *Chajidan* account continues with a sketch of the latter half of his career. According to this, Jukō's troubles followed him into his life in Zen, whose meditative practices and scholarly reading had a soporific effect upon him. Concerned about his excessive drowsiness, Jukō decided to consult a famous physician for help with his problem. He explained his inability to follow the orders of his superiors and his rootless life as a wanderer and finally told the doctor that not only meditation but the study of theology tended to put him to sleep. "You are," he said, "a famous physician. If you can find in the medical tomes of Japan or China a medicine to banish drowsiness, please prescribe it for me." Thereupon the doctor promptly launched into an exposition on the merits of tea along the lines of Eisai's *Kissa Yōjōki*. He explained that each of the five organs had its preferred taste, acid for the liver, pungent for the lungs, bitter for the heart, sweet for the spleen, and salty for the kidneys. Since the people of the day tended to have weak hearts and since the heart was prime among the organs, what they needed was the bitter taste of tea to nourish the heart. It was the weakness of the heart, he said, that lay at the root of the drowsiness that troubled Jukō. The priest was elated to learn of a cure and immediately ordered tea from Toganoo, which he regularly drank and enjoyed thereafter. He also read all of the Chinese classics of tea, including *Chajing* and *Chalu*. Jukō thus had direct exposure to information about Chinese methods of taking tea.[9]

There are also variant accounts of Jukō's life in other Edo era works. One, *Chanoyu Roku Sōshō Denki,* explains that there were two theories of Jukō's career as a priest, one that he was from Shōmyōji and the other that he was at Kōmyōji. At age twenty-five or so, after ten years at one or the other, it said he went to Kyoto and built a hut in the Sanjō area. There he studied flower arranging with Sōami [*sic*, probably Nōami]. A Kyoto aristocrat befriended him, introduced him to tea, and at Jukō's request, allowed him to view Chinese tea caddies. Jukō's natural talent led him to become a famous authority on the Way of Tea and, perhaps thanks to Nōami, he came to the attention of Yoshimasa, who summoned him to Higashiyama. According to this source, Jukō left the priesthood and built a tea pavilion near Rokujō Horikawa in the capital, where he took up residence.[10]

Edo era writers on *chanoyu* like the one just cited agree that Nōami helped bring Jukō and Yoshimasa together, but modern research has been unable to confirm the connection through contemporary sources.[11] One sixteenth-century source that discusses this relationship is *Yamanoue Sōji Ki*. Yamanoue Sōji essentially confirms the association with Yoshimasa in an account of him during this period. Moreover, he explains their meeting as the work of Nōami:

> Yoshimasa, living in seclusion in Higashiyama, devoted himself to amusement in all seasons and both morning and night. One evening, feeling plaintive while waiting for the moon and listening to the cries of the insects, he summoned Nōami, and had him read from the *Tale of Genji* a passage about a discussion on a rainy night. They talked about all their old pastimes from poetry and moon or flower viewing to balls, bows, fans, and the writing of poems using plant and insect names. Yoshimasa lamented that they had exhausted every single amusing topic from the past. It has already become cold, he said, and I am too old to take my hawks and go hunting in the snowy mountains. Surely, there is some unusual diversion for us to enjoy. Nōami listened and replied respectfully but with conviction that the kettle envies the wind in the pines. There is an entertainment, he said, that is interesting in any season.[12]

Sōji continues that at that point Nōami told Yoshimasa about Jukō from the Shōmyōji in Nara and said that the priest had delved deeply into the Way of Tea, having devoted himself to it from the age of thirty. He was, moreover, familiar with the tenets of Confucius. Nōami explained the new teachings to Yoshimasa and said that tea was a capital way to appreciate all sorts of famous utensils and ancient paintings.

He explained that Jukō's approach to tea was simpler than his own very formal style. Jukō had received from Ikkyū a scroll by the Chinese artist Yuanwu and would hang just that single piece in the alcove of his tea room and gaze at that alone. He had inscribed in his heart Ikkyū's teaching that "there is also Buddhism in *chanoyu*," and that is how he came to dedicate himself to its study. Jukō, who had been a priest since his childhood in Nara, had become acquainted with Ikkyū and as a result of their studies together had grown convinced that the ultimate ideal of tea lay in the world of Zen. He realized the unity of Zen and tea and understood the purity and religious ecstasy to be had from it.[13] Therefore, when Yoshimasa called Jukō to ask him about tea, the latter replied, according to *Wakan Chashi*, "Tea is not play; it is not technique; it is not entertainment."[14] Ideally, it is a means of purifying one's heart, and its religious content is foremost. Jukō did not, to be sure, ignore the more conventional preoccupations of tea men, such as the appraisal of the Chinese utensils that were so popular at the time, ownership of them, or skill in the service of tea. Yet the realm of Zen always remained the ultimate ideal toward which he strived.

Confucian aims were one part of the ideal he sought. As Nōami said, Jukō had studied the teachings of the Master, and this interest in Confucianism can also be found in the *Wakan Chashi* account. When he told Yoshimasa that tea was neither game, technique, nor entertainment, the shogun asked, "Why, then, do people do it?" Jukō responded, "Through *chanoyu* one exercises *li* [the Confucian virtue of decorum]."[15] According to this account, Jukō's tea involved preparing and serving food and drink with the ceremony that the Master recommended and was not merely the act of eating and drinking. He would draw water from a valley stream, kindle fine charcoal, use Chinese or Korean utensils, prepare a grass-thatched hut and collect rocks to lay out a garden that would convey the sense of remote mountains.[16] All of this was a reflection of Confucian ideals.

Chajidan also has an account of how Jukō came to employ the *daisu* shelf for tea.

> At that time there was a *daisu* at the Daitokuji in Murasakino, Kyoto, but no one knew how to use it. It was a tea stand that had come many years earlier as a present from Song China to the Shōfukuji, a Zen temple in Hakata in Kyushu. (Note: Ankokuzan Shōfukuji is in Hakozaki, Hakata, Chikuzen province. Its mountain gate has a tablet with a six-character inscription written by former emperor Go-Toba. It says, "First Zen Temple in Japan." Today's formal tea ritual using the *daisu* originated with this shelf.) This shelf was later sent to Hieizan and after that came to Daitokuji. When Jukō spied it, he proclaimed it could only be for tea and promptly began using it in his tea service.[17]

This is how Jukō came to use the *daisu* from the Shōfukuji in Hakata in his tea service. Both Nōami's *Kundaikan Sōchōki* and Sōami's *Okazarisho* mention it, and it was probably Jukō who first used it to hold the utensils for his preparation of tea.[18] It is, moreover, probably safe to conclude that Jukō was the first to create in this way a ceremonial service of tea with formal rules of preparation, for we further learn, "Jukō used the shelf for his brazier and kettle, the water supply jar, dipper stand, fire chopsticks, and waste water container; he laid out the tea room based upon this device and had his guests drink with due formality."[19] Thus he created a method of service built around the *daisu* that is not significantly different from the way we use it today.

At the Shōmyōji in Nara, there is a memorial tablet dedicated to Jukō and containing his posthumous name and the date "fifteenth day, fifth month, second year of Bunki, year of the elder brother of water and the dog [1502]." Since *Yamanoue Sōji Ki* has an entry "Jukō passed away at age eighty, perhaps [like] a snowy mountain,"[20] it is generally accepted that he died in 1502 at age eighty, that is, seventy-nine by Western reckoning.

Now that we have traced Jukō's career, we must not neglect the record that tells us most about his theory of the Way of Tea. That is the letter that he wrote to his main disciple, the Yamato magnate Furuichi Harima Chōin, which constituted the secret transmission of his teachings. This letter enables one to understand the spirit that Jukō injected into *chanoyu*.

> In this Way, chief among evils is the heart's overbearance, attachment to self. Begrudging the masterly and scorning beginners are thoroughly wrongheaded. You must approach the masterful, beseech their least word, and never fail to guide beginners. Critical above all else in this Way is the dissolution of the boundary line between things native and Chinese. This is vital, truly vital; attend to it with care. Further: These days mere beginners take up pieces of Bizen or Shigaraki, talking of the "chill and withered"; and they make a show of being "advanced and deepened" though ignored by everyone—it defies all utterance. "Withered" means owning splendid pieces, knowing their savor fully, and from the heart's ground advancing and deepening so that all after becomes chill and lean: it is this that has power to move. Further: Though it is so, the person wholly incapable must not turn contentious over the tools of the Way. And however artful one's motions, a painful self-awareness is crucial. Overbearance and attachment simply obstruct. And yet the Way lies unattainable if there's no overbearance at all also.

A dictum of praise states:
"Grow up heart's master, not heart mastered—."
words of an ancient[21]

One sees throughout this letter a connection between tea and linked verse, both of which enjoyed great popularity in Jukō's time and both of which Jukō understood thoroughly. He speaks of the spirit of tea clothed in the language of linked verse theory, and in this way he has produced the earliest statement about the essence of his tea art. According to the letter, the worst errors a tea practitioner could fall into were pride and obduracy. A person who thought only of himself would find his spirit intractably set in his own ego and become unfeeling for others. It was inexcusable, for example, either to envy those who were accomplished or to despise those who had just begun to practice tea. One should learn from the former and encourage the latter. It was also of major importance to strike a harmonious balance between Japanese and Chinese elements, so that one should devote great thought and effort to that end. Moreover, beginners, who imagined, to the scorn of others, that they could achieve the "cold and withered" taste so fashionable at that time simply by using plain-looking Bizen and Shigaraki pottery were being foolish. What was interesting in the practice of tea and would truly display the "cold and withered" taste was for a person first to have and appreciate good utensils and then to seek to enter the realm of the "cold and withered" in his own heart. Having said that, however, those who could find no satisfaction in either physical or spiritual matters might just as well give up merely amusing themselves with utensils. No matter how plain or coarse a utensil might be it was important to "take it to heart." It was wrong simply to feel pride or attachment without that sense of "taking it to heart." Still, one must not just negate his own ego completely, for the Way also meant that there were times when it was appropriate to feel a sense of self-confidence.

The Furuichi Harima to whom Jukō addressed this letter was a local magnate in Furuichi in Yamato province (modern Nara). He was a powerful adherent of the Kōfukuji and commanded a castle with a domain worth thirty thousand *koku*. At the same time he also held high office in the Buddhist hierarchy. *Yamanoue Sōji Ki* called him Jukō's foremost disciple and a famous man of tea with a collection of over thirty utensils.[22] Before becoming Jukō's disciple, however, his upbringing was not the sort to seem suitable to one who would devote himself to the

Nara School of the Way of Tea, which Jukō had founded. Readers who recall the previous chapter's reference from Kyōkaku's diary to the Furuichi baths might have surmised that already. The account of the bath had a date of 1469, while Furuichi Chōin was born in 1459, and that would mean he would have been about ten years old.

The same Furuichi Chōin also appears in *Daijōin Jisha Zōjiki* from time to time, for he was an acquaintance of its author, Jinson. For example, at least seven entries for the first month of 1482 mention tea contests or linked verse gatherings. Though one cannot always tell whether Chōin attended, on the twenty-sixth one finds, "Furuichi was host. . . ."[23] Of course, this may have been Chōin or his elder brother In'ei, but in any event one can easily imagine that the brothers were a part of that environment. A further entry for 1/26 identified Furuichi as the loser in a gambling party, while on 1/29 Chōin, mentioned by name, began a series of linked verse parties and served as the first host. In the same month three years later, the entry for 1/4 mentioned the first tea contest of the year "as usual" with three prizes. The following day Jinson noted the birth of a son to Furuichi Chōin, once again specifically named. Somewhat later in 1495, the first tea contest of the New Year, held on the fourth in seven rounds with fans and tissues as prizes, had the names of fifteen guests, one of whom was Fujichiyo, Chōin's son.[24] Thus, Chōin appeared as a regular participant in the tea contests, gambling, and verse parties of the Nara social circuit.

Jukō's transmission of the mysteries of tea to Chōin needs to be viewed in this light. That is, Chōin, the dilettante who had devoted himself to the pleasures and entertainments of his day, was now attempting to master the spirit of the grass hut style of tea, and the letter aimed to reshape the disciple's thinking about such entertainments. The first line of the letter explains principles common to the practice of all of the arts. Thus, Jukō first warned against "pride and obduracy of the heart," by which he meant that feeling of self-centeredness that could cause one to become set in his own ways. These constituted a kind of egoism that one needed to be careful of in all the arts. Zeami in his *Kadensho* enjoined the aspirant not to forget the spirit of the beginner, another expression of this same all-important idea. Pride and obduracy, after all, would bring progress in the arts to a halt. Concretely, in *chanoyu* one should neither envy the accomplishments of those who knew more nor should one look down upon the beginners, who knew less. Instead, one should associate with the accomplished and ask questions while at the same time, guiding the efforts of those who were just starting. Furthermore, by exhorting Chōin to blend Chinese and Japanese elements in his tea, he was encouraging him to use utensils of both Japanese and continental provenance and not to become fixed only on Chinese wares. Thus, in order to be able to master the grass hut style thoroughly, Jukō enjoined the disciple to banish the bathhouse tea parties and contests that his family had previously organized.

Thus far the letter contains a theory of practice that could apply to any of the arts, but from this point on Jukō began for the first time to discuss innovative principles that applied specifically to tea.

This amounted to a new theory of a Way of Tea that was unprecedented in either China or Japan, and it became the point of departure for the later "*wabicha*." One can see this innovation particularly in the references to the "cold and withered" taste. By belittling beginners who got ahead of themselves and used Bizen or Shigaraki wares in a vain effort to achieve the cold and withered fashion, he was condemning their pretense to seem more than they really were. Yet he was also saying that Bizen and Shigaraki tea bowls had that "cold and withered" quality. That style was to have a great impact on later ages. Yamanoue Sōji wrote, "The priest Shinkei [1406–1475] said of linked verse that the poems should be cold and withered; Tsuji Gensai said that Jōō always told him that the essence of *chanoyu* must become like that as well."[25] Thus, the "cold and withered" taste applied equally to linked poems, as seen in these words, and one can readily imagine that *renga* theorists like Shinkei exerted extraordinary influence on Jukō. "Cold and withered" or "cold and lonely" were terms that enjoyed the greatest esteem in *renga* circles as expressions of *yūgen* or *yūshin*, the subtlety and profundity that were considered the highest principles of poetic theory.[26] It is unclear whether the term "cold and withered" might have been familiar to any member of the intellectual classes of the day or whether its use would have been confined to those who were conversant with the theory of poetry. In any case, however, it would be entirely plausible that Jukō had read such theoretical works. We know that the Zen priests Ikkyū and Sōchō [1447–1532] were accomplished poets,[27] and Jukō may well have undergone religious training together with Sōchō under Ikkyū, though one cannot be certain since the dates of their Zen studies are not known. Nonetheless, it would seem not unusual for a single individual to be familiar with both arts, for references to tea regularly appeared in writing about poetry.

The poet Nijō Yoshimoto [1320–1388], for example, wrote in *Jūmon Saihishō* in 1383 a section on the theory of poetry in which he discussed the relationship between essential content and the mode of expression of that content in linked verse.

> It is ridiculous when one perceives that the cherry blossoms are wonderful and then laughs boisterously without a thought in one's head. It may seem relatively amusing to force a certain coarseness when that feels like the right thing to do. This is the way it is with the best tea, *honcha*. It may have a wonderful fragrance in and of itself, but it may not be perceived as wonderful if its presentation is unskillful. No matter that it comes from Toganoo or Uji, its splendid flavor will be lost if the preparation is poor.[28]

As one can see, he uses tea as an analogy, contrasting the essential fragrance and flavor of the best tea with unskillful preparation. For the history of tea, this is a valuable source, for its fourteenth-century date makes it one of the earliest references to the difference between *honcha* and *hicha*.

Moving to a slightly later period, we find Shōtetsu's [1381–1459] *Seigan Chawa* (*Shōtetsu Monogatari*). It is noteworthy that the author, though a *renga* poet, used the term "*chawa*," meaning "tea stories," in his title. Shōtetsu drew a distinction among levels of interest in poetry and based his explanation on similar distinctions among tea men. Since the work appeared in the middle of the fifteenth century, it suggests that such distinctions were already widely understood at that time. He wrote:

> There are different sorts of interests in poetry just as there are different types of fascination with tea. [In tea] there are first of all the *chasuki*, those who are mad about tea, who care most about its beautiful trappings and dabble in things like Chinese tea bowls, kettles and water supply jars. . . . There are also the tea drinkers. These are not necessarily concerned with the utensils but go to all sorts of ten-round tea contests to drink. They seem to know right away what sort of tea they are tasting. If it is Uji tea, they know that it was from the third crop or whether it was picked after the first day of the third month. If Toganoo tea, they can tell which field it grew in, this one from

Tobata, that one from Sagazama. . . . Finally, there are the tea devourers. They will drink any kind of tea. Good tea or dregs, they put it in a huge bowl and gulp it down. They do not know whether the tea is good or bad; they just want plenty of it.[29]

Thus he found three different types of tea aficionados, those who liked the utensils, those who enjoyed the distinctions of taste more than the trappings of tea, and those who simply liked to drink lots of it without caring how it tasted. Though omitted in this quotation, the author had included after each type of tea drinker a characterization of a comparable type of linked verse poet. Shōtetsu, himself a poet, seems to have had a fair degree of knowledge and experience with tea as well. It is interesting to compare Shōtetsu's types of tea lovers with the better-known classification found in *Yamanoue Sōji Ki*.

There are first the ones we call *chanoyumono*, the men of tea, who have a discerning eye [for utensils], are skillful at preparation, and make their way in the world as masters of *suki*. Next there are the persons called *wabisuki*, who own not a single piece but have all three elements of calm preparedness in the heart, creativity, and achievement. Finally, there are the ones we call the *meijin*. They have the three qualities of owning Chinese utensils and skill both at judging utensils and at preparation of tea. They will also have delved deeply into the Way. Matsumoto and Shino may both be called *chanoyumono*; Zenpō is a *sukimono*. Those who combine all these qualities and are *meijin*, ancient and modern, are Jukō, Insetsu, and Jōō.[30]

The first group, his *chanoyumono*, were persons who could judge the merits of tea utensils and who excelled at the performance of the service itself. They were able to make their living as teachers of *chanoyu*. The second he called *wabisuki*. They had no special Chinese wares but did have the three attributes of calm spirit, creativity, and technique. Finally, there were the *meijin* who did own Chinese utensils and were knowledgeable about their qualities. These also possessed spiritual preparedness, creativity, and technique, and they had tried to understand the philosophical foundations of the Way of Tea as well. Murai Yasuhiko has pointed out in *Chanoyu no Rekishi* the different bases for classification in the two sources just cited. In the former, by Shōtetsu, interest in utensils was the criterion for inclusion in the first group, the *chasuki*. The other two groups he divided according to how they drank the tea, perhaps reflecting the fad for tea contests current at that time. Yamanoue Sōji, by contrast, subdivided Shōtetsu's first group and stressed the importance of utensil ownership as well as the ability to judge their merits as major criteria for inclusion in his categories. Sōji's greater emphasis on utensils may have resulted from an increased interest in them as well as more widespread ownership of them.[31]

Sōchō, the *renga* poet, seems to have been conversant with *chanoyu*, as reflected in scattered references through his journal *Sōchō Shuki*. There were, for example, a series of entries beginning on 1526/8/11 that said: "Left Kyoto. Stayed one night at the Tsujinobō villa in Shirakawa, Uji. The twelfth at Tōunken. From the day before we have mostly done linked verses." The following day he wrote: "Just after dawn on the thirteenth, the boat sent from Fushimi [to meet me] pulled up by a bridge. There was also a [second] boat. They said it was from Tōunken, and various utensils were loaded on it so as to be ready for *chanoyu*. It was really entertaining." Later the same year he mentioned the famous Chōgetsu Tea Pavilion at Hōsenji: "While we were all in our cups, they brought more wine at Einō's Chōgetsuken at the Hōsenji by the Hiei Crossroads. Shōzō left for home, but I stayed and rested for a couple of days. The architecture is thought out in every detail, and there are even facilities for *chanoyu*. It is incomparable."[32] Jukō had already died in 1502, so he was not there then, but it seems quite possible that Sōchō's interest in tea had begun earlier, and we have already seen that both Sōchō and Jukō had studied Zen under Ikkyū.

One may conclude that many *renga* poets had an acquaintance with *chanoyu*, and some may have engaged in it under Jukō. It would, therefore, be entirely natural for him to resort to linked verse theory to interpret the tea art. One can infer, therefore, that the term "cold and withered" as it appeared in Jukō's letter to Furuichi Harima came originally from works on linked verse or from conversations with poets.

Some of the earliest appearances of the terms "cold and lonely" or "cold and withered" occurred in the works of the poets Shinkei and Sōgi. In *Hakuhatsushū*, Sōgi [1421–1502] wrote, "When a person who is just beginning the study of *renga* tries too hard to achieve a cold and lonely style, he will find it difficult to advance."[33] He continued by explaining that would-be poets should be cautious even though that effect may be their ultimate aim. He went on to write that beginners were trying deliberately to use "withered" phrases or "cold" phrases, with the result that they produced clumsy lines like these: "Wind blows through the lonely tree in the frost-cold field" or "Evening—in a withered tree on the peak of a hill a crow is crying." They would show enormous pride, as if to say I am the one who used this "cold and withered" language, but the result, said Sōgi, was meaningless and painful to listen to. He hated even to see the look on their faces. Instead a novice should select "more pleasant" subject matter like "young noblemen dressed in finery enjoying themselves beneath the cherry blossoms."[34] In other words, beginners should start with bright and flowery subjects that are exactly the opposite of the "cold and withered" effect. The tradition of *nō* drama similarly forbids neophytes to play the roles of elderly people. In effect, Sōgi was saying that the "cold and withered" feeling properly belongs to those who have entered the realm of great age.

Shinkei's opinions appeared in *Shinkei Sōzu Teikin* and completely supported the view of Sōgi. "When one is a beginner he should not enjoy the withered effect but [concentrate on that which] is correct and beautiful. . . . One will naturally gain 'withering' after one has deepened in age and skill."[35] Sōgi and Shinkei each used a variety of terms to express the "cold and withered" notion, but they both agreed on their prohibition of its use by novices. Shinkei further reiterated that a person would "naturally come to know the cold and withered effect in both its inner implications and its external manifestations after he had attained a [considerable] degree of skill."[36] In this case the term he used, "*hieyase*," was precisely the language of Jukō in his secret instruction to Furuichi Harima. A Shinkei disciple, Inawashiro Kensai [1454–1510], had written *Shinkei Sōzu Teikin*, and Furuichi Harima had received a copy. That was in 1488, so Jukō at sixty-five would already have entered the realm of advanced age. One can hardly imagine that his high disciple would have kept the book a secret. In that circumstance it would have been quite reasonable for Jukō to have employed the language of the *renga* poet in his letter. Indeed, it would have facilitated his explanation.

Jukō's letter initiating Furuichi Harima into the mysteries of tea had expressly forbidden beginners in the art to attempt the cold and withered style because it was inappropriate to their age and station. In doing so he used language that was reminiscent of Zeami's writing about *nō* drama, for the latter had also instructed his followers not to be premature in their attempts to take on roles more suitable to age. In the case of *chanoyu*, Jukō had seen the "cold and withered" style in pottery from Bizen or Shigaraki. Anyone who has had the opportunity to compare these wares, both produced in Japanese kilns, with Yōhen Tenmoku or Yuteki Tenmoku pieces from China will easily understand what a "withered" feeling they convey. Nishibori Ichizō, writing about Shigaraki and Bizen wares in *Nihon Chadōshi*, explained in concrete terms how they differed from the Chinese ceramics used theretofore. First of all, he said, they do not evoke a sense of beauty. Instead they arouse feelings of coarseness or roughness.[37]

Such Bizen and Shigaraki pieces had a feeling that was exactly the opposite of the bright, flowery style that the poets had recommended for novices. Their method of firing allowed the clay body to show through without glazing, leaving them with a sense of sobriety and restraint that young people could hardly appreciate. It was that sense that Jukō was calling "cold and withered."

In the Way of Tea, the correct approach to the "cold and withered" experience was first of all to take good utensils like antique Chinese wares and to study and appreciate them thoroughly. That would then serve as a foundation for entry into the realm of age and skill that would permit one to plumb the more complex aesthetic depths. This approach was analogous to the process in poetry in which people would write beautiful verses while they were young and refrain from attempting ones that were withered. However, this approach would only be a spiritual preparation for the entry into the cold and withered condition; it would not necessarily clarify what that condition was. Jukō was speaking only of the atmosphere surrounding Bizen and Shigaraki wares. Therefore, he was simply reiterating what the beginner needed to understand. It was important, he said, for the novice not to concern himself merely with utensils. One who sought the Way should strive only to advance farther along the path no matter what his level of age and experience. His final words in the letter then served as his conclusion: "Grow up heart's master, not heart mastered—."

This expression came from Buddhist spiritual practice. Much the same wording can be found in *Ichigon Hōdan* or *Hosshinshū*, and Genshin's well-known *Ōjōyōshū* contained the same sentiment in nearly identical phraseology.[38] That is, one must keep distractions and ego and earthly desires under control. This is but one example of the profound impact that Buddhism has exerted on all of the arts and Ways of Japan. Abandoning the attachment to ego meant being selfless, and that reflected once again the influence of nō. Zeami stressed the importance of *monomane*, impersonation.[39] Once the *nō* performer has donned his mask, he strives only to abandon his own persona, and having done so he may as easily become an old man as a young woman. There is no room left for one's own personality. The *nō* mask itself becomes one's persona.

The same is true in *chanoyu*. The world of tea also emphasizes *monomane*. It exhorts against egoistic attachment. Yamanoue Sōji writes:

> In Kyoto Rikyū made a tea room of [only] one and a half mats for the first time. It was unusual at the time, but the ordinary person would have been unable to use it at all. Rikyū was a *meijin*, an expert, so even if he turned mountains into valleys, made west into east, broke the rules of *chanoyu* or did as he pleased, he could achieve an interesting effect. If an ordinary person were to do as he did, it would not be *chanoyu* at all.[40]

This was a warning against ego, for he meant that if most people did just as they liked, the result would not be cold and withered. That is, they would not be able to achieve the *wabi* taste. Self-expression had to wait until one had attained a thorough familiarity with tea. Because Rikyū was a master, he could design a tiny room of one and a half mats. Yet beginners must never try that themselves, just as they must not use Bizen or Shigaraki ware. Only by abandoning self will they succeed in discovering the true Way and produce a Way for themselves. Only after reaching that stage can one act as he likes without exceeding the limits. It is at that point that one will discover the "cold and withered" style.

The following document reveals Jukō's thinking in actual practice. It was a letter he wrote in response to questions about tea practice to the same Furuichi Harima.

Concerning Your Inquiry

Item.   Your style should be natural so that it will not be obtrusive.

Item.   The flowers should convey a light feeling suited to the tea room.

Item.   The way to kindle incense is to keep it from being too obvious or overly perfumed.

Item.   Utensils should vary according to whether those [in attendance] are old or young.

Item.   Sitting in the tea room, the most important thing is that the spirits of both host and guests should be calm and in

> no way distracted from their concentration upon the
> occasion. Act so that your actions will not be evident
> to others.
>
> In this world, though rumors confound us,
> The fragrance of a petrinia flower may somewhere be found.[41]

This letter perhaps reflects a transitional stage in the development of *chanoyu*. Up until this point Jukō, much like Kan'ami and
Zeami in *nō*, may have been overly concerned to curry favor with the
aristocracy,[42] but one is conscious here that he was in the midst of trying to move to the grass hut style of tea from the old *shoin* style, which
had included many elements from the gorgeous tea contests earlier. He
may have been trying to distance himself from the arts of entertainment
in order to create a more spiritual Way. Thus, the letter served to cau-
tion Furuichi Harima, who was beginning to develop an awareness of
the changes from his background in tea contests. For this reason it emphasized the importance of conducting the tea service in a way that was
not ostentatious. Each item of the letter deliberately discouraged anything that was overt or gave a showy impression. The technique of tea
preparation, Jukō said, should be natural and not intrude. The number
of flowers should be appropriate and the incense, not overly fragrant.
Utensils should suit the age and station of the participants. His advice
was directly practical, stressing issues that were of the utmost importance for one who was attempting to create a style of *chanoyu* with the
tranquillity of the grass hut. All his advice aimed to achieve that tranquillity. Finally, he said that as one enters the tea room, the spirit must
be calm and one must leave extraneous concerns outside. In effect he
was emphasizing the unity of Zen and tea, for this is precisely the attitude of the Zen priest as he enters the temple hall to sit in meditation.
Moreover, this attitude may be the foundation for the *wabi* tea that was
to come into existence later.

In addition to the above, there is also the *Jukō Isshi Mokuroku*,
which seems to be a source for Jukō. *Yamanoue Sōji Ki* contains a version of it, but it is unclear to what extent Sōji's copy may reflect Jukō's
original teachings. Sōji commented on its provenance by saying that it
contained notes on what Jukō had learned from Nōami during practice
sessions while studying appraisal techniques. The resulting material
passed along to his disciples Sōshu and Insetsu without change, but
when it reached Jōō, the latter revised it completely and added further
material to it. "Jōō," said Sōji, "was a genius in his age, a leader and one

who revived *chanoyu* and caused it to flourish." Jōō passed the supplemented material on to his disciple Tsuji Gensai, including much secret matter as well. Jōō showed that "everything about the style of *chanoyu* was based on Zen." Sōji continued that thirty years had passed since his death and that Rikyū, also a Jōō disciple, had assumed leadership in the tea world.[43] What Sōji had written was a further revision based on his own ideas from what the venerable Rikyū had taught him during a period of over twenty years.

Kuwata Tadachika writes in *Yamanoue Sōji Ki no Kenkyū* that the so-called *Jukō Isshi Mokuroku* was originally little more than a listing of the names of famous antique tea utensils. To this simple catalog Jōō, Rikyū, and Sōji had added interpretations. Therefore, Kuwata argues that the only material that one can directly ascribe to Jukō himself would be the "twenty-one articles that were secretly and orally transmitted from Jukō."[44] For this reason, I should like to base this discussion only on that segment that one can construe as reflecting the thinking of Jukō about the spirit of tea. In this the most significant statement is the following: "Jukō said, 'It is best to have a magnificent steed in a straw hut.' Thus, it is good to have famous antique utensils in a rough tea room. Such an atmosphere will be even more affecting."[45]

Several modern scholars have commented on this quotation. Karaki Junzō in *Sen Rikyū* and *Chūsei kara Kinsei e*, on the one hand, states that *wabi* arose from the contrast between the rough and the splendid. Thus, the *wabi* of the present contrasts with the splendor of the past; the *wabi* within the individual contrasts to the glamor of the world; the *wabi* in oneself contrasts to one's own affluence. Kuwata, in *Ransei to Chadō*, on the other hand, interprets Jukō's assertion to be an expression of *sabi*, and the plain, straw tea room, of *wabi*. The fine antique utensils within represented luxury, rarity, and brilliance. The combination of the *wabi* in the same setting with the splendid constituted *sabi*. It was the combination of the sweet leisure of tea and the bitterness of tea. The flavor of tea, he says, was the *sabi* taste. The tea taste of the ordinary individual, in other words, should seek the *sabi* style. Clearly, these two define *wabi* in completely opposite ways. Yet Jukō was not providing a prescription for "*wabi*." He was, nonetheless, expressing the spirit of *chanoyu*, and we may conclude that Yamanoue Sōji himself considered that to mean *wabi*.[46]

Let us reflect upon what Jukō meant by "a splendid steed in a straw hut." It must have had something in common with the "cold and withered" taste and with the mixing of Chinese and Japanese utensils.[47]

That is to say, flowery and brilliant beauty must precede the cold and withered. This was as true of *chanoyu* as it was of Zeami's *nō*. In simple chronological order, the gorgeous tea contests lay in the immediate background. There was, moreover, the contrast between the glossy black Tenmoku bowl with its gold rim and the coarse Bizen and Shigaraki wares. Jukō himself did not speak of *wabi*, but it would not have been enough for him to have had the straw hut by itself. Neither would the magnificent steed have sufficed. The spirit of Jukō was to be found both in the glamor of the tea contests and in the cold and withered. "*Wabi*" would come later. Haga Kōshirō has claimed that the reason later ages venerated Jukō as a founder of *chanoyu* was that he was the first to move toward the *wabi* aesthetic and to create a style of tea based on the concept of *wabi* in contrast to the tea contests or even the *shoin* style of tea. Yet it is not at all clear, he says, to what extent Jukō was conscious of what he was doing. It may be that later tea men apotheosized him after the fact.[48] One can, nonetheless, recognize that Jukō made the tendency toward *wabi* tea more concrete.

Another individual who contributed to the trend toward *wabi* tea was Konparu Zenpō [1454–1520], a friend of Jukō. The following passage from *Zenpō Zōtan* also reflects Jukō's thinking: "Jukō used to say that he did not enjoy the moon without clouds. That was provocative. Once, a flower-arranging disciple of Ikenobō carried on in great detail about preserving cherry blossoms in salt and acted as though he thought that were truly fascinating, though in fact it was not."[49] Yamada Tōemon actually wrote the book based on conversations with Konparu Zenpō, so it is unclear whether Jukō said these words or not, but at least the book did attribute to Jukō the assertion "I do not enjoy the moon without clouds.[50]

This calls to mind the famous *Tsurezuregusa*. Nishio Minoru calls this classic by Yoshida Kenkō [ca. 1283–1350?] the epitome of literature on the aesthetics of style in the medieval era and says it was based on a new world view that differed from that in other literary works. Kenkō's aesthetic sense, he writes, revolved about a beauty of expectation, of recollection, and of imagination.[51] Kenkō's new sense of aesthetics found beauty in anticipation or in imperfection, which one can find in his statement "Are we to view the cherry blossoms only in full bloom, the moon only when it is cloudless? To long for the moon while looking on the rain, to lower the blinds and be unaware of the passing of the spring—these are even more deeply moving."[52] This aesthetic sense that saw the light of the full moon as wanting surely had an impact on Jukō's comment on the moon without clouds. Jukō took that idea, developed it, and applied it to *chanoyu*. To use only antique Chinese utensils would be as unsatisfying as the unclouded moon. They needed a leavening of Japanese pieces as well. This is also why he preferred "a magnificent steed in a straw hut." Later the idea spread throughout the world of tea and even reached the point that Okakura Kakuzō would refer to it as "essentially a worship of the Imperfect."[53] In the final analysis, Jukō's influence on *chanoyu* helped to give concrete expression to *wabi* tea with his contrastive aesthetic of the "magnificent steed in the straw hut" so different from the old tea contests, his cold and withered beauty from poetry, or his aesthetic of imperfection that despised "the moon without clouds."

One can see that Jukō's spirit as expressed in these famous lines was not yet exclusively a *wabi* taste by looking at Yamanoue Sōji's list of the utensils that Jukō had once owned.

Item.   Shōka.
        Leaf tea jar with a capacity of seven catties. Huang Qingxiang ware [imported from Luzon]. Black clay body with two types of clay. Whitish-red underglaze. "Qingxiang" written on it. Honored as one of the three most outstanding utensils together with Matsushima and Mikazuki. Even tea masters are astonished at the subtle flavor of tea stored in it. An old theory still passed by oral transmission is that Jukō was the original owner. Thereafter the jar went to Kondaya Sōtaku, then [Kitamuki] Dōchin, then up to Lord Nobunaga. In the confusion [of Nobunaga's assassination] Hori Kyūtarō rescued it and gave it to the Kanpaku [Hideyoshi].
Item.   Jukō Tea Bowl.
        Lost in the fire . . . [during Nobunaga's assassination]. Hishiode [celadon]. Color. Had twenty-seven spatula traces. Sōeki [Rikyū] sold it to [the daimyo] Miyoshi Jikkyū for one thousand *kan*. Satsumaya Sōsetsu [of Sakai] has a similar piece. There are oral traditions about this item.
Item.   Jukō Nabe Kettle.
        Price one thousand *kan*. Owned by Imai Sōkun [of Sakai], but Sōeki says he wonders if he still has it.
Item.   Jukō Censer.

Unique under Heaven. Used on an accompanying square base. Owned by Sōeki of Sakai.

Item. Yuanwu Scroll.

One item. Owned by Iseya Dōan of Sakai. This is the piece that Ikkyū gave long ago to Jukō. Ink hanging.

Item. Xuxi Painting [of a heron].

The above item owned by Jukō. Color on silk. . . .

Item. Momojiri. [Owned by the] Kanpaku.

Originally owned by Jukō. Bronze flower container. [Has official status as] Foremost under Heaven. Accompanied by five letters of explanation as well as a square base on which it sits.

Item. Nitta Shouldered Tea Caddy.

Jukō owned this. Foremost under Heaven. [Owned by the] Kanpaku.

Item. Nagezukin [tea caddy].

Originally owned by Jukō. Four spatula tracings with two on the opposite side. It has single horizontal lines impressed top and bottom. Glazed in the "avalanche" style with running glaze. Main glaze is a deep brown. At Jukō's first tea party he had the Nitta tea caddy, next [he had] the Sōgyū Bunrin [tea caddy], and finally the Konasu [tea caddy]. He traded this jar for the Yuanwu scroll. After [Jukō's] death it passed to Sōshu, and by his will he wanted tea to be served on memorial days for him with the Yuanwu scroll hanging and Nagezukin displayed with *hikuzu* [the leavings from a tea winnow] in it.

Item. Bunri [tea caddy]. Owned by the governor of Bungo.

Jukō formerly owned this. It is called *bunri* because it resembles the shape of a [plum] fruit. First-class utensil. Accompanied by square base.

Item. Bunrin [tea caddy owned by Tsuda] Sōgyū of Sakai.

Jukō formerly owned this. It is said to be in a *kantō* bag and to have a narrow mouth and good glazing. Accompanied by a square base.

Item. Jukō Konasu [tea caddy].

In a *kantō* bag; accompanied by a square base. Lost in the fire at Nobunaga's death. Jukō formerly owned this eggplant-shaped tea caddy. Next it went to [Furuichi] Harima. . . .

Item.   Jukō Dakioke [water supply jar].
[Owned by Tsuda] Sōgyū of Sakai.

Item.   Jukō Gōsu [lidded container].
[Owned by] Tsuda Sōgyū.

Item.   Jukō Dipper Stand with an Orange-shaped Mouth.
Lost in the fire . . . [during Nobunaga's assassination].[54]

From the above list extracted from *Yamanoue Sōji Ki*, Jukō's taste for Chinese tea caddies is apparent. One would have to consider these his "magnificent steed." Not only did Jukō enjoy these fine utensils, however. At the same time he would tether his steed to a "straw hut." In order to achieve the "cold and withered" style that was his ultimate ideal in tea, he would abjure pride and egotistic attachment to concentrate on the practice of the Way. Therefore, even though he participated in Nōami's formal, palace style of tea service, *Nanpōroku* depicts him as designing a tea house with a four-and-a-half mat room. It states: "Jukō designed a room of four and a half mats. It was a formal room whose walls were covered with extremely white paper of the highest quality. The ceiling was of clear cedar without knots. Shingles covered the roof, which was four-sided. Its tokonoma alcove was one *ken* wide [almost two meters]."[55]

Chajidan also discusses Jukō's taste in architecture and mentions a room in Nara just over three mats in size. Its Edo era owners claimed Jukō had designed it, but the work says:

In fact, however, in Jukō's day the smallest tea rooms were four and a half mats. There were no three-mat tea rooms. In the time of Jukō [the tea service was formal so that] they placed all their utensils on bases and used Tenmoku bowls on stands [all devices suitable only in a larger room]. The above tea room was probably [in reality] one that a Jukō follower such as Insetsu or Furuichi preferred.[56]

These sources tell us that there was already a developing trend in tea house architecture toward smaller and smaller rooms. There was already the embryonic sense that the small tea room was first of all a place for the practice of the Buddhist Way, as *Nanpōroku* would later say.[57]

8 Takeno Jōō and the Maturation of the Way of Tea

Murata Jukō's aesthetic sense, with its cold and withered beauty, its cloud-covered moon, and the contrast of "a magnificent steed in a straw hut" marked a sharp departure from the practice of tea as it had existed in the early medieval era. His contributions brought about the birth of a Way of Tea as distinct from the tea rituals of the temples, on the one hand, as from the tea entertainments of the parvenus, on the other. In order for a comprehensive art of tea to flourish, however, still further changes would have to occur. One of these changes would be the further refinement of the concept of *wabi* as an aesthetic ideal, and that was to be the work of Takeno Jōō, under whom the Way of Tea would mature.

Takeno Jōō, though not a direct disciple of Jukō, was a part of the tradition that he established. First, the Nara school of tea, with its "grass hut" style begun by Jukō, passed into the hands of Sōshu. According to *Yamanoue Sōji Ki*, "Sōshu was the heir of Jukō and received through his will his Yuanwu ink scroll, the great Shōka tea jar, and Nagezukin, his shouldered tea caddy."[1] Sōshu was a priest at the Sonkyōin of the Kōfukuji, but he had been a disciple of Jukō and his successor as a master of tea. He moved to Kyoto, and in the southern end of the city maintained a tea room of four and a half mats, which the linked verse poet Sōchō mentioned in his diary, *Sōchō Shuki*, (1526/8/15): "What we call Shimogyō [southern Kyoto] *chanoyu* has lately been termed "*suki*." Sōshu's house has tea rooms of four and a half mats and six mats, both of which are busy as people of all sorts come to learn from him."[2]

Other disciples of Jukō included Furuichi Harima, Shino Dōji, Matsumoto Shuhō, Awataguchi Zenpō, and Torii Insetsu. Among these

Zenpō was the one who continued the most austere grass hut style, and Yamanoue Sōji said of him: "All his life Awataguchi Zenpō of Kyoto had just a sake warmer that he used for everything—cooking food as well as making tea. This was the way Zenpō liked it. Jukō praised him as a man with grace in his heart."[3] In his classification of tea men Sōji had cited Zenpō as the exemplar of the "*sukimono*" type of *wabi* tea man. He represented one pattern of tea issuing from Jukō, while Dōji, Insetsu, Fujita Sōri, and Jūshiya Sōgo constituted a second. Sōji said of Shino Dōji, "Shino was a treasury steward of the shogun and had numerous pedestrian utensils; the family practiced the art of incense." The latter phrase referred to his belonging to the Shino School of the Way of Incense, but as a tea man Sōji disparaged him as having more quantity than quality in utensils. Dōji taught tea to Sōgo, and Sōji was just as thoroughly critical of him, remarking that "he had no eye at all; he had many little pieces but not a single good one."[4]

Whatever Sōgo's assets or lack of them as a tea man, however, it was he who passed Jukō's teachings on to Jūshiya Sōchin and Fujita Sōri and through those two on to Takeno Jōō. Jukō's disciples may not have moved much beyond the point their teacher had reached, for we have already seen Sōji's comment that Jukō's teachings "passed along to his disciples Sōshu and Insetsu without change." In the hands of Jōō,

Takeno Jōō (1502–1555), under whom the concept of *wabi chanoyu* became clearly defined. Collection of the Takeno family, Nagoya.

however, that was no longer the case. "Jōō," said Sōji, "was a genius in his age, a leader and one who revived *chanoyu* and caused it to flourish."[5] Even Insetsu, the Sakai tea man whom Sōji had called a *meijin*, had merely preserved Jukō's ideas about tea, but Jōō added the stamp of his own originality. Like most of Jukō's followers, Jōō was a townsman from the city of Sakai, but he rose above all the rest.

Sakai Kagami, an Edo period gazetteer about the city, has a special entry for Jōō. It says that he had been a resident of the Henomatsu quarter in Sakai whose knowledge of tea was so profound that he was venerated as a master of "Kyoto Inaka [country] *chanoyu*." He died of natural causes on 1555/10/29. The entry continues with a discussion of his family background, noting that he was a distant descendant of the Takeda family of samurai. His grandfather had died of wounds sustained in the Ōnin War, and his father, orphaned, had wandered about the country until he came to reside in the southern part of Sakai. It seemed, however, that Jōō could not settle down there, so he moved to Kyoto, where he ensconced himself next door to a place called Ebisudō. As an epithet for his house, and by extension himself, he used the name "Daikokuan." It was a complicated play on the name of his neighbor, for in the lineup of the Seven Lucky Gods whom Japanese celebrate each New Year, Ebisu and Daikoku were side by side. The former, depicted carrying a sea bream, and the latter, with his bags of rice and coins, together served as the patron deities of the material side of life. The account continues that, when he took the tonsure, he used the name Jōō Ikkan Koji as his Buddhist appellation.[6] From other sources we know that he had been born in 1502.

Sakai Kagami also covers his artistic career. It says that Jōō began by studying poetry. Initially when Lord Ōuchi came to Kyoto from his home in Yamaguchi, Jōō would call on him for instruction. Later his profound desire to know the Way of Poetry impelled him to seek out the poet Sanjōnishi Sanetaka (1455–1537), scion of an ancient and distinguished aristocratic lineage. After many years Sanetaka took his pupil's pleas to heart and gave him a copy of the *Kokinshū*, the famed imperial poetry anthology. Jōō's connection with tea was through Sōchin and Sōgo, both of whom lived nearby in the capital and had studied the Jukō tea tradition. Jōō went to their place and asked questions to clarify his doubts about particular points in tea lore. The *Sakai Kagami* concludes that after many years Jōō returned to Sakai, practiced *chanoyu*, and earned fame in that art.[7]

Jōō thus was a student of poetry, first with the daimyo Ōuchi of Yamaguchi and later with the aristocrat Sanetaka. Thanks to the wealth that the father had been able to accumulate in his generation and through the aegis of his family, he received a court appointment to Junior Fifth Rank, Lower Grade, and the title of Inaba no Kami, honors usually reserved for members of the samurai class. He was thirty when he took the tonsure in 1532. It was in Jōō's generation and as a result of his thinking that the concept of "*wabi* tea" came into increasingly clear focus. *Yamanoue Sōji Ki* comments on the origins of Jōō's *wabi*: "Until age thirty Jōō was a *renga* poet and from Sanjōnishi Sanetaka he learned of the preface to *Eika Taigai* [by Fujiwara Teika, 1162–1241]. [Later] he excelled at *chanoyu*, became a master, and was a certified initiate into its mysteries."[8]

Thus, we find that in addition to the *Kokinshū*, which *Sakai Kagami* said Sanetaka had given him, Jōō also had the preface to *Eika Taigai* as a means to learn the traditional secrets of poetry. Let us turn, therefore, and examine the relationship between Jōō and his aristocratic mentor.

Jōō, who was born in 1502, first studied with Sanjōnishi Sanetaka in 1525 at the age of twenty-three. His teacher would have been seventy. By that time circumstances seem to have reduced Sanetaka to a life of penury, and his diary, *Sanetakakōki*, had constant references alluding to his straits. A series of entries in the third month of 1520, for example, reflect his poverty. On 3/7 he wrote: "I let Ryōchin have my copy of *Genji*. He said the constable of Noto wanted it. As it was a secret treasure, I hated to let it go, but I was powerless to do otherwise."[9] Haga Kōshirō's interpretation is that, in order to eke out the family finances, Sanetaka had most reluctantly sold his privately held copy of *The Tale of Genji* to Hatakeyama Yoshifusa, the daimyo in Noto, for two thousand copper cash.[10] Related entries supporting that view followed. On 3/9 he wrote, "Discussed with Ryōchin paper supplies for *Genji*," and on the next day, "Today two thousand cash arrived as thanks from the constable of Noto."[11] The entry also suggests that he used the money to pay off his servants and used two hundred cash to buy more paper to make another copy as soon as possible. This was not, however, the beginning of Sanetaka's economic difficulties. On 1511/2/9, when he was fifty-six, he wrote that a certain Hayashi and a lady in waiting had quit his service. Every year, he said, "it grows worse—how awkward!"[12] Haga claims that the servants left because there was no way to pay them. A related entry appeared the following month on 3/6, noting that Sanetaka had written a will for Uesugi Sadazane, the daimyo in Echigo, the previous year. To his astonishment and joy, a messenger arrived with payment, and its appearance was not only a surprise but the sum was evidently more than expected, a long sword with cord and one thousand cash. Sanetaka said he hardly knew what to do, so he served the daimyo's emissary a cup of wine.[13] The diary's repeated protestations of pleasure on this occasion hint at how little he had to live on, but even that did not suffice, for just two months later on 5/28 he noted putting two sets of formal winter robes and some fabric into pawn for "four strings," that is, four hundred copper cash strung through their holes on four cords.[14] The poet seems still to have been able to enjoy tea, however. On 5/23 he noted that a certain Irie had invited him to tea. Sanetaka said he had a conflict and could not accept, so Irie sent tea sweets instead.

In the midst of all his financial difficulties, a new name appeared. On 1514/3/21 he wrote, "Sent a volume of *Eika Taigai* to Takeno." Two days later he noted: "Takeno came, but I did not receive him because of the lateness of the hour. He brought salt-cured fish and other food."[15] Since Jōō would have been just twelve in 1514, the Takeno who received Teika's treatise on poetry was probably his father, Nobuhisa. Takeno Nobuhisa after his years of wandering had settled in Sakai, where he prospered, thanks to the patronage of the military Miyoshi family, as a merchant dealing in leather, which he supplied for the making of armor. It hardly seems likely that he could have found the time by that point to polish his skills as a poet. Therefore, it must have been a case of Sanetaka's swallowing his pride and lending his prized volume to someone who could provide financial support. Haga has found, in fact, that Sanetaka's diary began to change at about his seventieth year. The entries relating to rents and other income from his various hereditary estates became astonishingly detailed. In his youth aristocratic pride meant that such mundane concerns as money had been beneath him, and in any event the family steward would have handled his financial affairs. Money might have been tight, but he still had enough. By the end of his life, however, his private finances became so desperate that pride no longer sufficed, and he was unable to keep up appearances. Poverty had touched off his interest in economic matters, obliging him to keep detailed records of income and expenses.[16]

Despite his circumstances Sanetaka was still able to entertain, and beginning in 1529 Jōō began appearing from time to time as a visitor. The entry for 1529/12/10 said: "Takeno came late in the evening and presented me one thousand copper cash quite unexpectedly. I granted him a cup of wine as thanks."[17] Ever the aristocrat, the terminology he used made it clear that the wine was a "grant" to one of a lower social station. Jōō for his part gave several kinds of gifts. In 1530, when Jōō would have been twenty-eight, Sanetaka lent him a copy of *Eika Taigai* on 3/21, and two days later Jōō returned with presents of fowl and salted fish, though he was too late to be received.[18]

Yamanoue Sōji had said that Jōō had been a *renga* poet until the age of thirty and that he became wise in tea, having studied *Eika Taigai* with Sanetaka. He had indeed thrown all his effort into the study of poetry and at about the age of twenty-eight had been rewarded with Teika's treatise. Clearly, too, as Sōji had also said, Jōō was wise in *chanoyu*. Yet there is some question whether Sanetaka would have admitted the merchant Jōō into the mysteries of the *Kokinshū* tradition, for he may have seen him just as a dabbler spending money on the arts. In any event there exists this corroboration that the latter did, in fact, receive *Eika Taigai*.

Jōō, who was said to have been thus enlightened, did, as Sōji suggested, change the *chanoyu* of Jukō. Let us consider how he changed it and how he further responded to the issue of "*wabi*." Sōji had listed Jōō together with Jukō and Insetsu as one of the greatest tea masters of all time, and he quoted Jōō's advice to tea men as follows:

In tea one can do either nothing at all or just that one thing. What Jōō told his disciples was that the human span has a limit of sixty years, and of these only twenty are spent in one's prime. Those who immerse themselves deeply in the study of tea will not gain skill in the [other] Ways. Even those who make a great effort in the other arts will probably remain unskilled. Nonetheless, he said, one should take calligraphy and literature to heart.[19]

While Jōō explains the necessity of pouring all one's effort into *chanoyu*, he says that one might also study calligraphy and literature. It was his own well-known interest in poetry that impelled him to write that. Yet as we shall see later, he did not use poetry to any remarkable extent in his practice of tea. For now, I prefer to look at his achievements as they relate to "*wabi*," which he was the first to use explicitly as an aesthetic term. As we have seen, *Yamanoue Sōji Ki* has what may be the earliest statement about it: "People of old said that after one has become a master of *chanoyu*, he should do only *wabi suki*, if he has only one set of utensils. The priest Shinkei said of linked verse that the poems should be cold and withered; Tsuji Gensai said that Jōō always told him that the essence of *chanoyu* must become like that as well."[20]

Tsuji Gensai was one of Jōō's leading disciples. The "people of old" in the quotation above probably referred specifically to Jōō. Yamanoue Sōji was saying that one should concentrate on *wabi* tea after becoming a master of the Way. The term *suki* here we may interpret to mean simply *chanoyu*. So what did he mean by "*wabi chanoyu?*" He meant the "cold and withered" style that Shinkei had called the heart of linked verse. Jukō himself had never actually used the term "*wabi*." Instead, he used words like cold and wizened or withered. Jōō, however, used "*wabi*" overtly for the first time and concluded that its essence was that "cold and withered" style.

Next, we must consider what Jōō's thinking was on the matter of "*wabi*." For this subject, there is the source popularly known as "Jōō Wabi no Fumi," Jōō's letter on *wabi*. The extant document addressed to Rikyū from Jōō is not in the latter's own hand but forms a part of a larger piece, *Sekishū Ryū Hiji Gokajō*. It is, nonetheless, a valuable source for the study of Jōō's concept of *wabi*. First of all it defines *wabi*.

> The word "*wabi*" is one that poets in the past used to write in their verses, but lately it has come to mean being straightforward, considerate, and not arrogant. Of the months of the year, the tenth most represents *wabi*. Lord Teika's poem expressed it well.
>
> The Month without Gods tells no lies.
> What more sincere than the first drops of an autumn shower?
> Whose are the honest tears that fall?
>
> Because he was Teika, he could compose such a poem. He was able to express in words what the rest of us feel but cannot articulate. This was Teika at his finest. One cannot improve upon this.[21]

Here Jōō defines the word "*wabi*" as the spirit that lay at the core of the Way of Tea, but it is unclear why he selected this particular term.

To be sure, as Jōō said, "the poets in the past" used the term frequently in their writing, but neither Jukō nor others like Sōshu or Sōchin had employed the word in the context of tea. One may speculate, however, that Jukō's grass hut style had spread, gradually replacing Nōami's older *shoin* tea, with the result that there ultimately came to be an identification of the grass hut style with a *wabi* sense that had come down from the past. That is, the picture of those whose fortunes had fallen in the world came to be viewed as one of *wabi*. This concept, however, took on its own independent status and became "*wabisuki,*" *wabi chanoyu.* Such, in any event, was Jōō's definition of the term.

Wabi, he said, was "straightforward, considerate, and not arrogant." Nishibori Ichizō in *Nihon Chadōshi* examined the idea of being "straightforward" or "honest" or "candid" and found that writers on Shinto since the Kamakura era had discussed this same term "*shōjiki*" in Japanese. It was, therefore, not necessarily an original idea, but Jōō's intent to align himself with Shinto thinkers was noteworthy. Nishibori found that the term "*tsutsushimibukai,*" "considerate," was similarly a Shinto concept and later became central to the thinking of the Edo Confucian scholar Yamazaki Ansai (1618–1682) in his writing about that religion.[22] *Yamanoue Sōji Ki,* as we have seen, had contended, "Because *chanoyu* comes from the Zen sect, it is chiefly the work of priests; Jukō and Jōō were both Zen [adherents]."[23] Yet in spite of that assertion, we have seen that not everything in tea came from Zen, in much the same way that Confucianism could not account for everything in the thought of ancient China. In using the terms "straightforward," "considerate," and especially "not arrogant," Jōō was seeking to define a style that was exactly the opposite of the gorgeous splendor of the tea contests like those of Sasaki Dōyo. It is easy to understand that since Jōō lived at a time when the excesses of the tea contest rounds and *unkyaku* tea parties were still fresh in the memory of tea men, he wanted to put as much distance as possible between his own style of tea and that of the past. One can see this also in his remark that the tenth month symbolized *wabi* better than any other time of the year. By the old calendar it was the time when both the showy cherry blossoms and the colorful autumn foliage had passed, leaving gaunt branches stark against the sky. This was the season of *wabi.* If we seek to learn how he came to that idea, we can get some help from one quite unusual passage, though of uncertain date, that shows that Jōō, too, indulged in tea in the bath house, as Furuichi had done. *Chōandōki* contains an account of his experience, as follows:

Once, coming out of the bath, Jōō had a tea service in the dressing room. As he was getting out of the tub, the idea occurred to him for the first time that he could use a bucket as a water supply jar, a rice server as his waste water container, and green bamboo as a lid rest. Jōō was the grandfather of the present priest Kōgetsu, and Sōka was Jōō's son. [The latter] was a fine man, and when I was young I had the opportunity to meet and know him.[24]

Chōandōki is a collection of anecdotes about tea, which Kubo Gondayū wrote in 1640, considerably later than Jōō's time, so it is not clear how old Jōō was when this happened. But it is certain that he retained a recollection of the previous age of splendor and was asserting that *wabi*, by contrast, was "straightforward, considerate, and not arrogant." In the final analysis these words contain no influence from Zen. Yet he did undergo the austerities of Zen training under Dairin Sōtō of the Daitokuji beginning in his thirties and received the Zen name Ikkan Koji at age forty-seven.[25] He would have been exposed, therefore, to a variety of influences on his style of tea. Nonetheless, in citing the tenth month as being most expressive of *wabi* or in saying that *wabi* was straightforward, considerate, and not arrogant, Jōō was acting under the influence of poetry. Thanks to his period of acquaintance with Sanetaka, he would often cite Teika's poetry to illustrate his thinking about tea, and here he was using the poet's statement about the honesty of the tenth month to explain *wabi*. In Japan, the tenth month by the old calendar corresponded to November today and had the poetic name of the "Month without Gods." The season with its bare, leafless trees often had cold, soft rains, which poets called "*shigure*." For Teika it had been a season without deception, and Jōō took that candor as a way to express the *wabi* sense, which was honest and circumspect.

Next, Jōō explained how tea was "straightforward, considerate, and not arrogant." Once one of his students observed that, originally, tea was served when one wanted tranquillity away from the cares of the world. When friends came to call, one would make tea and look for things like flowers to brighten the place and so relax. He asked Jōō to explain this way of serving tea, and the master replied to the student's satisfaction: "Let there not be a single act divided from heart and mind. This means that the foundation of the gathering is the attitude of offering hospitality [even] where mind does not precisely follow mind;

hence, it is an act that accords with what is right and proper without self-consciousness that is genuinely and unaccountably astonishing."[26] Jōō was explaining here the origin of the grass hut tradition of tea as opposed to *shoin* tea or tea contests. It came from tea served to friends in a quiet setting, decorated with flowers, far from the concerns of daily living. This was how Jōō explained the spirit of tea.

Jōō left his disciples a set of twelve precepts to clarify the mental attitude needed for the proper performance of *wabi* tea.

Item.   One should practice goodwill toward others.

Item.   One's manner should be correct and harmonious.

Item.   One must not be critical of the gatherings of others.

Item.   One must not be filled with pride.

Item.   Do not covet utensils owned by others.

Item.   It is entirely inappropriate to think of *chanoyu* only in terms of utensils.

Item.   One soup and three other dishes are suitable to the *kaiseki* meal. One should not exceed that amount even for special guests.

Item.   Men of tea may find utensils that have been discarded and use them for tea. How much more is this so for ordinary people.

Item.   Men of tea especially hate to be seen as such.

Item.   The man of tea observes a spirit of *wabi* and leads a life of quiet retreat. He should know the precepts of Buddhism and experience the feeling of Japanese poetry.

Item.   One should lead a secluded life and feel *sabi*. One should also strive for a middle Way, for one who appears too splendid is wanting and if too [*wabi*], simple or slovenly.

Item.   There should be no *chanoyu* that does not consider the heart of the guest; such would not be sincere tea. One's own *chanoyu* should be like this. Also, one should not impose upon one's guests or ask them for help.[27]

This was how Jōō expected his followers to conduct themselves in order to have the correct preparation of mind for the kind of tea he advocated. These were commandments by which he spelled out clearly the concept of "*wabi*" in actual practice. Yet to be straightforward, considerate, and not arrogant meant to be conscious of others. This was not tea that one could enjoy in isolation. It was a world where the distinction between self and others did not obtain. This was a new realm for tea. It differed from the tea of Lu Yu, which he enjoyed sequestered from what lay beyond his own walls. It differed as well from the tea rituals of the Zen temples of Kamakura era Japan. And it differed from the tea contests of the mid-Muromachi period. It was a Way of Tea that combined them all.

An ideal of *chanoyu* that governed the encounter between host and guest implied something new. It introduced into tea a spirit, which it had also in common with *nō*, that each occasion was special and unique. The phrase "*ichigo, ichie*" was a means for Jōō to suggest that one could never exactly duplicate the particular gathering of host and guest on any given occasion,[28] so one should concentrate on the occasion and abandon superfluous conversation about mundane matters. Jōō further insisted on "Five Resolutions for Beginners" that would serve as a spiritual preparation for *wabi* and *sabi* as opposed to the earlier cold and withered style. They were, "Be courteous; make full effort; practice *sabi*; practice *wabi*; be creative."[29] These were his keys to the successful conduct of tea.

The quintessence of tea, accordingly, lay in these principles. When he said, for example, that one "may find utensils that have been discarded and use them," he meant that one should develop the capacity to find and use such materials. When he spoke of leading "a life of quiet retreat," he was suggesting that a follower of the Way of Tea should live simply with a spirit of detachment in accordance with a full cognizance of Buddhist principles. The reason for mentioning Japanese poetry was that one should cultivate the refinement that would come from its mastery. That is, the true spirit of tea was one of compassion and of sensitivity to beauty. Even a broken old crock was worth saving and using to hold flowers, thus revealing their inner heart. Trying to discover something more than mere sufficiency in that which is imperfect or deficient was the spirit of tea. Through compassion and aesthetic sensibility one could open for the first time a new world of possibilities, but it was one of quiet detachment. This Way was, accordingly, a solitary Way. This was why Jōō said one should "lead a secluded life and feel *sabi*." The spirit of tea and the true import of the precepts of Buddhism were that one should be direct but gentle and detached without being deliberately withdrawn or secluded. His path to the true Way of Tea thus became deeper still. Naturally, since "men of tea especially hate to be seen as such," this was a different matter from knowing how to move ahead in the world.

One can see that the content of the pursuit of tea in this period was far more profound philosophically than it had been in the Heian or Kamakura eras. Completely new aesthetic values had given the ideal of tea a more systematic status. This new system informed all parts of tea from the tea room as a place for the conduct of *chanoyu* to the interaction between host and guest and even the utensils they used and the *kaiseki* meal.

9 Rikyū and the Fruition of the Way of Tea

The more profound concept of *chanoyu*, which Jukō and Jōō had helped to shape, saw its completion with the advent of Rikyū, who further refined it and provided it with a philosophical and aesthetic structure. Let us in these final pages trace the process by which Rikyū further deepened the concept of an art of tea.

Jōō, as a means of escaping the formality of the old *shoin* style of tea that still survived in his day, had embraced a *chanoyu* that was considerate and not arrogant, and used the word "*wabi*" as a way to express that whole concept. All of the arts at that time taught that the key to progress in their practice was to be fond of the Way. They used the verb "*suku*" or its noun form "*suki*," meaning "to like" or "to have a taste for" the Way. *Bunrui Sōjinboku*, which Shinshōsai Shunkei wrote in 1564, comments on that notion with a fairly complicated play on words:

> The term "*suki*" seems to be used in all the Ways to mean to en‑
> joy or have a fondness. The reason we have lately called
> *chanoyu suki* is that in it one assembles a numerous (*su*) collec‑
> tion (*ki*) of utensils. So *chanoyu* means having a big collection.
> Even a *wabi* person will assemble [at least] the following: brazier
> and kettle, base, water supply jar, waste water container, lid rest,
> tea caddy, tea bowl, tea whisk, tea scoop, tea cloth, fireplace, ad‑
> justable hook, charcoal holder, fire chopsticks, flower vase, pic‑
> ture, ink scroll, leaf tea storage jar, tea grinder, and the like.
> None of the other arts involves collecting so many instruments
> as *chanoyu*![1]

This comment came from a time less than ten years after Jōō's death in 1555. Nobunaga and Hideyoshi had hardly begun their ascent to the splendor of the Azuchi Momoyama age, and only dimly could one see an end to the turmoil and bloodshed of the day. By that time the term *suki,* which could have been used in any of the arts, had already come into general usage as a particular synonym for *chanoyu.* For amusing effect, people wrote the word with Chinese characters meaning "numerous" and "collection" instead of the usual characters. Despite the appearance of the *wabi* concept, the main force in tea at that time was among the townsmen of Sakai and Kyoto, and they furiously expended huge sums of money to assemble great collections of utensils. It was entirely natural that such a collection should have been a requisite for participation and that possession of famous, antique utensils should have been a condition for recognition as a *meijin,* a master. Even for a practitioner of *wabi* tea, a considerable collection of over twenty utensils from brazier and kettle on down to a grinder was necessary, as the quotation said. Thus, the same author continues, "Nowadays, people have come to use no Chinese utensils. That is a shame! Yet beginners and those who practice a *wabi* style have difficulty even getting charcoal and tea together. Therefore, how much more difficult it is to own Chinese wares. So they must enjoy their tea without them."[2] Once again, this suggests that the antique Chinese utensils were still considered necessary. However, the writer nonetheless felt obliged to recognize the widespread extent of *wabi* tea as well. For those who could barely afford charcoal and tea, there could still be pleasure in the *wabi* style without Chinese wares. He was, therefore, expressing the view that there was a compatibility between formal tea, using such utensils, and the "grass" style of informal tea without them. Indeed, one suspects that the trend toward the *wabi* style may have become the more prominent, for he goes on:

> Daimyo and men of means say that *suki* is interesting when done in the *wabi* fashion. [But] both the tea room and the food service only imitate poverty. That is not the way it should be. They should conduct themselves in a way more fitting to their wealth and station. In a play, for example, when an actor plays a beggar, one will not find him wearing rags. They should act in a way that appears more in keeping with their circumstances.[3]

The last sentence is noteworthy. Even in *nō* drama, Zeami had argued, an actor playing an old man should not appear stooped, for the audience could not appreciate it. Even though one might speak of imitating life, there was nevertheless the obligation to satisfy the theatergoer. In *chanoyu* as well, *Bunrui Sōjinboku* cautioned against a man of wealth straining to give the appearance of deprivation. *Wabi* seemed to refer in this case to a general appearance of poverty. In *The Book of Tea* Okakura Kakuzō said the Way of Tea was "essentially a worship of the Imperfect, as it is a tender attempt to accomplish something possible in this impossible thing we know as life."[4] For the "daimyo and men of means" of the day, however, the Imperfect was simply a toy for their entertainment, and that was what *Bunrui Sōjinboku* deplored. Okakura also said that true beauty was to be found by completing the incomplete within one's own heart. Of the three levels of formality in tea, there are formal, known as *shin*; semiformal, *gyō*; and informal, called *sō*, literally "grass." The "Imperfect," this *wabi* type of tea, which we have been discussing, would be the last level, the so-called grass style. *Bunrui Sōjinboku*, however, admonished tea aficionados to follow a style suitable to their social status. Thus, Jōō's *wabi* had at last moved to the forefront as an issue in tea. At this time, however, it remained honorable, genteel poverty, standing in opposition to the gorgeous splendor of the past.

Largely through the work of Jōō, tea had become overwhelmingly popular, so much so that Yamanoue Sōji could write, "A person who does not practice *chanoyu* can hardly be considered human. All the daimyo follow it, of course, and especially the townsmen of Nara, Kyoto, and Sakai have thrown themselves single-mindedly into it."[5] He continued that townsmen who had skill in the art and who also owned rare Chinese wares were much in demand even at the parties of daimyo, and that encouraged them to collect utensils all the more avidly. Throughout the era of unification from Nobunaga's first entry into Kyoto in support of Shogun Yoshiaki until Hideyoshi's triumph, the daimyo and their high retainers all excitedly pursued tea. For many, ownership of a prized tea utensil could bring as much joy and pride as holding a key fief. In the midst of this environment, the court conferred upon Jōō his position of junior fifth rank, lower grade, on account of his wealth, and his disciples among the merchants of Sakai began to accept situations as tea advisers to the military barons.

Jōō's disciples included, among members of the military class, Matsunaga Hisahide, who often entertained the Sakai tea men at his gatherings during the 1560s. Among his famous utensils were the tea caddy known as Tsukumogami and his Hiragumo kettle. The former, one of the most treasured pieces in tea, he later presented as a peace offering to Nobunaga, but the Hiragumo kettle he smashed to bits rather than see it fall into the hands of his enemies at the time of his death vainly defending Shigisan Castle. Other military disciples of Jōō were the Miyoshi family members Sōsan, Jikkyū, Chōkansai, and Shōgan. Hosokawa Yūsai, a samurai known for his accomplishments in poetry, also studied tea with Jōō. All of these enjoyed a close relationship with the townsmen of Sakai.

Turning to those Sakai tea devotees who practiced in the Jōō tradition, we find Tsuji Gensai, Imai Sōkyū, Tsuda Sōtatsu, and Sōgyū, as well as Tennōjiya Dōshitsu. Sen Rikyū was also a member of this cohort, a follower of Jōō. People such as these made up the governing council of Sakai. In 1568, when Nobunaga, in a bid to take Sakai under direct control, levied a tax of twenty thousand *kan*, so-called arrow money, one hawkish faction insisted that the city was wealthy enough to resist Nobunaga by force of arms. Sōgyū and Sōkyū, however, reportedly remonstrated with them and led the city safely through the crisis. Imai Sōkyū, particularly, assumed a leadership role in Sakai thereafter. Toyoda Takeshi argues that Nobunaga backed Sōkyū because he hoped to avail himself of the merchant's wealth. Later, in 1579, Nobunaga paid a visit to the city and specially attended a tea gathering that Sōkyū hosted. Nobunaga's generals also enjoyed Sōkyū's financial accommodation from time to time. During the Battle of Anegawa, Hideyoshi also wrote Sōkyū to report on the progress of the fighting and to request a supply of gunpowder and ammunition.[6]

Among the citizens of Sakai, Imai Sōkyū and Tsuda Sōgyū enjoyed a position of unquestioned affluence, but there was also another council member who had operated a seafood shop,[7] Yohei, the father of Sen Rikyū. As a child Rikyū had used the name Yoshirō; later, after studying Zen at Daitokuji with Dairin Sōtō, he changed it and became Sōeki, a name he used most of his adult life. *Sakai Kagami* had a special entry for him and reported that the family had lived for generations in Sakai and that he had resided in the southern part of town in the Imaichi quarter. Naturally, it commented on his tea:

> He began to study tea with [Kitamuki] Dōchin at the age of sixteen and made a name for himself [in that field]. When he was eighteen, Dōchin spoke of him to Jōō and said that Sen Yoshirō was devoting himself to tea and often came [to study]. [Dōchin

continued] his tea does not look bad, and his conversation is provocative. Jōō, therefore, concluded that they should have tea together. Years later Rikyū became as famous as Dōchin and Jōō and controlled how tea was performed throughout the land.[8]

As this indicates, Rikyū first studied with Kitamuki Dōchin, who practiced the Higashiyama style of tea that had come down from Nōami. Thereafter, he studied with Jōō in the Jukō tradition, and by conjoining these two strands, he was able to construct a new basis for the success of *chanoyu*. Then in 1570, according to *Imai Sōkyū Chanoyu Nikki Kakinuki*, Rikyū met Nobunaga for the first time and prepared tea before him.[9] In this way he ultimately took a place as tea adviser to Nobunaga as one of a group of three headed by Imai Sōkyū and Tsuda Sōgyū. *Shinchō Kōki*, a biography of Nobunaga, mentions several occasions when the three prepared tea for the general.[10]

Later, after Hideyoshi succeeded to Nobunaga's position, the three continued as advisers and came to be the three *chanoyu* masters of the land, each with a grant valued at three thousand *koku* of rice per annum, but the influence of Sōkyū and Sōgyū faded, while Rikyū's steadily pulled ahead. At about this time Rikyū also befriended the priest Kokei of the Daitokuji, and they shared their knowledge with each other, tea on the one hand, Zen on the other. After Hideyoshi's conquest of Odawara, Daitokuji placed a statue of Rikyū atop its Mountain Gate as thanks for his contributions toward the gate's rebuilding. The statue's location meant that anyone entering the temple, even Hideyoshi, would be obliged to pass under the statue, which was shod in footgear of Rikyū's own design. We are told that Hideyoshi took offense, and on the twenty-eighth day of the second month of 1591, he compelled Rikyū to die by his own sword at the age of sixty-nine.[11] *Yamanoue Sōji Ki*, as we have seen, named Rikyū as the successor of Jukō and Jōō, and stated that thirty years after Jōō's death, Rikyū became foremost in the art of tea. It was, therefore, Rikyū who was to complete the process of bringing "*wabi*" into *chanoyu*.

What was Rikyū's concept of *wabi* tea? Let us turn to *Nanpōroku* for an answer:

Jōō said that the spirit of *wabi chanoyu* might be found in a *Shinkokinshū* poem by Teika.

> As far as the eye can see
> Neither cherry blossom nor maple leaf.
> A hut of rushes by the shore.
> Dusk in the autumn.

He was using cherry blossoms and maple leaves as an analogy for the glory of the *daisu* shelf in a *shoin*. Having [first had the opportunity to] gaze long and fully at the cherries and maple foliage, one comes to the rush hut by the shore, a realm of emptiness. One who had not first seen the cherries and maples could not live in the hut at all. [But] because he has seen them, he can appreciate the rusticity and quietude of the hut. Jōō called this the true spirit of tea.

Sōeki also found another poem and would often write the two of them, for he believed they both embodied the spirit of tea. The other was by [Fujiwara] Ietaka [1158–1237], also in the same anthology.

> To those who long only for cherry blossoms
> How I'd like to point out the grass of spring
> In the snow of a mountain village.

One should keep this as well as the other poem in mind. The people of the world look at the distant mountain or the forest yonder and wonder when the flowers will ever bloom. From morning to night they gaze out at the distance. Not at all do they realize that the cherries and maples are within their own hearts but enjoy only the colors they can see with their eyes. The mountain village, like the rush hut by the shore, is a lonely place with a feeling of *sabi*. This year's snow covers last year's flowers and leaves rendering the village as desolate and barren as the hut by the shore.

Then, naturally, from the bleak void comes the act that evokes our feeling with nature moving at its own pace from stage to stage. Though the snow still covers all, with the approach of the warm breath of spring, here and there amid the white rise up truly green, green blades of grass. The true way of Nature moves without effort, like the two blades here and the three blades there. The spirit of the Way of poetry might be expressed in great detail, but these two poems serve to illustrate the Way of Tea of Jōō and Rikyū. This is what I have learned and committed to writing.[12]

The above passage provides an explanation that compares the *wabi* of Jōō's tea with that of Rikyū's style. Each of the two poems illustrates and defines their respective feelings about *wabi*. First, Teika's poem sets the brilliance of cherry blossoms and maple leaves against the quiet solitude of a rush hut by the shore and finds the hut to be more strongly evocative emotionally. Ietaka's poem contrasts the glory of flowers to the grass amid the snow of a mountain village and, similarly, sees the latter as preferable. *Nanpōroku* used the concept of *sabi* to describe both the rush hut by the shore and the mountain village, and this deserves attention. Jukō's straw hut to which the magnificent steed was tethered also had a quality of *sabi*. The straw hut, the hut of rushes, and the mountain village all shared a common character. *Nanpōroku*, furthermore, explicitly likened the cherry blossoms and maples to the splendor of the *daisu* or the *shoin*. Then, in contrast to their flowery grandeur, it cited the *sabi* dwelling of the rush hut. The *sabi* of the rush hut was what a person discovered by seeking quiet solitude after having known the flowers and maples and wanting something different. <u>Wabi was the feeling of longing for *sabi* by one who had seen flowery brilliance.</u> Thus it was quite natural that one who had not known flowers and maples would not be able to live in the rush hut. So it is with the *wabi* of the Way of Tea. Only one who has experienced the splendor of the *shoin* style will be able to appreciate the *wabi* of the grass hut style.

Let us examine for a time the Ietaka poem by which Rikyū explained *wabi*. The difference between the *wabi* of Jōō and Rikyū was one of mood. The former saw it in the season from late autumn to early winter, while the latter found it in the vernal grasses amid the snow from late winter to early spring. If this was the difference in their perception of *wabi*, how did they differ in personal style? *Yamanoue Sōji Ki* says: "Jōō died at fifty-three in the prime of his career in tea. We may liken his life to the cherries of Yoshino just past their peak, to the maple leaves after the passing of summer and the autumn moon."[13] To put it simply, Jōō died just after his career had peaked. He just reached autumn after having lived through spring and summer. Sōji also said, "Insetsu died at seventy and was like the season when autumn rains have begun and the leaves have scattered." "Jukō," he wrote, "died at eighty—perhaps a snowy mountain." Thus, he had reached the dead of winter. Finally, there was Rikyū, who had almost attained his seventieth year but still survived when Sōji wrote. "Sōeki's *chanoyu* is like a tree in early winter," he wrote, conjuring images of barren branches.[14] Thus, for all of the tea men, including Sōji, "*wabi*" was most akin to the season of winter. It is clear why Jōō thought of *wabi* as a rush hut contrasted to flowers and maples, why Rikyū saw it as a mountain village in much the same fashion. Still, his mountain village was not "a realm of emptiness," for it had its "grass of spring in the snow." The scene is one of young shoots emerging through the covering of snow. Let us consider how much more profound his concept of *wabi* tea was, given this definition. The preface to the memorandum section of *Nanpōroku* recounts, "Once Sōeki was talking about *chanoyu* at Shūun'an and said, 'Even though the *daisu* is the basis of tea, where the heart is concerned, the small, grass-style room is unequaled.' "[15] He was saying that the quintessence of *chanoyu* is *wabi* tea and that ideally one should practice it in "the small, grass-style room," by which he meant one of four-and-a-half mats or smaller. The following description of the ultimate ideal of *chanoyu* in the small room is found in the same source:

> *Chanoyu* in a small room means first of all to practice the austerities of Buddhism. To enjoy a splendid dwelling or a meal with rare delicacies is a trivial pleasure. A house suffices if it does not leak; a meal, if it satisfies hunger. Such is the teaching of the Buddha and the essence of *chanoyu*. We carry water, take firewood, boil the water, and make tea. Next we offer it to the Buddha, serve our guests and drink it ourselves. We arrange flowers and light incense. All of these are ways to pursue the teachings of the Buddha and his elders.[16]

The primary aim of *chanoyu*, *Nanpōroku* maintains, was to undergo spiritual training, and everything one did in it was a means to inquire into the teachings of the Buddha and the elders of the faith. Its initial act was to make an offering to the Buddha, and only after laying that spiritual basis could one serve one's guests and finally drink oneself. Though both Jukō and Jōō had considered *chanoyu* to be a "rejoicing in Zen and in the purity of the Law," this was an infinitely more thoroughgoing statement. It was no mere matter of disporting oneself in a world apart, for the world it sought was a far more profound one. It was not a rationalistic search for the quotidian benefits of a mystical medicine but religion in actual practice. *Nanpōroku* also explains: "The first act of the host is to carry water into the tea garden, and the first act of the guest is to use that water. Herein lies the cardinal principle of the dewy ground and the grass hut. This is the basin where both he who invites and he who is invited into the dewy ground can wash away the impurities of the world."[17]

There is no more accurate way to express the meaning of the water basin when one is invited as a guest to tea. The act of walking the garden path and then dipping the water from the basin releases one from the mundane by sweeping away the dust of life. The Japanese language has a particular term for the garden of a tea house, "*roji*," whose literal meaning is "dewy ground."[18] The Parables of the Lotus Sutra suggest its significance, for they say, "There is no peace in the Three Worlds; they are like a house in flames." But then the account continues, "One emerges from the house in flames to sit on the dewy ground."[19] This escape from the consuming passions of the world is the function of the tea garden. The space of the tea room itself to which one has been invited does serve, to be sure, as a place where host and guest can take food and drink tea, but it is also a hall for the conduct of Buddhist training. The establishment of this fundamental concept meant that *chanoyu* came to embrace a spiritual culture of an extremely high order. Spiritual preparation, therefore, is the function of the "dewy ground." But there is more. The need to arrange the utensils in the room naturally gives rise to guidelines for their use. *Nanpōroku* also says: "In the small room it is best for all the utensils to be incomplete. Some people hate for little things to be amiss, but I cannot understand their feelings at all."[20] This sentiment matches exactly Jukō's "cold and withered" realm that we have seen in his letters. From this sense of incompleteness comes a rule for the scroll, which hangs in the alcove. *Nanpōroku* continues: "There is no object more important than the hanging scroll, for that is what enables both host and guest to center their attention and to grasp the import of the occasion. An ink scroll is best. One will venerate its words and appreciate the virtue of its writer, a man of the Way or a priest. Do not display scrolls with secular themes."[21] The purpose of the scroll, which hangs in the tea room, as this explains, is to enable the participants to focus on what is to take place, so the host must select a scroll that will facilitate that spiritual function. Since secular content would impede the intended process, it is unacceptable. It is the scroll that naturally sets a criterion that will unify all aspects of the gathering from the selection of utensils to the conduct of the tea service and even the conversation between host and guests. It is a matter of "rules ruling without rules." So long as spiritual contemplation of the Way is within one's heart, everything will naturally come into its proper order.

The credibility of *Nanpōroku* has been called into question because its content is far too meticulously organized.[22] But be that as it may, Rikyū established *chanoyu* as a Way, and because of that fact, the tradition of tea has continued unbroken to the present and, further, retains its significance as a comprehensive cultural system.

Rikyū, in order to achieve a more pronounced *wabi* sense, began toward the end of his career to design tea rooms that were smaller than the four-and-a-half-mat size that had come down from Jukō. In this way he created an extreme form of the *wabi* that said, "A house suffices if it does not leak; food, if it satisfies hunger." *Yamanoue Sōji Ki* records:

> Jukō had a room of four and a half mats; Insetsu, one of six. Until Jōō's time the only ones to have three-mat rooms were *wabi* tea men who owned no utensils. Those who owned even one Chinese piece would build rooms of four and a half mats. Sōeki had a different concept. From his age twenty-five things remained as they were with Jōō, but in the last ten years, under the regime of the Kanpaku [Hideyoshi], people of all classes have used rooms of three mats or even two and a half. . . . In Jōō's time there was only one two-and-a-half-mat room in the whole land. [It belonged to] a man called Yamamoto Sukegoro, and because he was Jōō's disciple, the master gladly performed *chanoyu* [there]. This was tea in the *wabi* style. . . . In Osaka [Castle] Sōeki made a narrow three-mat room [termed narrow because the alcove was at one end], as shown in an attached chart. However, though a person who owns [good] utensils or a skilled practitioner of tea might do likewise, a beginner should not.[23]

Thus, one sees that tea rooms steadily grew more restricted in size. We saw earlier that "in Kyoto Sōeki made a tea room of [only] one and a half mats for the first time." This is considered the smallest feasible extent.[24] To suit the mood of the smaller room it was necessary to reduce the size of its entry as well. That became the *nijiriguchi*, the so-called crawling-in entryway, which is so low that one must enter on one's knees. In that connection, *Chadō Shiso Densho* relates, "Sōeki saw someone ducking into [the cabin of] a boat at Hirakata, Osaka, and thought that had an interesting flavor of *wabi*, so he made for the first time a small tea room with an entry for people to duck through."[25] The term "ducking" that appeared here was the earliest name for this low entry, thus testifying that Rikyū was its first designer. Up until that time people had simply entered from a narrow verandah, so it is evident how much more confining Rikyū's crawling-in entry was. Horiguchi Sutemi's research into tea room architecture is quite thorough on this matter, and his studies such as *Rikyū no Chashitsu* and *Chashitsu Kenkyū* reveal the following measurements:

1. Tōdaiji Jizōin, Jukō style, internal measurement of lintel: 5 *shaku* 6 *sun* 5 *bu* (2 meters)
2. Daitokuji Kōrin'an, Jōō style, internal measurement of lintel: 5 *shaku* 5 *sun* 2 *bu* (1.98 meters)
3. "Ducking" entry to six-mat room: 2 *shaku* 7 *sun* (94 cm.) high, 2 *shaku* 5 *sun* (88 cm.) wide
4. *Nijiriguchi* to four-and-a-half-mat room: 2 *shaku* 2 *sun* 5 *bu* (80 cm.) by 2 *shaku* 2 *sun* (79 cm.)
5. *Nijiriguchi* at Myōkian: 2 *shaku* 6 *sun* 1 *bu* (91 cm.) by 2 *shaku* 3 *sun* 6 *bu* (84 cm.)[26]

The first two, each measuring about two meters high, would easily admit an adult standing erect. By contrast, Rikyū's entries, the last three, were all under one meter. The highest, an entry to a six-mat room, was just ninety-four centimeters. Though evidently the crawling-in entry did not appear until relatively late in his career, it accorded well with the attitude of piety he sought to inculcate as well as the spirit of *wabi* by which he reduced action to its minimal level.

Entries were just one aspect of tea house architecture. There were other issues as well. Jōō in *Ikenaga Sōsa Chasho*, a letter to one of his Sakai disciples, indicated that rooms for *chanoyu* normally faced north. The reason was that the light from the other directions was too bright to permit one to appreciate the true appearance of the tea utensils.[27] Rikyū, however, favored a south-facing room. In fact, the light from the south does appear intense, but Rikyū oriented his tea rooms in that direction anyway. To block the light, he planted trees and shrubs outside the south wall. Rather than try to achieve the effect of *wabi* by making a dark tea room isolated from the light, he seems to have chosen to seek a greater sense of *wabi* by blocking part of the light while allowing part to spill through. One of Rikyū's favorite verses was by Sōgi:

> Moon in the evening.
> Can it be the sea I spy,
> Dimly through the trees?[28]

It relates to a traditional story about Rikyū to the effect that he disliked the direct view of the sea from his tea room in Sakai and planted trees to obscure it. That way he was able to catch just a glimpse of it through them. Rikyū employed this same tactic in the orientation of his tea rooms, no doubt hoping to intensify the mood of *wabi* thereby. Since Rikyū had said, "A house suffices if it does not leak; food, if it satisfies hunger," he may have been trying to express that sentiment in an objective fashion, as well as trying in a subjective way to experience the meaning of *wabi* in such a place.

Let us return to the tea garden, which was an inseparable extension of the tea environment inside. Two poems, traditionally attributed to Rikyū, sum up in a few words his most important teachings about the *roji*:

> House and dewy ground.
> Guest and host both joined as one,
> Share a cup of tea.
> In tranquil meditation,
> No margin divides their hearts.

> The *roji* is a way
> Apart from this bustling world
> And its many cares.
> How will that path sweep away
> The dust from within out hearts?[29]

It is important to understand that the act of entering the tea garden itself removed one from the mundane world outside. It is likely that the tea garden first assumed great importance after Sakai merchants began to practice *chanoyu*. The realities of merchant life obliged such people to grapple with problems of the most practical sort, and for them the tea garden represented a first step toward attaining spiritual peace and stability by bringing Zen into their lives and its spirit into their tea. *Zen-charoku* calls the *roji* "a place for the practice of Buddhist austerities and a realm of purification." It explains:

> Of the two characters with which the word "*roji*" is written, the first means "to reveal or expose." The second means "heart." Thus, together they mean "the revelation of one's essential being." We call it "*roji*," because it reveals the innate self as it truly is, apart from all one's evil passions. . . . Based on this definition, the significance of the tea room is that it is a hall of spiritual training where one reveals one's innermost essence, and we call it "*roji*." Thus, "*roji*" is one name for the tea room [itself].[30]

For Rikyū, who considered harmony, respect, purity, and tranquillity to be first principles of tea, the *roji* was a place of cleansing where one expunged the stains of the spirit. We have seen that the characters for *roji* can also mean "dewy ground," and there is a method of purifying the garden called the "three dews." *Nanpōroku* describes it in this way: "One sprinkles water over the garden once before the guests enter, once during the break in the middle, and once as the guests rise to leave at the end of the gathering, for a total of three times."[31] It was Rikyū's intent that, for their part, guests were to rinse the hands and mouth at the basin in the garden as a form of mental preparation for the occasion to cleanse their own impurities. It might seem unpleasant in cold weather, but the host was to fill the basin anyway. When it was hot, the water would seem refreshing to the guests. To pour the water into the basin without anyone's being aware was unsuitable; the host should pour it without hesitation before the guests' eyes. The process of filling and using the basin was an act jointly performed by both host and guests. In this fashion Rikyū sought to leap to a realm of religious freedom through the medium of tea. It was a matter of somehow transcending the mundane and impure by taking advantage of the forms of *chanoyu*. No matter what one may choose to call these cares of the world, whether "a house in flames" or impurities, their elimination must always be the foremost consideration. This concept was a fundamental principle of *wabi* tea.

The various artistic elements that compose tea, such as the tea house and garden, the utensils, and other appointments, must all conform to the spirit of *wabi* tea, for only in this way is it possible to achieve the particular significance of tea as a cultural system. Rikyū did not discuss this in a theoretical way but expressed the theory in the world of concrete form. Herein lies the historical significance of his *wabi* tea. *Nanpōroku* says:

> For a formal *shoin daisu* ritual one should arrange everything in the strictest order. The rule of the formal ceremony is one's gauge in all matters, whether it be an ordinary tea service, a grass-style tea in a small room, or the style of the garden. But ultimately one puts the gauge aside, forgets technique, and all comes down to thought without thought.[32]

The true art of *wabi* begins to function only when one can "put the gauge aside."[33] What emerges is extremely creative and free. One must not mistake the rule, but neither must one be wedded to it. It is the way of *wabi* tea to be free while still in conformity to the rule. To be able to perform in this way is the true spirit of tea.

So it is also with the selection of utensils for a tea gathering. Each piece must harmonize with all the others. Achieving this naturally requires an aesthetic sensitivity. The tea confections must accord with the utensil for their service; the scroll, with the flowers for the alcove. And the flower container will vary depending on the selection of flowers and the content of the scroll. For the tea bowl, tea caddy, and kettle as well, it is essential to preserve a harmonious unity throughout. One must perceive the heart of the host in every detail, and that means first to taste with the tongue, to appreciate with the eyes, and to pay heed to one's companions with the heart. In pursuing tea in this way one can begin to realize its ultimate ideal through the enjoyment of this realm of freedom.

The freedom of the concept of *wabi* tea meant many things. It meant the discovery of an aesthetic ideal that said that antique Chinese wares, though pleasing, were not the only source of beauty. Japanese wares made with creative craftsmanship might in fact excel. It meant the spirit of harmonizing Japanese and Chinese wares embodied in Jukō's dictum that one should mix pieces from both countries. It meant a creativity that could regard a grass hut as being more in conformity to aesthetic standards than a golden tea room. But, having said that, it also meant a revolution in values that said that no ordinary person should try to imitate that style. When that happened the distinction between rich and poor disappeared in tea. The Great Kitano Tea Party, which Hideyoshi held in 1587, was perhaps the most concrete illustration of that point. His edict summoning *wabi* persons, that is, *wabi* tea men, went as follows:

Item.　We hereby proclaim that there will be a grand tea party in the woods at Kitano for ten days beginning on the first of the tenth month, weather permitting. In connection with this, Lord Hideyoshi will display his entire collection of famed tea utensils without exception in order that devotees of *suki* may view them.

Item.　All devotees of *chanoyu*, whether they be warrior attendants, townsmen, farmers, or of even lesser station are to bring a kettle, a bucket, and a drinking vessel. Those without tea will be allowed to bring powdered grain [to prepare as a beverage].

Item.　As for tea huts, since the event will be in a pine wood, two tatami mats [should be appropriate]. However, *wabi* persons may simply spread worn-out mats or bags of rice straw. There will be no assignment of sites, which participants may select for themselves.

Item.　Not only Japanese but even persons from the continent may attend if their hearts are set on *suki*.

Item.　To permit all, including even those from distant areas, to view [the collection], the event will not begin until the first day of the tenth month.

Item.　Inasmuch as the arrangements detailed above have been made out of a feeling of compassion for men of *wabi*, those who do not attend will hereafter be prohibited [to practice *chanoyu* or] even to prepare powdered grain [to drink]. This prohibition will apply equally to those who participate in the gatherings of those who do not attend.

Item.　For all men of *wabi*, no matter who they are or from what distance they may have come, it is hereby decreed that Lord Hideyoshi will personally prepare tea for them.[34]

Theories abound as to Hideyoshi's motive for this affair. Though I cannot discuss them all here, we can say that he aimed at cultivating the *wabi* tea men, and that was the reason for his planning a mass tea party inviting "all devotees of *chanoyu*, whether they be warrior attendants, townsmen, farmers, or of even lesser station . . . to bring a kettle, a bucket, and a drinking vessel" with or without tea.

An innovative concept of tea made it possible to create an entirely new beauty and to discover new values. Such a creation of a new aesthetic sense would not have emerged from the tea fancies of the literati, from formal tea ceremonies at the court, or from the stylish but vulgar tea entertainments of the parvenus.

The establishment of a conceptual basis for *chanoyu* had been a sine qua non for this revolution in values, and the three tea pioneers had increasingly satisfied the precondition. The new concept of tea had begun to germinate with Jukō and then grew steadily under Jōō to burst into flower with Rikyū. The transformation of values, moreover, did not stop with aesthetics. Social values also changed. So long as one stood on the dewy ground safe from the flames of the three worlds, so long as one stood before the grass hut, distinctions of wealth or poverty, high station or low, no longer mattered. All such considerations belonged to the dust of the world and could be swept away. The samurai had to set his two swords aside and commoners could sit in the grass hut as his equals. Such a spirit belonged to the Way of the Buddha, for whose sake one could reject such mundane considerations. Since differences of wealth and class belonged to the world outside, they had no place inside the grass hut. The values of the ordinary world lost their currency. Rikyū's grass hut style rose in the public estimation to such an extent that *Nanpōroku* could say the people venerated it as "more holy than the discipline of a temple." This is why it said his influence was such that "the people of the land, thus, followed his pure style."[35]

What was Rikyū's intent in thus raising up the ideal of his simple, unaffected style of tea? What lay at the root of these least formal methods of conducting a service of tea? Why, indeed, did he promote such a movement? It is necessary to probe to the heart of these questions, and for an answer we need to examine two sets of issues. One is related to what lay within Rikyū himself, and a second set to the demands of his times.

The first of these issues was his world view, rooted in what we might call a profound religious experience internal to Rikyū. He conceived of tea in the grass hut as a means of practicing the austerities of Buddhism. That ultimate ideal, therefore, provided cohesion to whatever he did. In his essential being he subordinated himself to the Way of the Buddha. Everything served that end, whether garden or tea house, utensils, or human relationships. It was Buddhism that brought him to the realization that utensils that were incomplete, especially those that were not rare or valuable, could cease to be incomplete despite their incompleteness. This led him to the theory that, though Chinese utensils were acceptable, Japanese ones were as well and might even be more pleasing aesthetically. Thus was it possible to come to the discovery that commonplace objects, made by nameless craftsmen and held in the hands of nameless peasants, could have a value as great as the rarest of treasures.

In short, an extremely positive, active spiritual movement wrought a revolution in the established values of the day. What rendered this possible was Rikyū's personal religious experience. We may think of it as a religious movement mediated by grass-hut style tea or as a means of achieving a spiritual revival by imparting a philosophical content to an aesthetic of life that consisted of the most advanced forms of *chanoyu* of the day and of the enjoyment of tea. *Chanoyu* was an activity performed for the purpose of drinking a cup of tea, but that was far from being all there was to it, for it was Rikyū's intent to rise to a higher realm of religion by means of that activity. In so doing he added a glorious new chapter to the history of the Way of Tea, one that brought a revolutionary systematization of *chanoyu*. This was how the simple act of drinking tea became a means of ascending to a separate, higher sphere. I have spoken in the introduction of a spiritual entertainment in a world apart among humanity. Indeed, elements of entertainment do pervade the performance of tea, but at the same time it is imperative that those elements serve its ultimate purpose of spirituality. Precisely for this reason, one's first step into the tea garden must also be a first step into that sphere apart so that the elements of entertainment will serve the spiritual purpose.

Each of the separate acts of taking tea is a real, concrete step, whether it be the drinking of the tea, the appreciation of utensils, or the conversation in the tea room between host and guests. Indeed, the flavor of the tea prepared there proves to be extraordinarily delicious when one tastes it. A broken tea bowl differs from an antique one from China. That is true in the sense of its real, concrete appearance. Nonetheless, when it comes to the entertainment value of tea—or more precisely— when it comes to the entertainment value of tea for the purpose of achieving the ultimate ends of tea, the broken bowl will harmonize perfectly with the other elements. A broken bowl in a grass-thatched house just strong enough not to leak will become an integral part of the occasion and naturally accord with the spirit of the garden as well. It is not a question of the perfection of each element, the tea house, the garden, the utensils. Rather, when this universe comes to its performance, one will discover in each thing itself the role it plays in the composition of the whole. Accordingly, the conventional value of the individual item itself becomes meaningless. To put it in its most extreme form, whatever is on hand will do, if that is all one has. It was to making a coherent system of such an ideal of tea that Rikyū devoted his life.

It was, however, a formidable path. Indeed, one wonders how far he succeeded in realizing that ideal or in gaining its general acceptance. In the section of *Nanpōroku* devoted to materials on Rikyū written after his death, the following appears:

> There are, however, a number of fears. The more people who study *chanoyu*, the more teachers there will be, each pursuing his own direction. In their associations with daimyo or the nobility they may treat the grass hut as if it were a *shoin*. Without concern for its essential character, people who like to eat and drink may turn the grass hut into a venue for [mere] bacchanals. It is odious to contemplate that they may say they like *wabi*, all the while ignoring its spirit. Teachers who make their living from tea may cater to the tastes of the daimyo and think only of organizing large and numerous parties. Men of wealth will love this sort of thing, and the teachers will be most fortunate. When it comes to *chanoyu* motivated by avarice, even now there are many cases of unimaginable behavior, and there may be no way to prevent its becoming even worse in the future. [Rikyū said] he would like to be born again a hundred years later to see just how far tea in the common world might have fallen.[36]

The obvious trenchancy of Rikyū's criticism makes one realize how difficult it was to propagate his ideas. Daimyo and wealthy merchants professed a fondness for the grass hut but all the same forgot what it really stood for. They did not truly enjoy *wabi* tea, for it kept them from enjoying the drinking parties of the sort *Kissa Ōrai* portrays. Rikyū expressed his fears for the direction tea might take in the following statement from *Nanpōroku*. It is an especially poignant lamentation: "In less than ten years people will abandon the true Way of Tea. But after it has declined, they will believe, on the contrary, that it is flourishing. Sadly, it will all become reduced to a vulgar amusement and even now is already deplorable."[37]

What of the second issue mentioned above as relevant to Rikyū's ideal of grass hut tea? We must now take up the demands of the age in which he lived. The era beginning in the late Muromachi period was a time when temporal authority counted for everything and a lust for power was the dominant mood. Yet it was also a time, by contrast, that saw an awakening of a humanistic spirit. One often finds the Momoyama era compared to the Renaissance in Europe, but the role of tea in this period was performed in the context of a movement that was critical of humanism and secularism. The golden tea room that Hideyoshi built was only three mats in size, but it was reputed to have had floor mats with a covering of red fabric called orangutan skin, edging of gold brocade, and stuffing of wadded silk. Gold foil covered the ceiling, walls, and the latticework of the shoji. Truly it was the picture of dazzling brilliance.[38] It was also the product of authority and wealth. Thus it was natural for a general criticism of such a movement to emerge. Rikyū's tea room of one and a half mats was a mere shack compared to Hideyoshi's room of gold. If the golden room was the product of power, Rikyū's was the product of powerlessness. Both of these might be thought of as tea rooms. The golden room, the product of power, might enjoy the higher evaluation in the world at large, but that worldly value, precisely because it was a worldly value, would become an obstacle when one considered the purpose of a tea room to be the pursuit of the austerities of Buddhism. The one-and-a-half-mat room, so worthless in the eyes of the world, might in fact hold greater significance. Insofar as the trend of the times would permit such an interpretation of relative value, one must also regard this as a relevant movement.

Rikyū's pursuit of the ultimate ideal of tea in the face of the tea room of gold further purified the ideal and made it more thoroughgoing. It established that ideal as a Way of *Wabi* Tea.

Conclusion

So far in this volume we have examined the differences in and transformation of *chanoyu* in China and Japan through each of several epochs. The permutations in the drinking of tea from the age of Emperor Shennong in China until Sen Rikyū during the Momoyama era in Japan were many. The changes in the service of tea after the origin of the grass hut tradition of *chanoyu* with Murata Jukō were especially pronounced, and no doubt the most decisive development was the creation of orderly procedures for the preparation of tea, which the Japanese call *temae*. The *temae* for *chanoyu*, which Rikyū perfected, were ways to prepare tea that were founded in aesthetics and differed from the reclusive tea style of Lu Yu, from medicinal tea, from the service of tea in temples in Baizhang's China and in the early middle ages in Japan, as well as from gambling tea. I wish to turn in conclusion to a consideration of the significance of these *temae*.

If one looks at *chanoyu* from the standpoint of the traditional arts and treats it as one field of those arts, the core of it would be its "*sahō*," its "rules" or ceremonial aspect, and one may consider it to be the most traditional of the comprehensive art forms. To examine the devising of the rules of tea service is tantamount to studying the creation of *chanoyu* itself. The *sahō* reflected the ages that produced them. It is widely recognized that Murata Jukō began the process, Takeno Jōō developed it, and Rikyū perfected it. However, in one's search for the origins of these rules, one cannot ignore the eras prior to Jukō.

Let us set aside for the time the gambling tea that had gained popularity among the warrior class during an age of warfare and consider the *shoin* style of tea service that emerged in the Muromachi era, particularly in the regime of Yoshimasa. Yoshimasa assembled a collection of famous Chinese utensils, treasures, and paintings, which were called "*karamono*." He displayed them, used them, and encouraged *chanoyu* among the elegant noble class, and it is clear that there existed rules for the use of those wares. We cannot, however, ascertain what those rules were. All we can discover, by looking at such works as *Kundaikan Sōchōki* or *Okazarisho*, is that they paid due attention to the appreciation of Tang and Song paintings as well as to the collection of various types of Chinese utensils and the way they were kept, displayed, and arranged. We can, moreover, prove from these records that there was already an elementary protocol for the taking of tea. We have been able to make educated guesses about the use of the *daisu* shelf in *shoin*-style tea because its handling, together with illustrations, has been handed down to the present. Each *shoin* at the time had its own placement of the shelf, but we have learned that in a formal, south-facing *shoin*, there was a raised level before which the service was conducted. For tea in particular there were two mats in an adjoining room. The placement of the shelf was on the left of this area as one faced it. Opposite, a folding screen of two or six panels adorned with gold dust surrounded the space and was high enough to conceal a Tenmoku tea bowl sitting on a stand on top of the shelf. On the south edge of the preparation space, there was a door called a "*mohiki no ōdo*." This door corresponded to the host's entrance to a modern tea room. Two helpers would carry the tea implements as far as the outside of this door, and, while one held them for a time, the person who was preparing tea would release the fastening of his *hakama* about the ankles and cleanse his hands at a basin for that purpose on the verandah. He would then take the tea implements, which had been brought earlier, and carry them to the shelf, proceeding from the door drawing the formal skirts of his *hakama* along like a train. All of this activity, including the washing of the hands, was easily visible from the raised area. This space we consider to be the origin of the modern preparation room and the host's entrance. Though the forms may have changed over the years, they have retained a fundamental importance in *chanoyu*. It is noteworthy that Rikyū and his disciple Nanbō, despite the emphasis they placed on the grass hut tradition of tea, nonetheless saw fit to commit these earlier forms to writing.

Quite apart from this *shoin* tea tradition of the nobility, we also have the grass hut style of Murata Jukō, which existed at the same time but separate from it, and it is that to which we should now turn our consideration. The latter was tea for commoners, in stark contrast to the *shoin* tea that we believe the aristocrats practiced at Higashiyama. It moved tea from the Zen monastery into the market square. Though we believe Jukō's tea shared elements of Zen, there is, alas, no extant evidence to inform us of the sort of tea rules that he created. About all we can do is to surmise their style based on our understanding of the sorts of tea settings and implements he preferred, his accomplishments in the light of the age in which he lived, and his associations with Yoshimasa and with Ikkyū. The tea of the Zen temple was fundamental to Jukō's practice, and this in turn rested upon the service of tea using the tea shelf, the *daisu*. Though his tea for commoners grew from the Zen temple and was religious in intent, his tea ideal in part still embraced the nobility's concern for famous utensils and art objects, as we can see from his extensive collection of such treasures, including the Jukō Bunrin or his Zhao Chang painting. With respect to the way in which he performed tea as well, there seems to have been a duality of origin stemming in part from Zen but also from the tea of utensil collectors, which was an inseparable element of the *shoin* tradition. That such duality survives even today after the fruition of *wabi* tea testifies to the strongly rooted universality of the traditional arts. At the same time it explains Jukō's place later as an honored progenitor of *chanoyu* who found a spiritual basis for skillfully amalgamating and uniting these disparate strands of tea usage even after the Muromachi era, when the cleavage between nobility and commoner became especially pronounced.

Though Jukō laid the foundation for the Way of Tea and advocated *wabi* practices, however, he did not go so far as to complete the all-important *sahō*, the rules for the preparation of tea. As tea spread from Jukō through his direct disciples Sōgo and Sōchin of the Jūshiya house and on to Takeno Jōō, it attained a new crest of achievement. In this transition the *wabi* tendencies of tea became even more pronounced under Jōō than they had been under Jukō. Jukō's formal tea room of four and a half mats gave way to the semiformal room of similar size that Jōō preferred. The latter in concert with Rikyū decided on the measurements for a sunken hearth in the room and had one built. Thereupon they devised rules for the preparation of tea in that new space.[1] Jōō freed himself from the confines of the *daisu* shelf and created the so-called *fukurodana* of black wood and expressed his spirit of tea with rules to suit that architectural device. There was a little verse that made a play on the literal meaning of *fukurodana,* "bag shelf," and the bags of riches associated with the god Daikoku, whose name Jōō had adopted.

> My name is Daikokuan
> So I keep my secrets in a *fukurodana.*[2]

Jōō, however, occupied only a preliminary and transitional stage in this process and was not the one to complete the work. It remained for Rikyū to succeed to this final opening of the Way, as one can see in the famous "Wabi no Fumi," which Jōō is said to have presented to Rikyū. It shows that he entrusted his own incomplete practice to Rikyū, in whom he found wisdom. It says in part: "You are no ordinary man for you have ears that hear and eyes that see that you may perceive that which is perceivable. Your brilliant virtue is unclouded. Though I take pleasure in tea, understanding it with my heart, I am unable to articulate it with my tongue. The clumsy expression of the essence of this Way in words can only sound shallow."[3]

It is now time to direct our attention to the era of the perfection of tea and to Rikyū himself. The Ietaka poem conveyed well the direction of Rikyū's tea:

> To those who long only for cherry blossoms
> How I'd like to point out the grass of spring
> In the snow of a mountain village.[4]

One can see that Rikyū moved actively toward the *wabi* taste, disdaining artificiality and directly approaching the true essence and nature of *wabi.* The transition in the forms of the tea tradition from the founder Jukō through Jōō to Rikyū quite naturally produced changes as well in both the spiritual aspects and the performance of the service of tea. Thus by learning how Rikyū practiced *chanoyu,* one can work back to discover its underlying principles. I should like now to take such an approach, using citations from *Nanpōroku.*

In referring to the rules for the conduct of the tea service, it is customary in the Way of Tea to use the phrase "*kiku sahō,*" literally, "standard etiquette." These rules govern not only the design of the tea room and the adornment of its alcove, but also the garden outside. In this sense one can say that everything about tea practice follows these rules. Without such rules *chanoyu* would lose its structure. Rikyū had such an aim when he said that *chanoyu* is simply to know the essentials of boiling water, preparing the tea, and drinking it. He did not mean that one should simply casually or thoughtlessly drink tea. Rather he meant that one should take it in conformity with standards and that even the act of drinking should follow the ordained methods. Indeed, one must conclude that the creating of these rules was the essential element in the establishment and completion of *chanoyu* and the Way of Tea for they were, in effect, the expression of the spirit of tea and its actual implementation in practice.

> The Higashiyama style is the basis of all of the various ways of preparing tea in the *shoin*. In [tea for] each of the four seasons, in celebratory services or for poetry gatherings or *kemari* kick ball sessions, or in each of the various festivals through the year, each in its own way can be splendid, inexpressibly magnificent. . . . Sōeki said you are not to pass on secrets about these affairs to others.[5]

One cannot today follow precisely the rules for *shoin*-style ceremonies, because there are no venues for which those rules have been adapted in today's world. But to the extent one can, one ought to be aware of how the great alcove, the *shoin* alcove, or the *chigaidana* shelves were decorated. In this way one can sense one's part as heir to traditional culture.

"'Even though the *daisu* is the basis of tea, where the heart is concerned, the small, grass-style room is unequaled,"[6] Rikyū taught. Periodically he would emphasize that one's true intent should lie in the small grass tea room of four and a half mats or smaller but that formal tea service using the *daisu* stand was the ultimate basis of tea etiquette. He shared the following view:

> As the *daisu* ritual is the most splendid, one should never be inattentive to it. It is the most formal of the styles and the basis of the *chanoyu*. In the adornment of the tea room, there are the three levels of formality, *shin*, *gyō*, and *sō* [formal, semiformal, informal], and even at practice one should dress appropriately with the laity in *kamishimo* and clerics in *kesa* or *juttoku* surplices.[7]

Rikyū emphasized that one must always remember the basics and cited examples from the past, including the idea that persons of noble status and high rank were to wear formal clothing and that the shogun Yoshi-masa usually wore *kariginu* as befitted the occasion.

Rikyū, moreover, often found religious foundations for his tea practice. In devising his rules, he drew widely from a variety of sources, selecting the best features of each. He frequently relied on the Zen work *Zen'en Shingi* but not only on Zen, for he also used esoteric Buddhist sources and the *Yijing* as well. The most momentous change he wrought, though, was to conceive of the ultimate in simplicity. He finally created the so-called *hakobi no hirademae*, a way of preparing tea that employed the most economical of actions and the bare minimum of implements. In it the host carried the fresh water supply vessel into the tea room and placed it directly on the tatami mat, eschewing furnishings of any kind.

Rikyū's role as the perfecter of the Way of Tea meant that none of the earlier styles of serving survived beyond him and that all of those that have come down to the present are ones that were completely transformed by his *wabi* taste. All contemporary styles of tea service can thus be traced either directly or indirectly to Rikyū himself.

When one interprets tea precepts narrowly and treats them as codes of behavior, one can define them as having two aspects, one based on the guest or guests, the other on famous tea implements and trea-sures of art. One can see elements of each in the rules for serving tea. With respect to the former, there are rules for entertaining a person of high rank, a small group of guests, or large gatherings. Inasmuch as the entertainment of noble guests was a common feature of the Way of Tea from its beginnings into the early Tokugawa era, reflecting the age in which it was born, the influence of that style of practice runs deep, and training in the Way of Tea today inevitably touches upon it. In such a ceremony one places a *daisu* shelf in the tea room and makes the tea in a Tenmoku tea bowl. Indeed, as this type of ceremony is focused on the high rank of one's noble guest, the bowl may only be of the Tenmoku type, the most formal. Japanese had collected such Tenmoku bowls, originally from China, from the Kamakura era on and soon incorpo-rated them into *chanoyu*, where they were used for the nobility and set on a stand when handled. Rules for this type of service became central to the ritual. In his era, however, Rikyū created the *nijiriguchi*, the low entrance through which one crawls into the tea room, so that the *wabi* tea of the grass hut might emphasize human equality. In this way each guest could be welcomed in a fashion that transcended the social status of the feudal age with its clear distinctions of class. For this purpose he also changed the rules for serving tea, and though the *daisu* enjoyed continued respect, he stressed the performance of a more democratic style of service.

With respect to the latter strand, that style of tea that focuses on the tea implements, there has been an unbroken tradition from the very beginning of the Way of Tea down to the present day. Indeed, from one point of view one might argue that the rules for the service of tea grew out of the need to handle such implements. *Chanoyu* defined rules for dealing with implements of each type, be it a *daisu*, a Chinese tea caddy, or a Tenmoku tea bowl. As a result, *chanoyu* has contributed to the protection of the valued cultural objects of the past and to their survival into the present. Thus the Way of Tea has performed a key service for society and has contributed greatly to traditional culture.

The precepts of tea service comprise three elements, namely, "position," "action," and "order." Position is one of the earliest principles established in tea service, and it is based on the use of the *daisu* shelf. A square rule, like that used by carpenters, is the standard for placement, and one positions the implements following a rule of "five yang, six yin," striking the proper balance between those fundamental elements. Using the precept of "two even, one odd" or "two odd, one even" as a basis, one should determine changes in position of the elements of the service with reference to the three structures of alcove, seats, and shelf.[8] For example, in using a brazier without a *daisu* shelf, one positions it in just the same place as if the *daisu* were there, and the board on which it rests must also conform in its position as well. Similarly, one places the water supply jar, the tea caddy, and the tea bowl as precisely as if one had used a carpenter's square, but by dint of practice one comes to be able to square without the square, to rule without the rule. One can ascertain the precise position naturally and intuitively, thanks to a sharp, refined sense of place. Rikyū's satirical jingle had it this way:

> You practice five over and six across
> Until at last you lay it out by heart.
> Wonder of wonders
> You find you can measure out five over and six across
> Without measuring at all.[9]

In the same vein as position is the harmonizing of utensils with respect to size, color, and the like. One matches large with small and small with large to find a neutral balance. "Rikyū always used to say that it is best for utensils to suit, and since he was a large man, small, gentle things suited him." This statement offers corroboration that the low, narrow host's entrance to the tea room made Rikyū, with his large frame, appear modest by contrast. Similarly, "for old men, lovely elegant utensils are best." The combination reflects the *wabi* taste of a single flower on the twig of a withered tree and strikes a balance among elements. For utensils, too, one contrives to appeal to the senses so that a large brazier belongs on a small board and a small one, on a large board. Though there are set standards for the way one positions oneself in the tea room, "in posture there should be a degree of latitude according to the individual."[10] Thus, there is provision that one's posture ought not be unnatural to one's own character. One should develop a personal style in conformity to a modern sense and structure and adapted to one's own internal "ruler," though it can be displayed freely only after one has experienced the prescribed forms.

Next is "action." To think of beauty in the conduct of one's life as well as in the slightest movement is also an essential element of the performance of *chanoyu*. Beauty of action is an expression of the heart, and it emerges as a result of assiduous practice. In the early days of the Way of Tea, Jukō preached a "cold and withered" beauty, but Jōō emphasized the spiritual aspect and spurned the stress on performance or movement in favor of a restrained, unprepossessing form. The age of Rikyū inherited this thinking and regarded the performance of tea to be an expression of "consideration," an expression of the *wabi* sense. Rikyū, steeped in the precepts of Zen, used them as a basis for heightening the ideal of directing all inward and penetrating to the heart of the void. He sought to use movement as a device to enter the realm of the nonself. When *mu*, nothingness, lives within the man of tea, when it infuses his actions, his performance of tea is no mere formality but is the height of freedom. A true beauty of movement comes into being, and he is thereby able to inspire his viewers and allow them to experience the *wabi* taste of tea without the burden of words. In the simple act of preparing tea, he can admit his companions into the realm of tranquillity through the beauty, which, though withered, shows through an artless gentleness.

It is said that true beauty is to be found when a person completes in his or her own mind that which is incomplete. When one considers that action is an expression of spirit, then the way to bring one's actions to a peak of perfection is to refine the heart that lies within. Accordingly, seeing a person's performance of tea will allow one to judge the character of the performer. Yamanoue Sōji said, "Chanoyu should take novel forms from year to year, but one should learn from that which went before." It is quite natural that there should be changes through the ages.[11]

Finally, there is "order." Just as there is an order to the days and months and to the flow of nature, so there are sequences that must remain inviolate. Any given performance of tea has its own sequence of procedures, and each of these in turn has its own internal pattern. There is, moreover, a proper order for moving through each of the stages of practice as well, and to disrupt this current is to invite disaster. When the sequence is on track, one knows naturally what to do, and there will be a seamless flow in performance. There will be an artless modulation of movement just as if one were following the rhythm of a silent verse.

Position, action, and order provide the structure of the performance of tea and preserve its integrity. On this account, the Way of Tea, like all of the other traditional art forms, retains even today the system of secret conventions to which one can gain access only by dint of hard, unstinting practice.[12] This system has exerted a great influence and has, in turn, helped to protect the traditional character of the way of tea. If these conventions were to be thrown open, no doubt the traditional character of the arts would become subject to the buffeting of ephemeral trends in thought and ultimately would survive only as fragments of the past.

Finally, I should like to take up three *temae* that constitute the basis of all tea practice. These are the *sumidemae* for laying and lighting charcoal, the *koichademae* for preparing thick tea, and the *usuchademae* for thin tea. All other aspects of tea service, no matter how arcane, come down to these three. Though all are essential to any tea gathering, the preparation of thick tea is, by common agreement, the single most fundamental of them. The laying of the charcoal is to ensure that the water will be right for the making of the thick tea; the serving of the *kaiseki* meal prepares the stomach for it; then, after the thick tea is made, the thin tea completes the process. The whole purpose of *chanoyu* is the sharing of this bowl of thick tea among the guests.

The laying of the charcoal varies according to the season, as does its timing within the flow of the procedure. During the cold months the tea room has a sunken hearth for the fire, while in the warmer months there is a brazier for that purpose. Practitioners of *chanoyu* know well that there are three steps in this process. In the cold months when using the sunken hearth, the host will light the charcoal as soon as the guests have entered the room and exchanged their initial greetings. There will already be three small bits of charcoal that the host will have lighted to start the fire; this is the first step. A thin mantle of ash on the charcoal will express wordlessly the host's sense of anticipation in welcoming those who are to partake of his tea. In the second step the host will spread moistened ash in the hearth and then place the charcoal on the lighted bits within. Positioning the pieces precisely according to pattern helps to create a lovely image of a fire on withered wood in a village in winter. The pattern used is one that the early tea masters conceived based on their keen sense and experience. The host will provide the *kaiseki* meal while the guests enjoy the fragrance and faint sound of the fire as it spreads to the fresh charcoal. This, too, is based on precept, principally from the food section of the *Zen'en Shingi*. At last, as the meal draws to a close, the steam escaping from the kettle will be just at its peak, sounding like the wind in the pines.

In summer the host defers the lighting of the charcoal until after serving the meal and clearing away the trays. The hotter weather means that the guests do not need any additional heat from the fire. Moreover, it is the practice for them not to observe the charcoal in the brazier but simply to view the shape of a bed of ash, which the host has prepared in it before lighting the fire. The host will have devoted enormous effort to shaping the ash, and doing so properly takes the utmost training to learn. One can enjoy the fresh, lively workmanship that has gone into it and at the same time appreciate the care and depth of concern that it reflects. There is a science to the shaping of the ash so that the fire not only heats the water but also lasts through to the end.

The third step for charcoal is the final rekindling of the fire after the thick tea service. To be sure that the kettle will be boiling properly during the following service of thin tea, the host will add charcoal to the fire as well as water to the kettle. This process also helps to sustain the interest of the guests. Even though the kettle may be boiling as strongly as before after the thick tea service, the host should nevertheless rekindle the charcoal so that the guests can take several cups of thin tea and still continue to enjoy the sound of the wind in the pines from the fireplace. The host should provide for every eventuality so that the kettle will sing until the very end and the guests' interest will not flag.

This is the charm of *chanoyu* and lends it its air of cultivation. In this last laying of charcoal, unlike the first, strict rules do not apply, and the host may exercise a degree of judgment about how the fire is burning and how much longer it must last. During the colder months when the sunken hearth is in use, there are times when the guests may be asked to rekindle the fire. On these occasions the host first clears the hearth and purifies it. Though a guest may add charcoal as he or she likes, it is considerate to put in somewhat less than the host might, for that is a way of expressing the thought that no extravagance is necessary. During the warmer season when using the brazier, it is proper to invite the guests' help for the first lighting of the fire. In such a case, the charcoal should be laid according to the prescribed fashion, and each guest in turn may then move to the brazier to view and appreciate it. The first laying of charcoal sets the stage for the thick tea service that follows, and the latter is to prepare for the thin tea. In each case the kettle should boil vigorously until the very end so that the guests may enjoy the occasion.

It goes without saying that the thick tea is the basis of *chanoyu*: "In that realm we call the dewy ground one enters a world of purity. This simple grass hut, which comprehends the universe in a space of two mats, cleanses and clarifies. One realizes at last that bringing the wood and the water is a means of experiencing the austerities of the Way and that in this bowl one can sense truth."[13] In *wabi* tea, as this passage suggests, the tea can be the means by which host and guests share what is in their hearts directly. One has only "to carry water, bring firewood, boil the water, and make tea. Next one offers it to the Buddha, to one's guests, and at last partakes of it oneself."[14] Throughout the ages from the most primitive times, human beings have pledged their hearts and bound themselves together with vows taken with food and drink. The Eucharist in Christianity, the partaking of food in Shinto, and the offering of tea to the Buddhist patriarchs are all such ceremonies. In *chanoyu* this religious, primeval communion through food and drink proceeds another step further. It takes on a wisdom and consciously employs a methodology bolstered by theoretical foundations. The crux of this thought is the bowl of thick tea, which the guests share among themselves. All the devices of *chanoyu* are organized for the sake of this object.

All of the preparation, training, wisdom, and mastery that go into the making of a bowl of thick tea and serving it to guests are in no way easy. For the guest as well, the experience of participating in a unique occasion and receiving the tea is a multifaceted one that involves comprehending the surroundings, the utensils and their arrangement, together with the intentions of the host. There is a fixed pattern in which the guests, after taking the sweet for thick tea following the *kaiseki* meal in the first half of the service, walk out into the garden. In treading on the dewy ground they redirect the mind, refresh the mouth, and renew both body and spirit. All of this directs them toward the thick tea to be prepared in the main service that is to come.

The *Roji Seicha Kiyaku*, attributed to Rikyū, says: "The rocks and trees in the garden are simply as in nature. Any who find this incomprehensible should leave forthwith."[15] The purpose of the break to allow the guests to reenter the garden is to encounter nature so that one may consider the significance of the rocks and trees, banish the accumulated worldly dust of the spirit, and free oneself from the passions of life. The respite in the garden marks a transition from the subdued yin of the first half to the bright yang of the second. The tea room will be set for the thick tea with flowers in the sacred alcove and a water supply jar and tea container resting on the mat where the host will prepare it. At this most critical moment of the entire experience, the host and guests will cease their conversation and confine their speech to defined greetings and commentary so that the host can proceed wordlessly with his task. As the first guest takes the initial sip, the host will enquire how it tastes. The answer given, the proceeding continues in silence. The host, who has been so absorbed in the single aim of making a delicious cup of tea that he hardly dared breathe, knows he has succeeded when he learns that the tea is right. To do what the host has done requires enormous training.

The way in which tea is made has passed through many stages from the earliest days to the present, and though its traditional, fundamental principles have remained immutable, its method of expression has undergone ceaseless renewal and innovation, reflecting changes in the times. Indeed, the single most essential task for the Way of Tea in the future will be to find approaches that are ever fresh but still firmly rooted in tradition.

Notes

Foreword

1. Quoted in Kumakura Isao, "Sen no Rikyū: Inquiries into His Life and Tea," in *Tea in Japan: Essays on the History of Chanoyu*, eds. Paul Varley and Kumakura Isao (Honolulu: University of Hawai'i Press, 1989), p. 42.
2. Ibid., p. 35.
3. Sen Sōshitsu XV, "Reflections on *Chanoyu* and Its History," in *Tea in Japan*, p. 238.
4. I have taken the information for this paragraph from the Urasenke Homepage on the Internet.
5. Kakuzō Okakura, *The Book of Tea* (New York: Dover Publications, 1964), p. 2.

Introduction

1. Tachibana Jitsuzan, *Kochū Rodan*. This work was published as part of *Chaji Shūran*, edited by Saeda Ryakuō. The collection itself comprises four volumes and contains unpublished works acquired at booksellers. The contents are not necessarily in chronological order, and editorial policy called for the omission of works published elsewhere. Volume 1 contains *Kochū Rodan*; Volume 2, Kobori Enshū's *Daiyūshi Shōsoku Hyakkajō, Enshū Kō Chanoyuki, Takuan Oshō Chanoyu Ichimai Kishōmon*, and *Seikan Zenji Chaji Jūrokkajō*; volumes 3 and 4, *Shōfū Zatsuwa*.

   The section on *roji* in *Kochū Rodan* states: "'*Roji*' is the name that we give to that tranquil place that sits at the boundary of the grass hut. In the Parables of the Lotus Sutra there appears the line that the powerful emerge from the house in flames in the three worlds to sit on the open [dewy] ground. The *roji* was also called the 'white cow' [i.e., enlightened person] or the 'white [pure], open ground.' People have gone so far as to apply this term 'white' because there one leaves behind the dust and impurities of the world and attains the void in which the heart is cleansed. When this is so, the rocks, trees, and nature of the garden become an external expression of the essence that is within the heart. In this superb place not a bird cries and the trees are deep like those in a forest. Thus to have such a wonderful, natural place amidst the dwellings of a city is a rarity. For this reason, even though the space be confined, we plant trees, cultivate clumps of bamboo, and enjoy the dews of morning and evening. We stroll under the moon or through the snow. It naturally reminds us of a lovely field or a vine-covered wall. It is not a place that is suited to crowds, but one where we may love the forest without flowers and await the arrival of a friend of the heart, sweeping the snow from the stepping stones. It is difficult to express [its beauty] adequately." Tachibana Jitsuzan, *Kochū Rodan*, in Saeda Ryakuō, ed., *Chaji Shūran*, vol. 1, pp. 10–11.

2. Tachibana Jitsuzan, ed., *Nanpōroku*, in *Chadō Koten Zenshū*, ed. Sen Sōshitsu, vol. 4, pp. 3–4. Cited hereafter as *Nanpōroku*. *Chadō Koten Zenshū* is cited hereafter as CKZ. For another translation, refer to Dennis Hirota, ed., *Wind in the Pines: Classic Writings of the Way of Tea as a Buddhist Path*, pp. 217–218.

3. *Nanpōroku*, p. 3. See also Hirota, p. 217.

4. Ibid.

5. Li Zhao, ed., *Tang Guoshi Bu*, vol. 2, p. 4. This work covers the period from 713 to 824. As explained in the translator's preface, traditional East Asian publications have printing on one side of a sheet of paper, which is then folded with the unprinted side in. The loose sides are bound at the spine, and the fold is out. Page numbers (if any) appear on the fold, but these do not have a uniform page numbering system. Page numbers in citations of such works are to the entire folded sheet, called "*chōme*" in Japanese.

6. Zhao Lin, ed., *Yinhualu*, part 3, pp. 6–7. The work comprises six parts. Part 1 contains records of the court; parts 2 and 3, of the officialdom; part 4, of persons out of office; part 5, the classics and history; and part 6, miscellany.

7. Ouyang Xiu, ed., *Jigulu*, in *Shuofu*, ed. Tao Zongyi, vol. 1, p. 102. This is in the section on tea in the part on economics and livelihood.

In *Xintangshu*, volume 18, part 196, there is information about ceramic statues of Lu Yu, who was worshiped as the god of tea. One of the twenty-four veritable dynastic histories, *Xintangshu* is a chronological account of the Tang. Rensong of the Song ordered Ouyang Xiu, Song Qi, and others to compile it in 1010. Ouyang Xiu, Song Qi, et al., eds., *Xintangshu*. Cited hereafter as *Xintangshu*.

Tang Guoshi Bu, vol. 2, p. 4, contains an account similar to that in *Xintangshu*.

Datang Chuanzai says that Lu Yu enjoyed tea and was the first to create ways to process it. In houses where tea was sold, it states, they made ceramic statues of him and placed them among the utensils. When tea sold, all was fine. Hongjian wrote *Chajing* in two [sic] volumes. Later people made statues of him and worshiped him as a god. When trade was good, they worshiped him, but they poured hot water from the kettle over him when it was not. *Datang Chuanzai*, in *Shuoku*, case 1, vol. 6, p. 2 (pages not numbered sequentially).

8. Eisai, *Kissa Yōjōki*, in CKZ, vol. 2, pp. 9, 12, 13, and pp. 28, 31, 32. Note that there are variant texts, as will be explained in Chapter 4. The author has consulted the earlier of the two main textual lines, but the translator of this volume has supplied references to both. CKZ supplies two versions, the first, dated 1211, is on pp. 4–23, and the second, dated 1214, is on pp. 24–40. Both versions are cited hereafter as *Kissa*. *Isei Teikin Ōrai* is variously attributed to Kitabatake Genne and Shaka Kokan, though both are doubtful. The date of compilation is also unknown, but it clearly falls between 1373 and 1386. It is numbered among the finest of the copybook genre. It contains twelve exchanges of letters, one for each month of the year, and is filled with general information about the world of its day. *Isei Teikin Ōrai*, in *Gunsho Ruijū*, ed. Hanawa Hokiichi, vol. 9, part 140, pp. 472–473. Cited hereafter as *Isei*. *Gunsho Ruijū* is cited hereafter as *Gunsho*.

Chapter 1: The Advent of Lu Yu and *The Classic of Tea*

1. Lu Yu, *Chajing*, in CKZ, vol. 1, pp. 89–118. Cited hereafter as *Chajing*. The "autobiography" of Lu Yu in Li Fang, ed., *Wenyuan Yinghua*, vol. 5, p. 4194, refers to the work as *Chajing*, using a variant form of the second character, but Feng Yan, ed., *Fengshi Wenjianji*, in *Gaudo Sōsho*, vol. 17, part 6, p. 1, refers to it as "a treatise on tea by the man of Chu, Lu Hongjian." It is unclear, however, whether "a treatise on tea" was intended to be a title, that is, a proper noun. Perhaps we should consider *Chalun* (Treatise on Tea) to be a variant title. *Wenyuan Yinghua*, an anthology of literature in one thousand parts, is one of the Four Great Works of the Song. Li Fang et al. compiled it at the order of Taizong in

987. (It is cited hereafter as *Wenyuan*.) *Fengshi Wenjianji* was compiled during the Tang dynasty in ten volumes (referred to hereafter as *Fengshi*). During the Tianbao era (742–756) in Xuanzong's reign, Feng Yan was a student, hence a contemporary of Lu Yu. See also John Blofeld, *The Chinese Art of Tea*, pp. 4–10.

2. *Chajing*, p. 91.

3. Ibid., p 108. Translation from Lu Yu, *The Classic of Tea*, trans. Francis Ross Carpenter, p. 122 (cited hereafter as Carpenter). Shennong was one of the three legendary emperors of the Chinese foundation myth. According to the myth, he tasted various plants and thereby discovered their medicinal properties.

4. Mitani Sōchin (1665–1741), *Wakan Chashi*, published in 1728, is a history of tea in China and Japan. It contains biographies of Lu Yu and Murata Jukō as well as entries on tea houses and gardens. Reprinted as *Wakan Chashi Yakuhon*, edited by Takaya Tsunetarō. Another Edo period work that traces tea drinking back to Shennong and Fu Yi is *Chadōgaku Riyū* by the eleventh Urasenke Iemoto, Gengensai, ms. in private collection of the author.

5. The Duke of Zhou was the younger brother of the Zhou king Wu. The duke was a paragon of Confucian virtue. Mitani, *Wakan Chashi*, p. 1. *Erya* is one of the Thirteen Classics. It explains the characters used in classical writing and consists of nineteen sections including sections on natural, geological, and biological phenomena.

6. Daiten, *Chakyō Shōsetsu*, vol. 1, p. 9 (hereafter cited as Daiten). Note that this is an Edo era woodblock edition, and the page number refers to the ninth *chōme*. Daiten (1719–1801) was a priest of the Rinzai sect of Zen from Ōmi province. A resident of Shōkokuji in Kyoto, he followed the Ogyū Sorai school of ancient learning.

7. Matsushita Satoru, *Nihon no Cha*. The author was a specialist on agriculture who studied the origins, taxonomy, and distribution of tea using field studies and scientific analysis.

8. *Bencao Gangmu* is a Ming era biological study by Li Shizhen dated 1578. Its fifty-two parts cover over 1,890 types of soils, gems, rocks, herbs, birds, animals, fish, insects, and so on. Vol. 3, part 32, p. 1870, contains the section on tea.

9. Aoki Masaru, *Chūka Chasho*, p. 1.

10. Wang Bao's patron, Xuandi of the Han dynasty, appointed him to the office of imperial censor, but he was censured for his association with theories of Taoist immortality.

11. Yano Jin'ichi, "Cha no Rekishi ni Tsuite," in *Chadō*, ed. Sen Sōshitsu and Sen Sōshu, vol. 1, pp. 32–114.

12. *Fengshi*, part 6, p. 1.

13. *Xintangshu*, vol. 18, part 196, p. 5611.
14. *Wenyuan*, vol. 5, p. 4194.
15. Xin Wenxiu, comp., *Tang Caizizhuan*, vol. 1, part 3, p. 10. *Tang Caizizhuan* contains biographies of Tang literary figures. In China the work has been scattered and lost and so is incomplete, but the Gozan edition in Japan is complete and has been reimported into China. Nunome Chōfū has studied it in detail.
16. *Xintangshu*, section on retired officials. The final lines, which mention Turkic Uighur peoples coming to trade tea for horses, also appear in the *Fengshi*, part 6, p. 2.
17. *Wenyuan*, vol. 5, p. 4194. Shi Jiaoran was a Tang dynasty priest of the illustrious Xie clan, a descendant of Xie Lingyun. His works include *Rushi Jiaoyouzhuan*, *Neidian Leiju*, and *Haonaozi*.
18. Shi Jiaoran, "Jiaoranji," in *Quan Tang Shi*, vol. 23, p. 9211.
19. Morooka Tamotsu, "Rikuu to Chakyō," in *Chadō*, ed. Sen Sōshitsu and Sen Sōshu, vol. 1, pp. 196–199.
20. Cited in ibid., p. 176.
21. The titles in Chinese are *Junchenqi*, 3 vols.; *Yuanjie*, 30 vols.; *Jiangbiao Sixingpu*, 8 vols.; *Nanbei Renwuzhi*, 10 vols.; *Wuxing Liguangji*, 3 vols.; *Huzhou Cishiji* in a single volume; and *Zhanmeng*, 3 vols. Other works no longer extant include *Huichalun* (mentioned above), *Guzhushan Chaji* (2 vols.), *Shushanji*, *Lingying Tianzhu Ershiji*, *Huqiushanzhi*, *Lishanji*, *Shuipin*, *Tang Wusengshi* (1 vol.), and *Jiaofanglu*. Ibid., pp. 199–200.
22. *Fengshi*, part 6, p. 1.
23. Li Fang et al., eds., *Taiping Guangji*, vol. 2, p. 1514. (Cited hereafter as *Taiping*.) *Taiping Guangji* was a five-hundred-volume collection of legends compiled by subject in the Song era by Li Fang and others. Dated 983, it covered the Han through Five Dynasties eras.
24. Quoted in Morooka, pp. 151–152; *Tang Guoshi Bu*, vol. 2, p. 4; *Taiping*, vol. 2, p. 1514.
25. Morooka, pp. 121–122.
26. Aoki Masaru, *Chūka Chasho*, pp. 2–3. Guo Pu appears in *Chajing* as Guo Hongnong. Jingchun was his epithet; he was from Wenxi in Hedong and served as an official of Yuandi of the Eastern Jin dynasty. A scholar of great erudition in literature, he was killed by Wang Dun but posthumously honored with the title and name Hongnong, which meant "one who extended agriculture." Du Yu was a literatus who enjoyed an official career serving as magistrate in Runan, as General of the Right in the Yongxing era (307–313), and as principal of the state academy. In the source cited here, the tea was from Shu, as was the case with Wang Bao's tea noted earlier. *Fengshi Wenjianji* in volume 6 also notes that tea picked early was called *cha* and that picked late was *ming*.

27. *Chajing*, p. 91. The quotation is from Carpenter, p. 59.
28. The first in Japan to deal with the issue of the characters with which "tea" was written was probably Okabe Haruhira [Kuzune], in *Chaki Zeigen*.
29. *Chajing*, pp. 91–92. See also Carpenter, p. 60.
30. *Chajing*, p. 92. Translation from Carpenter, pp. 60–61.
31. Literally, the phrase he used said that tea was not inferior to *tihu*, pure butter, or *ganlu*, sweet dew, which naturally fell from Heaven in times of righteous rule and great peace.
32. *Chajing*, pp. 92–93; Carpenter, pp. 62–66. Quotation from Carpenter, p. 66.
33. Daiten, vol. 1, p. 17, fourth *chōme* of main text.
34. *Chajing*, pp. 93–94; Carpenter, pp. 66–68.
35. *Chajing*, pp. 94–95; Carpenter, p. 70.
36. *Chajing*, p. 95. Quotation from Carpenter, pp. 70–71.
37. *Chajing*, p. 95. Quotation from Carpenter, p. 71.
38. *Chajing*, p. 95; Carpenter, pp. 72, 74.
39. *Chajing*, p. 95.
40. Nunome Chōfū, CKZ, vol. 1, p. 19. Note the phrase does not appear as such in Carpenter.
41. Huang Furan, in *Quan Tang Shi*, vol. 6, p. 2181.
42. Ibid., vol. 8, p. 2820.
43. *Chajing*, pp. 96–97; Carpenter, pp. 77–78.
44. *Chajing*, p. 97. See also Carpenter, pp. 79–80.
45. *Chaji*, vol. 2, compiled by Yu Zheng of Nanchang during the Ming era. Cited in Takahashi Tatsuo, *Chadō*, p. 17. See also Blofeld, pp. 11–13.
46. *Chajing*, pp. 97–101. See also Carpenter, pp. 80–90.
47. *Chajing*, pp. 101–102. Quotation from Carpenter, pp. 90, 92.
48. *Chajing*, pp. 102–103. See Carpenter, p. 93–99.
49. *Chajing*, p. 104.
50. *Chajing*, p. 105; Carpenter, p. 105.
51. *Chajing*, p. 105. See Carpenter, p. 105, 107.
52. *Chajing*, p. 105. See Carpenter, pp. 107, 109.
53. *Chajing*, pp. 105–106.
54. Ibid., p. 106.
55. Ibid., p. 107; Carpenter, pp. 115–116.
56. *Chajing*, p. 107; Carpenter, pp. 116, 118.
57. *Chajing*, p. 107. See Carpenter, p. 118.
58. *Chajing*, pp. 107–108. See Carpenter, pp. 118, 119.
59. *Chajing*, pp. 107–115.
60. *Guangya* (ten volumes) was compiled by Zhang Yi of the Wei era. It was intended to supplement *Erya*.
61. *Chajing*, p. 109.

62. Ibid., p. 110. Fu Xian, son of Fu Xuan, was an official of Wudi of the Jin dynasty. His epithet was Changyu, and he came from Niyang. This account from *Sili Jiao* is essentially the same as another in *Fu Zhongchengji*, an anthology of famous writings of one hundred three writers from the Han, Wei, and Six Dynasties periods.

63. Zuo Si, epithet Taichong, cited in *Chajing*, p. 110.

64. Liu Jingsu, ed., *Yiyuan*, cited in *Chajing*, p. 112.

65. *Chajing*, p. 112. The original presumably was a work called "Guangling Qilaozhuan." Wen Tingshi's supplement to the Jin literary catalog in the Qing period says it was cited in *Taiping Yulan*, vol. 867, but it is not known to be extant.

66. *Chajing*, pp. 116–117.

67. Ibid., pp. 117–118. See Carpenter, pp. 118, 149–150.

68. *Chajing*, p. 118; Carpenter, p. 151.

69. *Chajing*, p. 118. See Carpenter, p. 152.

Chapter 2: Tea in China after *The Classic of Tea*

1. Xu Zhao, epithets Daoyun, Lingyun, Shanmin, was fond of tea and skilled in poetry. He was a member of the Yongjia faction of scholars in the Song era and author of *Fanglangxuanji*. See Xu Zhao, *Fanglangxuan Shichao*, in Nagasawa Kikuya, ed., *Wakokubon Kanshi Shūsei: Sōshūhen* vol. 4, p. 72.

2. Zhang Youxin, *Jianchashuiji* (*Senchasuiki*), in *Chūka Chasho Zenshū*, ed. Nunome Chōfū, vol. 1, p. 150. (Cited below as *Jianchashuiji*.) This work seems to have been referred to as *Shuijing*, the classic of water, for *Taiping Guangji* makes reference to it in that way. *Taiping*, vol. 4, p. 3201. The author's epithet was Kongzhao.

3. Morooka, pp. 218–219.

4. Ibid., pp. 219–221.

5. *Jianchashuiji*, pp. 150–151.

6. Morooka, p. 218.

7. "Wei Suzhouji," in *Quan Tang Shi*, vol. 6, p. 1994.

8. Ji Zhong in ibid., vol. 21, p. 8511.

9. *Taiping*, vol. 3, p. 298.

10. Cai Xiang, *Chalu* [*Charoku*], in CKZ, vol. 1, pp. 205–214. Cited hereafter as *Chalu*.

11. Kanda Kiichirō, "*Charoku* Kaidai," in CKZ, vol. 1, pp. 215–219.

12. *Chalu*, p. 207. Dingwei was a scholar of the Song dynasty who passed the government examinations in 992. We know little of the *Chalu* apart from the title. See notes to *Chalu*, CKZ, vol. 1, p. 197.

13. Ibid., pp. 207–208.
14. Ibid., p. 209.
15. Ibid., pp. 209–210.
16. Ibid., pp. 210–211.
17. Ibid., pp. 211–213.
18. Su Shi's poem is included in the *Chaji,* a two-volume collection of tea-related poems compiled in the Ming period by Yuzhen, and included in his compendium titled *Chashu,* which has a preface dated Wanli 40 (1612). The Naikaku Bunko copy of the *Chaji* is included as no. 18 in Nunome Chōfū, ed., *Chūka Chasho Zenshū,* vol. 1; the poem appears on p. 228. Su Shi, a poet and author who lived during the Song dynasty, is counted as one of the eight great men of letters of the Tang and Song periods. His epithets were Zizhan and Dongpo, and his works include *Chibifu, Dongpoci,* and *Dongpozhilin.*
19. Saeki Futoshi, ed., *Daikan Charon,* in *Chadō,* ed. Sen Sōshitsu and Sen Sōshu, vol. 13, pp. 13–14.
20. *Daguan Chalun [Daikan Charon],* in CKZ, vol. 1, p. 247. See Blofeld, pp. 15–17, 31–38.
21. *Daguan Chalun,* in CKZ, vol. 1, p. 248.
22. Ibid., pp. 248–249.
23. Ibid., pp. 249–253.
24. Ibid., pp. 253–256.
25. Fukushima Shun'ō, "*Chokuju Hajō Shingi* Kaidai," in CKZ, vol. 1, pp. 371–374.
26. *Baizhang Qinggui [Chokuju Hajō Shingi],* in CKZ, vol. 1, pp. 341–370.

Chapter 3: Tea in the Heian Era

1. Kūkai, *Shōryōshū* [also *Seireishū*], in *Nihon Koten Bungaku Taikei,* vol. 71, p. 242 (cited hereafter as NKBT). *Shōryōshū* is a collection in ten volumes of Kūkai's poems, public writings, and inscriptions assembled by his disciple Shinsai. Takahashi, pp. 14–15, cites *Hiesha Shintō Himitsuki,* which says that Saichō brought tea seeds from China, but that is extremely doubtful. The character *tu,* which sometimes meant tea, had previously appeared in several places in the *Shōsōin Monjo,* but in each case it should be understood to mean "bitter herb" rather than "tea."
2. Daiten, vol. 1, p. 1. Daiten cited *Ōgishō* for his entry. *Ōgishō* was a book of poetry by Fujiwara Kiyosuke from about 1124 to 1144. See Fujiwara Kiyosuke, *Ōgishō,* in *Nihon Kagaku Taikei,* ed. Sasaki Nobutsuna, vol. 1, pp. 222–370. *Tōdaiji Yōroku* covered the period from 1106 to 1134

and contained documents linking Emperor Shōmu to tea. See Kangon et al., comps., *Tōdaiji Yōroku*, ed. Tsutsui Hidetoshi. Daiten wrote *Chakyō Shōsetsu*, as has been mentioned before, in the mid-Edo period. Ichijō Kanera's *Kuji Kongen* was completed in 1422. These cannot be taken as reliable sources for the drinking of tea in the Nara era. Kanera is also known as Kanenaga and Kaneyoshi.

3. Ichijō Kanera, *Kuji Kongen*, vol. 2, pp. 9–10.

4. Yanagita Kunio also had a theory, not based on documentary evidence, that tea was autochthonous in Japan. Yanagita Kunio, *Mura to Gakudō*, p. 124.

5. Sugawara no Michizane, comp., *Ruijū Kokushi*, in *Shintei Zōho Kokushi Taikei*, vol. 5, p. 173. *Ruijū Kokushi* was an imperially commissioned history of two hundred volumes completed in 892. It classified the Five Histories from the *Nihon Shoki* to the *Buntoku Jitsuroku* according to the subjects of Shinto, the emperors, imperial consorts, annual events, officials, and so forth. The entry in *Nihon Kōki* for 815/4/22 contains a similar account. It says that on the lake was a boat, which the emperor boarded, and further rounds of song and dance took place. The emperor distributed gifts to the officials according to rank. *Nihon Kōki*, in *Shintei Zōho Kokushi Taikei*, vol. 3, p. 132 (cited hereafter as SZKT).

6. Ono no Minemori, comp., *Ryōunshū*, in *Gunsho*, 3d rev. ed., vol. 8, p. 454.

7. Ibid.

8. Chou Ying was a painter of the middle Ming era, skilled at both polychrome paintings and ink sketches. A native of Taicang in Jiangsu, he was also known by the epithets of Shifu and Shizhou.

9. *Ryōunshū*, p. 458.

10. Yoshimine no Yasuyo, comp., *Keikokushū*, in *Gunsho*, vol. 8, p. 504. *Keikokushū*, compiled by Yoshimine no Yasuyo in 827, was imperially commissioned and the earliest comprehensive anthology of Chinese-style poetry in Japan. Only six of twenty volumes are extant.

11. Ibid., p. 508.

12. Fujiwara no Fuyutsugu et al., comp., *Bunka Shūreishū*, in *Gunsho*, vol. 8, p. 479. *Bunka Shūreishū* is an anthology of Chinese-style poetry compiled in 818 by Fujiwara no Fuyutsugu and others on the order of Emperor Saga.

13. Ibid., p. 480.

14. Murai Yasuhiko, *Chanoyu no Rekishi*, pp. 45–49.

15. *Keikokushū*, pp. 436–437.

16. Miyako no Yoshika, "Chōshimei," in Fujiwara no Akihira, comp., *Honchō Monzui*, in SZKT, vol. 29 *ge*, p. 292. *Honchō Monzui* was a col-

lection of poetry in Chinese style, covering the ninth to eleventh centuries. It consisted of 428 works in fourteen volumes.

17. Yoshishige no Yasutane, "Banshu Sanshū Yakuōji o Sugite Kan Ari," in ibid., p. 242.

18. Sugawara no Michizane et al., *Kanke Bunsō*, in NKBT, vol. 72, pp. 343, 391. *Kanke Bunsō* was an anthology of Chinese-style poetry by Sugawara no Michizane (845–903), completed in 900. 12 volumes.

19. Sugawara no Michizane et al., *Kanke Kōshū*, in ibid., p. 515. *Kanke Kōshū* was an anthology of Chinese-style poetry. 1 volume. Completed in 903, it contains thirty-eight poems presented to Ki no Haseo by Sugawara no Michizane as the latter faced death.

20. Takahashi, pp. 124–126, discusses the powdered and infused tea division.

21. *Engishiki*, in SZKT, vol. 26, pp. 147, 590. *Engishiki* detailed regulations covering court ceremonies and systems during the early Heian era. Comprising fifty volumes in Chinese, it was completed in 927. See Takahashi, pp. 21–23.

22. Minamoto no Takaaki, *Saikyūki*, in *Shintei Zōho Kojitsu Sōsho, Saikyūki*, vol. 1, pp. 200, 233. This may also be read *Saigūki* or *Seikyūki*. Other variant names also possible. Minamoto no Takaaki (913–982), the author, recorded court practices and usage, including ceremonial matters, during the reign of Emperor Murakami. Written in Chinese style.

23. Murai, pp. 56–57

Chapter 4: The Ethos of the *Kissa Yōjōki*

1. Shunjōbō Chōgen (1121–1206) studied Shingon at Daigoji and later Pure Land Buddhism with Hōnen. He traveled to Song China three times between 1167 and 1176.

2. *Azuma Kagami*, in SZKT, vol. 32, pp. 709–710. This is a historical work of the Kamakura period. 52 vols. One of Japan's earliest collections on the military class.

3. *Kissa*, pp. 23, 39.

4. Ibid., p. 22.

5. Ibid., pp. 22, 39.

6. Ibid., pp. 23, 39.

7. Ibid., p. 5, has the former and p. 23 has the latter inscription. See p. 25 for the second version.

8. Mori Shikazō, "*Kissa Yōjōki* Kaidai," in CKZ, vol. 2, pp. 126–141, has a discussion of textual variants.

9. Kikō Daishuku, *Shoken Nichiroku*, p. 153. *Shoken Nichiroku* is a diary of a sojourn in Sakai from the fourth month of 1484 to the end of 1486. Cited hereafter as *Shoken*.
10. *Kissa*, pp. 4, 24.
11. *Fusō Ryakki*, in SZKT, vol. 12, p. 292.
12. Taga Munehaya, ed., *Shūgyokushū*, pp. 542, 549, and 495, respectively.
13. Jien, *Gukanshō*, in SZKT, vol. 19, p. 63. See Delmer M. Brown and Ishida Ichirō, trans. and eds., *The Future and the Past*, p. 20, and *passim*.
14. Kujō Kanezane, *Gyokuyō*, vol. 3, pp. 550, 551, 620, 930, 944. *Gyokuyō* covers the period from 1164 to 1200.
15. Haga Kōshirō, *Chūsei Bunka to sono Kiban*, pp. 63–92.
16. *Kissa*, pp. 4, 24.
17. Ibid.
18. Ibid., pp. 4–5, 24–25. Translation in Tsunoda Ryusaku et al., eds., *Sources of Japanese Tradition*, vol. 1, pp. 283–284.
19. *Kissa*, pp. 5–6, 25–26.
20. Ibid., pp. 8–9, 27–28.
21. Ibid., pp. 9, 29.
22. Ibid., pp. 10, 29.
23. Ibid., pp. 10–11, 29–30.
24. Ibid., pp. 11, 30.
25. Ibid., pp. 11–12, 30.
26. Ibid., pp. 12–13, 31.
27. Ibid., pp. 13, 32.
28. Mori, pp. 141–149.
29. *Kissa*, pp. 13, 32.
30. Ibid., pp. 13, 32.
31. Ibid., pp. 13–14, 32.
32. Ibid., pp. 15, 33.
33. Ibid., pp. 15–23, 33–39.
34. Ibid., pp. 20–21, 38–39.
35. Ibid., pp. 21–22, 39.

Chapter 5: Tea in the Temples of the Medieval Era

1. The year 1214 was the date of the second variant. As noted above, the date of the earlier text was 1211.
2. *Isei*, p. 473.
3. *Gundari Myōō Hō*, ms. in Kanazawa Bunko cited in Hayashiya Tatsusaburō and Murai Yasuhiko, *Zuroku Chadōshi*, p. 99. Photo of the ms., p. 100.

4. *Yūgaku Ōrai,* in *Zoku Gunsho Ruijū,* ed. Hanawa Hokiichi (hereafter cited as *Zoku Gunsho*), vol. 13 *ge,* p. 1149, has the following: "Tea, which originally came from the immortals, at last crossed over to Japan. It is the ancestor of all beverages as well as of all medicines." It goes on to provide a list of the merits of tea that almost completely duplicates those on Myōe's Ashiya kettle. The order is slightly different, and "Heaven and the devil will do as one wills" replaces Myōe's eighth advantage of tea. It ends with the rhetorical question that, as the philosophers of old drank it, how can we today not? Cited hereafter as *Yūgaku.* See Nagano Hiroshi, "Juttokugama," in *Kadokawa Chadō Jiten,* ed. Hayashiya Tatsusaburō, vol. 1, p. 607; and Tanihata Akio, "Cha no Juttoku," in ibid., vol. 1, p. 900.

5. See *Shōbōgenzō: Zen Essays by Dōgen,* trans. Thomas Cleary.

6. Furuta Bonsen, ed., *Eihei Genzenshi Shingi,* vol. 1, p. 78.

7. *Sōtōshū Zensho Shingi,* p. 348.

8. Ibid., pp. 349, 354–357.

9. Ibid., p. 369.

10. *Taiheiki,* ed. Gotō Tanji and Okami Masao, in NKBT, vol. 36, p. 252. Cited hereafter as *Taiheiki.*

11. Nagashima Fukutarō, *Chadō Bunka Ronshū,* vol. 1, pp. 343–352.

12. Cited in Murai, p. 75.

13. Ibid., pp. 72–78.

14. *Teikin Ōrai,* in *Zoku Gunsho,* vol. 13 *ge,* p. 1141.

15. *Yūgaku,* vol. 13 *ge,* pp. 1149–1150.

16. Murai, pp. 72–78.

17. *Kanmon Gyoki,* in *Zoku Gunsho,* vol. *Hoi 2 jō,* p. 397. Cited hereafter as *Kanmon.* Note that all page numbers hereafter are in vol. *Hoi 2 jō* unless otherwise indicated.

18. Hayashiya and Murai, p. 132. The phrase in Japanese, *"ippuku issen,"* can be seen in a picture scroll in ibid., p. 200; Hayashiya Tatsusaburō, *Chūsei Bunka no Kichō,* p. 137.

19. Tsuji Zennosuke, ed., *Daijōin Jisha Zōjiki,* vol. 10, p. 145. Cited hereafter as *Daijōin.* Such sales of tea were sufficiently popular to make their way into Kyōgen comedies. An outstanding example is "Tsūen," about the selling of tea at Uji Bridge. See Hayashiya, p. 132.

20. *Daijōin,* vol. 1, pp. 105, 117, 204, 290, 351, 358, 442; vol. 2, p. 14; vol. 7, pp. 2, 38, 68, 126, 206.

21. Ibid., vol. 1, pp. 109, 121, 202, 237, 307, 312, 332, 345, 348, 350, 353, 357, 359, 381, 390, 391, 411, 442, 457; vol. 2, pp. 36, 40; vol. 6, pp. 490, 492; vol. 7, pp. 2, 17, 37, 38, 52, 86, 87, 90, 95, 122, 179, 239, 240.

22. Ibid., vol. 6, p. 491.

23. Citations to *Gion Shugyō Nikki* can be found in Miyaji Naoichi, ed., *Yasaka Jinja Sōsho*, vol. 1, p. 106. Cited hereafter as *Yasaka*.
24. Ibid., p. 230.
25. Tsuji Zennosuke, ed., *Rokuon Nichiroku*, vol. 1, pp. 271–314. Cited hereafter as *Rokuon*.
26. Kanazawa Bunko, ed., *Kanazawa Bunko Komonjo*, vol. 1, p. 99. *Kanazawa Bunko Komonjo* contains numerous documents related to tea. Kumahara Masao in *Kamakura no Cha* has examined these in detail. He has found that there were fifty items related to gifts of tea, and the majority, thirty-five, were Sadaaki's. See Kumahara, p. 57.
27. Kanazawa Bunko, ed., vol. 1, p. 98.
28. *Shoken*, p. 104. *Shoken Nichiroku* contains scattered references to tea. The entry for 1484/8/18 (p. 26) mentions a group of priests that took tea after a ceremony; 1485/1/23 (p. 51) mentions taking tea as a tonic; 2/29 (p. 59) mentions sending powdered tea as a gift; 3/17 (p. 63) and 1486/1/14 (p. 127), ceremonial presentations of tea to the deities; 1486/1/29 (p. 134) and 2/11(p. 138), taking packs of tea on visits; 3/15 (p. 153), previously cited, mentions a book on mulberry and tea; and 5/7 (p. 178) mentions twenty packs of bitter tea.
29. *Rokuon*, vol. 2, pp. 65, 101, 127, 190.
30. *Saihokushū*, in *Gozan Bungaku Zenshū*, ed. Murakami Kankō, vol. 1, p. 57.
31. *Kūkashū*, in ibid., vol. 2, p. 83.
32. Ibid., p. 98.

Chapter 6: The Vogue of Tea Contests

1. *Isei*, p. 474.
2. Dohi Tsunehira, *Shunsō Rōwa*, in *Nihon Zuihitsu Taisei Daisanki*, vol. 10, p. 432. *Sekiso Ōrai*, in *Gunsho*, vol. 9, p. 505, said, "Of late, Uji is [the more] admired. Though Toganoo has declined in popularity, its name remains." The latter work is attributed to Ichijō Kanera [1402–1481].
3. *Taiheiki*, vol. 36, pp. 252–253.
4. Ibid.
5. Ibid., p. 253.
6. Ibid., p. 357.
7. *Kissa Ōrai*, in CKZ, vol. 2, pp. 166–167. The description that follows is on these same pages.

8. Linked verse, called *renga* in Japanese, influenced *chanoyu* in a variety of ways and was especially important in shaping the aesthetics of the tea art, as the text discusses below. Linked verse grew out of *waka* or *tanka*, the traditional form of Japanese prosody, which contained stanzas of three lines of five, seven, and five syllables each, the upper unit, and two lines each with seven syllables, the lower unit. It became the practice to link stanzas with new units of three and two lines with content related to the previous ones. Individual poets could compose new links to their own verse, or, more commonly, pairs or groups of poets could alternate in supplying units. Linked verse parties commonly produced hundred-stanza sequences or ones of a thousand stanzas. Later, *haikai*—a similar linked verse form—led to the development of the familiar *haiku*, which can be thought of as the upper unit of a linked verse stanza and has three lines of five, seven, and five syllables.

9. *Kissa Ōrai*, p. 167.

10. Ibid., pp. 167–168.

11. *Kanmon*, vol. *Hoi 2 ge*, pp. 58, 112.

12. Ibid., p. 117.

13. "Nijō Kawara Rakugaki," in *Kenmu Nenkanki*, in *Gunsho*, vol. 25, p. 504.

14. The character *shu* (types) can also have the pronunciation *chu*. In the expression "ten *types* of incense," the Oie School of the Way of Incense customarily uses the latter pronunciation, while the Shino School uses the former. How it would have been pronounced at the time discussed here is unclear.

15. *Kenmu Shikimoku*, in *Gunsho*, vol. 22, p. 34.

16. Hayashiya, pp. 134–146, contains detailed information on the tea gatherings called "*chayoriai*."

17. *Isei*, p. 474. Another source, *Yūgaku Ōrai*, calls tea an elixir to nourish health, a miraculous means of prolonging life, and goes on to say that at that time all persons, whether rich or poor, high or low in social station, were using tea as a means of amusement. Then it lists major production areas including Toganoo, Murōji in Yamato, Hannyaji in Nara, Ise, Tango, Uji, Hamuro, Ninnaji, Daigo, Ishiyamadera, Kawagoe in Musashi, Seki in Suruga, Hattori in Iga, Kawai in Ise, and Hiei in Ōmi. It also lists four types of teas imported from China: Mohanci, Tiantai, Jianxi, and Furan. *Yūgaku*, p. 1148.

18. *Kanmon*, pp. 4, 6.

19. [Gyōyo], *Ainōshō*, ed. Masamune Atsuo, p. 86.

20. Ibid.

21. Nakahara Moromori, *Moromoriki*, vol. 1, pp. 11, 18, 82, 94, 134.

22. *Yasaka*, pp. 48, 56, 64.

23. *Taiheiki*, vol. 36, pp. 357, 444.

24. Takahashi, pp. 36–37, is my source for material from *Hakudō Zuihitsu*, whose present owner is unclear. One should note, moreover, that *Hakudō Zuihitsu* is thought to be from a considerably later period than the events it recounts.
25. *Yasaka*, pp. 1–91, *passim*.
26. Ibid., pp. 9, 25, 35, 38, 39, 43, 47, 48, 53, 56, 58, 59.
27. Ibid., pp. 103, 104.
28. Ibid., pp. 136, 153, 159–160.
29. Ibid., pp. 161, 162, 163.
30. The chart on which Chart 2 is based appears on the back of a page in the Yoshikawa family's copy of the *Genkō Shakusho*. See Hayashiya and Murai, p. 136.
31. *Daijōin*, vol. 1, pp. 307, 314, 320, 326, 446; vol. 2, pp. 48, 221, 413. See also vols. 3–5, *passim*.
32. Nakahara Moromori, vol. 1, pp. 127, 128, 130, 133, 134, 135, 138.
33. *Yasaka*, pp. 38, 53.
34. Ibid., p. 65.
35. Ibid., p. 59.
36. Ibid., pp. 69, 71, 76, 79.
37. *Kanmon Gyoki* contains numerous examples, e.g., pp. 6, 85, 112–116, 207–211, 284, 329, 377, 416, 418, 470, 477, 479, 480, 481, 482, 498, 499, 500, 501. See also *Mansai Jugō Nikki*, in *Zoku Gunsho*, vol. *Hoi* 1 *jō*, pp. 196–197, 219. On 1422/1/20, its author noted: "Today I was invited to dinner at Sairinji. Five of us, including Umetsu Hōshi and Azechi Hōkyō, suggested a drink of wine. We had tea [also]. Everything was as we usually enjoy it." On the same date a year later the diarist wrote: "Today I went to the Sairinji and took along a little money for refreshments. This is what we do every year. [Afterward] we were all obliged to have a ten-round tea contest."
38. *Kanmon*, p. 6.
39. Ibid., p. 8.
40. Musō Soseki, *Muchū Mondō*, pp. 165, 169–170.
41. Nagashima Fukutarō, *Cha no Koten*, pp. 36–48.
42. *Kanmon*, pp. 8, 9–10.
43. Ibid., p. 26.
44. Ibid., pp. 85, 87, 254, 498.
45. Yamada Takao, ed., *Genna Sannen Ban Kagakushū*, p. 101. Cited as *Kagakushū* below.
46. Thesis "Murata Jukō to Chakai no Dentō," published in Horinouchi Tajirō, *Chadōshi Jokō*, p. 90.
47. Kyōkaku, *Kyōkaku Shiyōshō*, unpublished portion of original ms. in the Naikaku Bunko archives, n. p.

48. *Kagakushū*, p. 94.
49. *Kyōkaku Shiyōshō*, whose original is in the Naikaku Bunko, employed an unusual character for the term translated here as "inferior." The precise meaning is open to question, but I have followed the standard interpretation, which is that it is a variant for a character meaning "miscellaneous" and by extension "inferior."
50. Hayashiya, p. 139.

Chapter 7: Murata Jukō and the Birth of the Way of Tea

1. Yamanoue Sōji, *Yamanoue Sōji Ki*, in CKZ, vol. 6, p. 95. Cited hereafter as *Sōji Ki*.
2. *Sōjiki Ki*, p. 96. *Nanpōroku*, p. 86, maintains that Nōami and Sōami devised the *shoin* style of tea service at Yoshimasa's mountain retreat in Higashiyama. That claim does not fit the facts, however, as the mountain villa was built after 1482, while Nōami died in 1471.
3. Nōami, *Kundaikan Sōchōki*, in CKZ, vol. 2, pp. 283–322.
4. Sōami, *Okazarisho*, in CKZ, vol. 2, pp. 407–434.
5. Kuwata Tadachika, *Nihon Chadōshi*, p. 65.
6. Kubo Gondayū, *Chōandōki*, in CKZ, vol. 3, p. 361.
7. Mitani, p. 8.
8. Nanshūjo, *Chajidan*, vol. 1, p. 8.
9. Ibid., vol. 1, pp. 8–9.
10. Endō Genkan, *Chanoyu Roku Sōshō Denki*, pp. 12–13.
11. See Theodore Ludwig, "Chanoyu and Momoyama: Conflict and Transformation in Rikyū's Art," in *Tea in Japan*, ed. Paul Varley and Kumakura Isao, pp. 71–100.
12. *Sōji Ki*, p. 51. As noted above, Nōami died in 1471, while Yoshimasa was still in his thirties. Also, he built the mountain retreat in 1482, so the source may not be entirely accurate in detail.
13. Ibid., pp. 51–52.
14. Mitani, p. 8.
15. Ibid., p. 8.
16. Whether the Edo era writer was correct in ascribing such a simple style to Jukō is open to question. Korean utensils in particular are problematical. The earliest references to the use of Korean utensils in *chanoyu* date from the middle of the sixteenth century, and mention of them did not become common until the end of the century. Korean utensils were used for tea, however, at least by the tenth century, as noted in *Engishiki* above. Moreover, Akanuma Taka, "Chūmon no Kōraijawan," in *Kōrai-*

jawan: Gohon to sono Shūhen, pp. 91–92, indicates that recent archae-
ological evidence shows more Korean ware in fifteenth- and early-six-
teenth-century sites than was previously thought to exist.

17. Nanshūjo, vol. 1, p. 10.
18. Nōami, *Kundaikan,* in CKZ, vol. 2, pp. 283–322; Sōami, *Okazarisho,* in
    ibid., pp. 407–460.
19. Nanshūjo, p. 10.
20. *Sōji Ki,* p. 99. A record in Daitokuji Shinjūan notes the fifteenth day of
    the fifth month as a time to commemorate Jukō. Presuming he is the
    same person, that corroborates the theory that he died on 1502/5/15.
21. Murata Jukō, "Jukō Furuichi Harima Hōshi Ate Isshi," in CKZ, vol. 3,
    pp. 3–4. This letter is known as "Kokoro no Fumi" (Letter of the
    Heart). English translation by Dennis Hirota, "Heart's Mastery: The
    Kokoro no fumi, The Letter of Murata Shukō to His Disciple Chōin,"
    in *Chanoyu Quarterly,* no. 22 (1979), p. 10. See Hirota, p. 198, for a
    freer, more artistic translation. For a philosophical interpretation of it,
    see Kurasawa Yukihiro, "Jukō no Cha no Shisō—Nihon no Geijutsu
    Shisō Kenkyū no Uchi," *Kenkyū,* vol. 40, pp. 18–58; vol. 42, pp. 31–50;
    vol. 45, pp. 1–42; vol. 46, pp. 24–65.
22. *Sōji Ki,* p. 96.
23. *Daijōin,* vol. 7, p. 263.
24. Ibid., vol. 7, pp. 253, 255, 260, 262, 263, 264; vol. 8, p. 138; vol. 10,
    p. 438.
25. *Sōji Ki,* p. 97. Shinkei may also be called Shingyō.
26. *Yūgen* and *yūshin* are terms used by medieval poets and dramatists in
    their aesthetic commentaries. The former, especially, most often asso-
    ciated with Zeami, the *nō* theoretician, was used to describe an elegant,
    ethereal quality in literature. In poetry Shinkei stressed this quality of
    beauty. *Yūshin* literally meant "having heart" and referred to a serious,
    elegant quality in poetry as contrasted to *mushin,* "not having heart,"
    the quality of lighter, more comical verse.
27. Murata Tahei, *Ningen Ikkyū,* pp. 213–215.
28. *Jūmon Saikishō,* in NKBT, vol. 66, p. 114.
29. *Shōtetsu Monogatari,* in NKBT, vol. 65, p. 230.
30. *Sōji Ki,* p. 52.
31. Murai, pp. 174–177.
32. *Sōchō Shuki,* in *Gunsho,* vol. 18, pp. 299–300, 304–305.
33. Sōgi, *Hakuhatsushū,* in *Zoku Gunsho,* vol. 17 *ge,* p. 1113.
34. Ibid.
35. Inawashiro Kensai, *Shinkei Sōzu Teikin,* in *Zoku Gunsho,* vol. 17 *ge,*
    p. 1121.
36. Ibid., p. 1125.

37. Nishibori Ichizō, *Nihon Chadōshi*, p. 68.
38. *Ichigon Hōdan*, in *Zoku Gunsho*, vol. 28 *ge*, p. 287; Kamo no Chōmei, *Hosshinshū*, in *Kōchū Kamo no Chōmei Zenshū*, p. i (pages not sequential, first page of preface).
39. Zeami, "Monomane Jōjō," section within *Fūshikaden*, in *Nihon Shisō Taikei*, vol. 24, pp. 20–27, and "Mazu sono Mono ni Yoku Nari, Sate Yoku sono Waza wo Niseyo," section within *Kakyō*, in ibid., p. 86.
40. *Sōji Ki*, pp. 101–102.
41. Yabunouchi Chikushin, *Genryū Chawa*, in CKZ, vol. 3, pp. 472–473. *Sōji Ki*, p. 97, said much the same thing as the fourth item, "after one has become a master of *chanoyu*, if he has only one set of utensils, he should do only *wabi suki*." Elsewhere, he said one's style of *chanoyu* should change from year to year so as to be novel. See Hirota, p. 199.
42. "Jo Ha Kyū no Koto," in Zeami, *Kakyō*, pp. 90–93.
43. *Sōji Ki*, p. 53.
44. Kuwata Tadachika, *Yamanoue Sōji Ki no Kenkyū*, p. 32.
45. *Sōji Ki*, p. 101.
46. Karaki Junzō, *Sen Rikyū*, p. 107; Karaki Junzō, *Chūsei kara Kinsei e*, p. 47; Kuwata Tadachika, *Ransei to Chadō*, pp. 40–44.
47. Komiya Toyotaka, in *Cha to Rikyū*, p. 10, stresses the contrast between the straw hut and the magnificent steed, but it should be understood as the blending of disparate elements.
48. Haga Kōshirō, *Sen Rikyū*, pp. 53–54.
49. Yamada Tōemon, *Zenpō Zōtan*, in *Nihon Shisō Taikei*, vol. 23, ed. Hayashiya Tatsusaburō, p. 480.
50. In *Kissa Zatsuwa* there is an anecdote called "Baika Ichiu," "Universe in a Plum Blossom," that captures Jukō's spirit of tea. It also shows how Jukō valued allusions that would leave a charming aftertaste. The phrase "universe in a plum blossom," coincidentally, comes from a poem, "Snows deep in the wood out front. Last night the branches blossomed." Jukō changed the plural branches into a single branch and then treated the single branch as "the "universe." Plum blossoms bloom early enough to open in the snow. Chachikushi, *Kissa Zatsuwa*, in *Zoku Gunsho*, vol. 19 *ge*, p. 523.
51. Nishio Minoru, *Chūseiteki na Mono to sono Tenkai*, p. 270.
52. Yoshida Kenkō, *Tsurezuregusa*, in NKBT, vol. 30, p. 201. Translation in Donald Keene, trans., *Essays in Idleness*, p. 115
53. Okakura Kakuzō, *The Book of Tea*, p. 4.
54. *Sōji Ki*, pp. 55–83. The term "*kantō*" generally refers to fabric woven in a striped pattern.
55. *Nanpōroku*, p. 52.

56. Nanshūjo, vol. 1, p. 13–14.
57. *Nanpōroku*, p. 3.

Chapter 8: Takeno Jōō and the Maturation of the Way of Tea

1. *Sōji Ki*, p. 96. In addition, Sōshu passed on to Prince Takachika of the Shōren'in the methods of appraising Chinese wares, which Jukō had learned from Nōami. Sōshu's death date is unknown, though he was active from the 1520s through the 1560s.
2. *Sōchō Shuki*, in *Gunsho*, vol. 18, p. 300.
3. *Yamanoue Sōji Ki* said: "Jukō had many disciples among the men of Kyoto and Sakai. To my knowledge these included Matsumoto, Shino, Dōtei, Zenpō, Furuichi Harima, Saifukuin, Insetsu. . . . In his tradition also were Sōshu, Sōgo, Zenkō, Fujita, Sōtaku, Jōteki, and Jōō." *Sōji Ki*, pp. 52, 63.
4. *Sōji Ki*, p. 96.
5. Ibid., p. 53.
6. *Sakai Kagami*, in *Naniwa Sōsho*, ed. Funakoshi Masaichirō, vol. 13, p. 62. This is a reprint of an original published in 1684.
7. Ibid., pp. 62–63.
8. *Sōji Ki* , p. 98.
9. Sanjōnishi Sanetaka, *Sanetakakōki*, vol. 5, p. 706.
10. Haga Kōshirō, *Sanjōnishi Sanetaka*, pp. 165–166, 179–180. Cited hereafter as Haga, *Sanetaka*.
11. *Sanetakakōki*, vol. 5, p. 706.
12. Ibid., vol. 5, p. 462.
13. Ibid., vol. 5, p. 475.
14. Ibid., vol. 5, p. 515.
15. Ibid., vol. 5, p. 679.
16. Haga, *Sanetaka*, pp. 182–183.
17. *Sanetakakōki*, vol. 8, p. 56.
18. Ibid., vol. 8, pp. 120, 121.
19. *Sōji Ki*, p. 91.
20. Ibid., p. 97.
21. Takeno Jōō, "Wabi no Fumi," in *Shinshū Chadō Zenshū*, ed. Kuwata Tadachika, vol. 8, p. 17. Cited hereafter as Takeno. *Sekishū Ryū Hiji Gokajō* is in the Diet Library. See Hirota, p. 208. See Mary Elizabeth Berry, *The Culture of Civil War in Kyoto*, pp. 277–278, for a brief discussion of *wabi*.

22. Nishibori, pp. 132–133.
23. *Sōji Ki*, p. 95.
24. *Chōandōki*, pp. 362–363.
25. Dairin Sōtō (1480–1568) was the ninetieth head of Daitokuji, successor to Kogaku Sōkō, and teacher of Zen to both Jōō and Rikyū.
26. Takeno, p. 17. Translation from Hirota, p. 208.
27. Takeno Jōō, *Jōō Montei e no Hatto*, in CKZ, vol. 3, p. 50.
28. The phrase *"ichigo, ichie"* expresses the uniqueness of any particular gathering, and the sentiment appeared in Takeno Jōō's "Mata Juttai no Koto," in *Sōji Ki*, p. 94. In the nineteenth century Ii Naosuke emphasized the idea in *Chanoyu Ichieshū*, in CKZ, vol. 10, pp. 331–421.
29. *Chaki Meibutsushū*. This was a secret transmission in one volume from Yamanoue Sōji to his disciple Kuwayama Shigeharu. In the food and drink section of *Zoku Gunsho*, vol. 19 *ge*, p. 494.

Chapter 9: Rikyū and the Fruition of the Way of Tea

1. Shinshōsai Shunkei, *Bunrui Sōjinboku*, in Sen Sōshitsu and Sen Sōshu, eds., *Chadō*, vol. 12, p. 31. There remains some doubt whether 1564 was the date of its composition, but this is thought to be a relatively early work on *chanoyu*.
2. Ibid., p. 31.
3. Ibid., p. 32.
4. Okakura, pp. 4, 35–52.
5. *Sōji Ki*, p. 52. For a treatment of the sixteenth-century "tea scene," see Berry, *Culture*, pp. 259–284.
6. Toyoda Takeshi, *Sakai*, pp. 80–90, citing Imai family documents. See V. Dixon Morris, "The City of Sakai and Urban Autonomy," in George Elison and Bardwell L. Smith, eds., *Warlords, Artists, and Commoners: Japan in the Sixteenth Century*, pp. 23–54.
7. The probate of Rikyū's will showed property related to a wholesale fish business.
8. *Sakai Kagami*, p. 64.
9. *Imai Sōkyū Chanoyu Nikki Kakinuki*, in CKZ, vol. 10, p. 21.
10. Kuwata Tadachika, ed., *Zōtei Shinchō Kōki*, p. 186, mentions Rikyū as host for Nobunaga.
11. I have made the decision here not to delve too deeply into biographical research on Rikyū. The following authors have pursued this study: Kuwata Tadachika, Nishibori Ichizō, Takeuchi Yasushi, Karaki Junzō, Haga Kōshirō, Murai Yasuhiko.

12. *Nanpōroku*, pp. 16–17. Note the poems that expressed the spirit of Jōō and Rikyū, respectively, can also be found in *Sakai Kagami*, pp. 63, 64. See also Hirota, pp. 233–234; Steven D. Carter, trans., *Waiting for the Wind: Thirty-Six Poets of Japan's Late Medieval Age*, pp. 13, 41. Ietaka is also called Karyū.

13. *Sōji Ki* , p. 99.

14. *Sōji Ki* , pp. 99–100.

15. *Nanpōroku*, p. 3. See Hirota, p. 217.

16. *Nanpōroku*, p. 3. See Hirota, p. 217.

17. *Nanpōroku*, pp. 3–4. See Hirota, pp. 217–218.

18. Originally, the characters for the term for the tea garden, *roji*, meant simply "pathway." However, characters meaning "open, dewy ground" replaced the original term in order to express the spiritual sense that the tea garden was more than just a narrow walkway or passage, that it served to help one attain a higher, spiritual dimension.

19. Sakamoto Yukio and Iwamoto Yutaka, eds., *Hokekyō*, vol. 1, p. 198. *Hokekyō* may also be pronounced *Hokkekyō*.

20. *Nanpōroku*, p. 10. See Hirota, p. 226.

21. Ibid.

22. Various theories have questioned the extent to which *Nanpōroku* can be considered authentic or reliable. One cannot, however, consider it to be spurious in its entirety. The *Nanpōroku* that we have today should be considered an original work redacted by Tachibana Jitsuzan. The portions of the work that are cited here are among those that are most reliable.

23. *Sōji Ki*, pp. 100–102.

24. There are several types of floor plans of the one-and-a-half-mat room. Horiguchi Sutemi, *Rikyū no Chashitsu*, p. 325. However, Konnichian, the tea room at Urasenke, probably best captures its spirit today.

25. Matsuya Hisashige, *Chadō Shiso Densho*, ed. Kumakura Isao, p. 54.

26. Horiguchi, *Rikyū no Chashitsu*, pp. 117, 119. See also Horiguchi Sutemi, *Chashitsu Kenkyū*.

27. *Ikenaga Sōsa Chasho*, in CKZ, vol. 3, p. 68.

28. Cited in Yabunouchi Chikushin, *Genryū Chawa*, in CKZ, vol. 3, p. 433.

29. *Nanpōroku*, pp. 417, 449.

30. *Zencharoku*, in CKZ, vol. 10, p. 304. There was a copy of *Zencharoku* by the Edo priest and tea man Jakuan Sōtaku, a disciple of Takuan, dated 1715/10/11. It had the title *Takuan Oshō Shi Chajinki*, but in 1828 it was published with the title *Zencharoku*. *Cha Zen Dōichimi*, a work in the same tradition, is attributed to Sen Sōtan, though the factualness of this is doubtful.

31. *Nanpōroku*, p. 5. See Hirota, pp. 220–221.

32. *Nanpōroku*, pp. 211–212.

33. *Nanpōroku*, p. 212, mentions the *kane*, a kind of carpenter's square, as a complicated way of determining the placement of utensils in the tea ceremony. This mention is one point that raises doubts about its reliability. Rikyū's advice to "put the gauge aside" has a greater ring of truth.

34. *Kitano Ōchanoyu no Ki*, in CKZ, vol. 6, p. 3. For translations see Mary Elizabeth Berry, *Hideyoshi*, p. 190, and Louise Allison Cort, "The Grand Kitano Tea Gathering," *Chanoyu Quarterly*, no. 31 (1982), p. 18. As the quotation indicates, the affair was originally scheduled to last for ten days commencing on the first of the tenth month, but it was canceled after only one day.

35. *Nanpōroku*, p. 308.

36. Ibid., pp. 265–266.

37. Ibid., p. 267.

38. The diary of Kamiya Sōtan and letters of the daimyo Ōtomo Sōrin contain information about the golden tea room. Sōtan's diary for 1587/1 mentions having tea at Osaka with Sumiyoshiya Sōmu serving, using utensils that were "golden." On 1592/5/28 *Sōtan Nikki*, his diary, indicates that Hideyoshi had a tea party in Nagoya in Kyushu for the daimyo in a "golden tea room of three mats." Kamiya Sōtan, *Sōtan Nikki*, in CKZ, vol. 6, pp. 162, 268–269. Sōrin letter of 1584/4/6 in Takita Manabu, ed., *Hennen Ōtomo Shiryō*, p. 74.

Conclusion

1. *Nanpōroku*, p. 299, says: "Upon consultation with Rikyū a tea room of two mats was completed. The sunken hearth was designed to the measure of the *daisu*. It was the first pit to measure one *shaku* four *sun* (48.5 cm.). Thereafter, it was also used in four-and-a-half-mat rooms. In the [slightly smaller] 'country size' four-and-a-half-mat room, the sunken hearth is one *shaku* three *sun* (45.5 cm.), while in [slightly larger] Kyoto rooms it is one *shaku* four *sun*."

2. Sen Sōsa, Sen Sōshitsu, and Sen Sōshu, eds., *Rikyū Daijiten*, p. 599.

3. Takeno, p. 17. See also the translation in Hirota, pp. 208–209.

4. Cited in *Nanpōroku*, p. 17.

5. *Nanpōroku*, p. 85.

6. Ibid., p. 3; Hirota, p. 217.

7. *Nanpōroku*, p. 205.

8. *Nanpōroku*, p. 213, says, "The alcove is the alcove; the seating, the seating; the shelf, the shelf; two even and one odd, two odd and one even."

9. Ibid., p. 219.

10. Ibid., p. 284.
11. *Sōji Ki*, p. 97.
12. Note that the traditional Japanese arts, including *chanoyu*, restrict the study of advanced elements of the arts to those who have mastered the elementary stages first. Such advanced aspects, often the more esoteric ones, are closely held secrets to which only the most knowledgeable may gain admission.
13. *Nanpōroku*, p. 265.
14. Ibid., p. 3; Hirota, p. 217.
15. *Kochū Rodan*, in CKZ, vol. 4, p. 415. Translation from Hirota, p. 240.

Bibliography

Akanuma Taka. "Chūmon no Kōraijawan." In *Kōraijawan: Gohon to sono Shūhen*, edited by Chadō Shiryōkan. Kyoto: Chadō Shiryōkan, 1992.

Aoki Masaru. *Chūka Chasho*. Tokyo: Shunjūsha, 1962.

Azuma Kagami. In *Shintei Zōho Kokushi Taikei*, edited by Kuroita Katsumi et al., vols. 32–33. Tokyo: Yoshikawa Kōbunkan, 1964–1965.

Berry, Mary Elizabeth. *The Culture of Civil War in Kyoto*. Berkeley, Los Angeles, London: University of California Press, 1994.

———. *Hideyoshi*. Cambridge: Harvard University Press, 1982.

Blofeld, John Eaton Calthorpe. *The Chinese Art of Tea*. London: Allen & Unwin, 1985.

Brown, Delmer M., and Ishida Ichirō, trans. and eds. *The Future and the Past*. Berkeley and Los Angeles: University of California Press, 1979.

Carter, Steven D., trans. *Waiting for the Wind: Thirty-Six Poets of Japan's Late Medieval Age*. New York: Columbia University Press, 1989.

Cort, Louise Allison. "The Grand Kitano Tea Gathering." *Chanoyu Quarterly*, no. 31 (1982): 15–44.

Daiten. *Chakyō Shōsetsu*. 2 vols. Kyoto: Sasaki Sōshirō, 1773.

Dōgen. *Shōbōgenzō: Zen Essays by Dōgen*. Translated by Thomas Cleary. Honolulu: University of Hawai'i Press, 1986.

Dohi Tsunehira. *Shunsō Rōwa*. In *Nihon Zuihitsu Taisei Daisanki*, vol. 10. Tokyo: Yoshikawa Kōbunkan, 1977.

Eisai. *Kissa Yōjōki*. In *Chadō Koten Zenshū*, edited by Sen Sōshitsu, vol. 2, pp. 4–23(dated 1211) ; 24–40 (dated 1214). Kyoto: Tankōsha, 1956.

Elison, George, and Bardwell L. Smith, eds. *Warlords, Artists, and Commoners: Japan in the Sixteenth Century*. Honolulu: University Press of Hawai'i, 1981.

Endō Genkan. *Chanoyu Roku Sōshō Denki*. Kyoto: Izumiya Mohei, 1702.

Engishiki. In *Shintei Zōho Kokushi Taikei*, edited by Kuroita Katsumi et al., vol. 26. Tokyo: Yoshikawa Kōbunkan, 1965.

Feng Yan, ed. *Fengshi Wenjianji*. In *Gaudo Sōsho*, vol. 17. N.p., 1756.

Fujiwara Kiyosuke. *Ōgishō*. In *Nihon Kagaku Taikei*, edited by Sasaki Nobutsuna, vol. 1, pp. 222–370. Tokyo: Kazama Shobō, 1969.

Fujiwara no Akihira, comp. *Honchō Monzui*. In *Shintei Zōho Kokushi Taikei*, edited by Kuroita Katsumi et al., vol. *29 ge*. Tokyo: Yoshikawa Kōbunkan, 1965.

Funakoshi Masaichirō, ed. *Naniwa Sōsho*. 17 vols. Tokyo: Meicho Shuppan, 1978.

Furuta Bonsen, ed. *Eihei Genzenshi Shingi*. 2 vols. Kyoto: Izumoji Bunjirō, 1884.

Fusō Ryakki. In *Shintei Zōho Kokushi Taikei*, edited by Kuroita Katsumi et al., vol. 12. Tokyo: Yoshikawa Kōbunkan, 1965.

[Gyōyo]. *Ainōshō*. Edited by Masamune Atsuo. *Nihon Koten Zenshū*. Tokyo: Nihon Koten Zenshū Kankōkai, 1936.

Haga Kōshirō. *Chūsei Bunka to sono Kiban*. Vol. 4 of *Haga Kōshirō Rekishi Ronshū*. Tokyo: Shibunkaku Shuppan, 1981.

———. *Sanjōnishi Sanetaka*. Tokyo: Yoshikawa Kōbunkan, 1960.

———. *Sen Rikyū*. Tokyo: Yoshikawa Kōbunkan, 1963.

Hanawa Hokiichi, ed. *Gunsho Ruijū*. 29 vols. Tokyo: Zoku Gunsho Ruijū Kanseikai, 1929–1934.

———. *Zoku Gunsho Ruijū*. Third revised edition, 86 vols. Tokyo: Zoku Gunsho Ruijū Kanseikai, 1957–1959.

Hayashiya Tatsusaburō. *Chūsei Bunka no Kichō*. Tokyo: Tōkyō Daigaku, 1953.

———, ed. *Kadokawa Chadō Jiten*. 2 vols. Tokyo: Kadokawa Shoten, 1990.

Hayashiya Tatsusaburō, and Murai Yasuhiko. *Zuroku Chadōshi*. Kyoto: Tankōsha, 1980.

Hirota, Dennis, ed. *Wind in the Pines: Classic Writings of the Way of Tea as a Buddhist Path*. Fremont: Asian Humanities Press, 1995.

Horiguchi Sutemi. *Chashitsu Kenkyū*. Tokyo: Kashima Kenkyūjo Shuppankai, 1969.

———. *Rikyū no Chashitsu*. Tokyo: Kashima Kenkyūjo Shuppankai, 1977.

Horinouchi Tajirō. *Chadōshi Jokō*. Kyoto: Takagiri Shoin, 1947.

Ichijō Kanera. *Kuji Kongen*. 3 vols. Kyoto: Heirakuji, 1694.

Isei Teikin Ōrai. In *Gunsho Ruijū*, edited by Hanawa Hokiichi, vol. 9, part 140, pp. 469–495. Tokyo: Zoku Gunsho Ruijū Kanseikai, 1932.

Jien. *Gukanshō*. In *Shintei Zōho Kokushi Taikei*, edited by Kuroita Katsumi et al., vol. 19. Tokyo: Yoshikawa Kōbunkan, 1964.

Kamo no Chōmei. *Kōchū Kamo no Chōmei Zenshū.* Edited by Yanase Kazuo. Tokyo: Kazama Shobō, 1971.

Kanazawa Bunko, ed. *Kanazawa Bunko Komonjo.* 6 vols. Yokohama: Kanazawa Bunko, 1952–1954.

Kangon et al., comps. *Tōdaiji Yōroku.* Edited by Tsutsui Hidetoshi. Tokyo: Kokusho Kankōkai, 1971.

Kanmon Gyōki. In *Zoku Gunsho Ruijū,* edited by Hanawa Hokiichi, vols. *Hoi 2 jō* and *ge.* Third revised edition. Tokyo: Zoku Gunsho Ruijū Kanseikai, 1957–1959.

Karaki Junzō. *Chūsei kara Kinsei e.* Tokyo: Chikuma Shobō, 1961.

———. *Sen Rikyū.* Tokyo: Chikuma Shobō, 1963.

Kikō Daishuku. *Shoken Nichiroku.* In *Dai Nihon Kokiroku,* edited by Tokyo Daigaku Shiryō Hensanjo. Tokyo: Iwanami Shoten, 1953.

Komiya Toyotaka. *Cha to Rikyū.* Tokyo: Kadokawa Shoten, 1956.

Kujō Kanezane. *Gyokuyō.* Edited by Kurokawa Shindō and Yamada An'ei. 3 vols. Tokyo: Kokusho Kankōkai, 1907.

Kūkai. *Shōryōshū.* In *Nihon Koten Bungaku Taikei,* vol. 71. Tokyo: Iwanami Shoten, 1965.

Kumahara Masao. *Kamakura no Cha.* Kyoto: Kawahara Shoten, 1948.

Kurasawa Yukihiro. "Jukō no Cha no Shisō—Nihon no Geijutsu Shisō Kenkyū no Uchi." *Kenkyū,* vol. 40, pp. 18–58; vol. 42, pp. 31–50; vol. 45, pp. 1–42; vol. 46, pp. 24–65. Kobe: Kobe Daigaku, 1967–1970.

Kuwata Tadachika. *Nihon Chadōshi.* Tokyo: Kadokawa Shoten, 1954.

———. *Ransei to Chadō.* Tokyo: Heibonsha, 1957.

———. *Yamanoue Sōjiki no Kenkyū.* Kyoto: Kawahara Shoten, 1957.

———, ed. *Shinshū Chadō Zenshū.* 9 vols. Tokyo: Shunjūsha, 1956.

———, ed. *Zōtei Shinchō Kōki.* Tokyo: Shin Jinbutsu Ōraisha, 1965.

Li Fang, et al., eds. *Taiping Guangji.* 5 vols. Beijing: Xinhua Shudian, 1959.

———. *Wenyuan Yinghua.* 6 vols. Beijing: Xinhua Shudian, 1966.

Li Shizhen. *Bencao Gangmu.* 4 vols. Beijing: Xinhua Shudian, 1978.

Li Zhao, ed. *Tang Guoshi Bu.* 3 vols. Tōto [Edo, Tokyo]: Yamasaki Kinbei, 1782.

Lu Yu. *The Classic of Tea.* Translated by Francis Ross Carpenter. Boston: Little Brown, 1974.

Matsushita Satoru. *Nihon no Cha.* Nagoya: Fūbaisha, 1969.

Matsuya Hisashige. *Chadō Shiso Densho.* Edited by Kumakura Isao. Tokyo: Shibunkaku, 1974.

Minamoto no Takaaki. *Saikyūki.* In *Shintei Zōho Kojitsu Sōsho.* 2 vols. Tokyo: Yoshikawa Kōbunkan, 1952.

Mitani Sōchin. *Wakan Chashi*. Reprinted as *Wakan Chashi Yakuhon*, edited by Takaya Tsunetarō. Osaka: Takaya Tsunetarō, 1914.

Miyaji Naoichi, ed. *Yasaka Jinja Sōsho*. 2 vols. Kyoto: Kanpei Taisha Yasaka Jinja Shamusho, 1942.

Morooka Tamotsu. "Rikuu to Chakyō." In *Chadō*, edited by Sen Sōshitsu and Sen Sōshu, vol. 1, pp. 115–260. Tokyo: Sōgensha, 1977.

Murai Yasuhiko. *Chanoyu no Rekishi*. Kyoto: Tankōsha, 1969.

Murakami Kankō, ed. *Gozan Bungaku Zenshū*. 5 vols. Tokyo: Shibunkaku, 1973.

Murata Tahei. *Ningen Ikkyū*. Tokyo: Chōbunsha, 1963.

Musō Soseki. *Muchū Mondō*. Kyoto: Naigai Shuppan Insatsu, 1934.

Nagasawa Kikuya, ed. *Wakokubon Kanshi Shūsei: Sōshūhen*. 10 vols. Tokyo: Koten Kenkyūkai, 1975–1979.

Nagashima Fukutarō. *Chadō Bunka Ronshū*. 2 vols. Kyoto: Tankōsha, 1982.

———. *Cha no Koten*. Kyoto: Tankōsha, 1978.

Nakahara Moromori. *Moromoriki*. Edited by Fujii Sadafumi and Kobayashi Hanako. 11 vols. In *Shiryō Henshū: Kokiroku-hen*. Tokyo: Zoku Gunsho Ruijū Kanseikai, 1968–1982.

Nanshūjo. *Chajidan*. 2 vols. Kyoto and Edo: Nishimura Ichirōemon, Nakagawa Mohei, Nishimura Genroku, 1760.

Nihon Kōki. In *Shintei Zōho Kokushi Taikei*, edited by Kuroita Katsumi et al., vol. 3. Tokyo: Yoshikawa Kōbunkan, 1966.

Nishibori Ichizō. *Nihon Chadōshi*. Osaka: Sōgensha, 1940.

Nishio Minoru. *Chūseiteki na Mono to sono Tenkai*. Tokyo: Iwanami Shoten, 1961.

Nunome Chōfū, ed. *Chūka Chasho Zenshū*. 2 vols. Tokyo: Kyūko Shoin, 1987.

Okabe Haruhira [Kuzune]. *Chaki Zeigen*. Kyoto: Biroka, 1853.

Okakura Kakuzo. *The Book of Tea*. 1906. Reprint, Rutland and Tokyo: Charles E. Tuttle Company, 1956.

Ono no Minemori, comp. *Ryōunshū*. In *Gunsho Ruijū*, edited by Hanawa Hokiichi, vol. 8, pp. 449–466. Third revised edition. Tokyo: Zoku Gunsho Ruijū Kanseikai, 1960.

Ouyang Xiu, Song Qi et al., eds. *Xintangshu*. 20 vols. Beijing: Zhonghua Shuju, 1975.

Quan Tang Shi. 25 vols. Beijing: Xinhua Shudian, 1960.

Ramirez-Christensen, Esperanza. *Heart's Flower: The Life and Poetry of Shinkei*. Stanford: Stanford University Press, 1994.

Saeda Ryakuō, ed. *Chaji Shūran*. 4 vols. Kyoto: Ishida Taiseisha, 1986.

Sakamoto Yukio, and Iwamoto Yutaka, eds. *Hokekyō*. 3 vols. Tokyo: Iwanami Shoten, 1962.

Sanjōnishi Sanetaka. *Sanetakakōki.* 21 vols. Tokyo: Zoku Gunsho Ruijū Kanseikai Taiyōsha, 1958–1963.

Sen Sōsa, Sen Sōshitsu, and Sen Sōshu, eds. *Rikyū Daijiten.* Kyoto: Tankōsha, 1989.

Sen Sōshitsu, ed. *Chadō Koten Zenshū.* 12 vols. Kyoto: Tankōsha, 1956.

Sen Sōshitsu, and Sen Sōshu, eds. *Chadō.* Reprint. 15 vols. Tokyo: Sōgensha, 1977.

Shuoku. 6 cases. Shanghai: Wenming Shuju, 1915.

Sōtōshū Zensho Kankōkai, ed. *Sōtōshū Zensho Shingi.* Tokyo: Kōmeisha, 1931.

Sugawara no Michizane, comp. *Ruijū Kokushi.* In *Shintei Zōho Kokushi Taikei,* edited by Kuroita Katsumi et al., vols. 5–6. Tokyo: Yoshikawa Kōbunkan, 1965.

Sugawara no Michizane et al. *Kanke Bunsō.* In *Nihon Koten Bungaku Taikei,* vol. 72. Tokyo: Iwanami Shoten, 1966.

———. *Kanke Kōshū.* In *Nihon Koten Bungaku Taikei,* vol. 72. Tokyo: Iwanami Shoten, 1966.

Taga Munehaya, ed. *Shūgyokushū.* Tokyo: Yoshikawa Kōbunkan, 1971.

Taiheiki. Edited by Gotō Tanji and Okami Masao. In *Nihon Koten Bungaku Taikei,* vols. 34–36. Tokyo: Iwanami Shoten, 1960–1962.

Takahashi Tatsuo. *Chadō.* Tokyo: Ōokayama Shoten, 1935.

Takita Manabu, ed. *Hennen Ōtomo Shiryō.* Oita: Takita Yuki, 1968.

Tao Zongyi, ed. *Shuofu.* 10 vols. Shanghai: Shanghai Guji, 1986.

Toyoda Takeshi. *Sakai.* Tokyo: Shibundō, 1957.

Tsuji Zennosuke, ed. *Daijōin Jisha Zōjiki.* 12 vols. Tokyo: Kadokawa Shoten, 1964.

———. *Rokuon Nichiroku.* 6 vols. Tokyo: Zoku Gunsho Ruijū Kanseikai, 1961.

Tsunoda Ryusaku, Wm. Theodore deBary, and Donald Keene, eds. *Sources of Japanese Tradition.* 2 vols. New York: Columbia University Press, 1958.

Varley, Paul, and Kumakura Isao, eds. *Tea in Japan: Essays on the History of Chanoyu.* Honolulu: University of Hawai'i Press, 1989.

Xin Wenfang, comp. *Tang Caizizhuan.* N.p., n.d.

Yamada Takao, ed. *Genna Sannen Ban Kagakushū.* Tokyo: Shinseisha, 1968.

Yamada Tōemon. *Zenpō Zōtan.* In *Nihon Shisō Taikei,* vol. 23, *Kodai Chūsei Geijitsuron,* edited by Hayashiya Tatsusaburō. Tokyo: Iwanami Shoten, 1973.

Yanagita Kunio. *Mura to Gakudō.* Tokyo: Asahi Shuppansha, 1945.

Yoshida Kenkō. *Essays in Idleness.* Translated by Donald Keene. New York: Columbia University Press, 1967.

————. *Tsurezuregusa.* In *Nihon Koten Bungaku Taikei,* vol. 30. Tokyo: Iwanami Shoten, 1957.

Yūgaku Ōrai. In *Zoku Gunsho Ruijū,* edited by Hanawa Hokiichi, vol. 13 *ge,* part 362, pp. 1144–1158. Third revised edition. Tokyo: Zoku Gunsho Ruijū Kanseikai, 1957–1959.

Zeami. *Fūshikaden.* In *Nihon Shisō Taikei,* vol. 24, *Zeami, Zenchiku,* edited by Omote Akira and Katō Shūichi. Tokyo: Iwanami Shoten, 1974.

————. *Kakyō.* In *Nihon Shisō Taikei,* vol. 24, edited by Omote Akira and Katō Shūichi. Tokyo: Iwanami Shoten, 1974.

Zhao Lin, ed. *Yinhualu.* N.p., n.d.

Index

About the Author

Sen Sōshitsu XV is the fifteenth-generation Iemoto of the Urasenke *chanoyu* lineage, headquartered in Kyoto, Japan. Born in 1923 as the eldest son of the fourteenth generation in the Urasenke family line, he is a direct descendant of Sen Rikyū. After graduating from Dōshisha University with a B.A. in economics and serving in the Imperial Naval Air Force during the Pacific War, he took Buddhist vows under the guidance of Gotō Zuigan Rōshi, 503d chief abbot of Daitokuji temple, whose calligraphy appears on the front of this book. In 1991, he was awarded the degree of doctor of philosophy by the government of the People's Republic of China for successfully defending his dissertation "*Chakyō* to Wagakuni Chadō no Rekishiteki Igi" (The *Chajing* and Its Historical Impact on the Japanese Way of Tea) at Nankai University. It was the first such degree ever granted by that government to a noncitizen. Other publications by Dr. Sen include *Tea Life, Tea Mind*, which has been translated into five different languages, and the foreword and afterword to the 1989 Kodansha International edition of the classic *The Book of Tea* by Okakura Kakuzō. In 1989, Dr. Sen was named Person of Cultural Merits by the Japanese government. He holds posts at a number of universities the world over, and, to ensure the furtherance of a global appreciation of the culture and traditions of Japan, he has endowed the Sōshitsu Sen XV Distinguished Professorship of Traditional Japanese History and Culture at the University of Hawai'i, and the Sōshitsu Sen XV Distinguished Lectures on Japanese Culture at the Donald Keene Center of Japanese Culture, Columbia University.